Formal Representation of
Human Judgment

Formal Representation of Human Judgment

Editor
BENJAMIN KLEINMUNTZ

Department of Psychology
Carnegie-Mellon University
Pittsburgh, Pennsylvania

Contributors for this Volume

RAYMOND B. CATTELL, University of Illinois
WARD EDWARDS, University of Michigan
EDWARD A. FEIGENBAUM, Stanford University
BERT F. GREEN, Jr., Carnegie-Mellon University
JOHN R. HAYES, Carnegie-Mellon University
PAUL J. HOFFMAN, Oregon Research Institute
BENJAMIN KLEINMUNTZ, Carnegie-Mellon University
JOSHUA LEDERBERG, Stanford University
ALLEN NEWELL, Carnegie-Mellon University
HERBERT A. SIMON, Carnegie-Mellon University
RICHARD K. SUMNER, Carnegie-Mellon University

*The third of an annual series of symposia in the
area of cognition under the sponsorship of
Carnegie-Mellon University*

JOHN WILEY & SONS, INC.
New York • London • Sydney

To Dalia,

and to Don, Ira, and Oren

Preface

This volume consists of presentations made at the Third Annual Symposium on Cognition. The announced topic for this year was formal representation of human judgment, and the participants were selected because they have, in various ways, contributed toward the formalization of human thinking.

The conference, which was held at Carnegie Institute of Technology (now Carnegie-Mellon University) on April 13 and 14, 1967, once again succeeded in attracting a wide audience of interested persons, and as in the past two years consisted of contributions from highly regarded scientists from within the topic domain. With the exception of Joshua Lederberg, who considers himself a microbiologist and whose work in genetics earned him the Nobel Award in Medicine (1958), the symposium participants regard themselves as behavioral scientists.

The order of presentations and the participants were as follows: On the morning of April 13, acting as chairman and organizer of the symposium, I opened the meeting by announcing the topic area and by explaining briefly that the purpose of these symposia is to stimulate research on cognition. This was followed by papers presented by Paul J. Hoffman and Ward Edwards. A discussion of these papers by Bert F. Green, Jr., concluded the morning. The afternoon's presentations consisted of papers by Raymond B. Cattell and myself; and these were discussed by Robert Glaser.

On the morning of the following day, Herbert A. Simon presented his paper, and this was followed by a joint presentation of a paper by Joshua Lederberg and Edward A. Feigenbaum.

Allen Newell then concluded the formal session by discussing the morning's papers. The conference was shifted, in the afternoon of April 14, to a large room which permitted free interaction among the participants themselves and between participants and interested faculty and graduate students. This informal session was chaired by Allen Newell, and was attended by an interdisciplinary group of persons drawn from the computer sciences, chemistry, metallurgy, physics and psychology. The very final setting of the conference, attended by a handful of interested viewers, was in the teletype room of the Computation Center. There, Joshua Lederberg and Edward Feigenbaum, hooked-up to the Computation Center at Stanford University, demonstrated the way their computer program solves structural problems in organic chemistry.

Essentially the participants' papers, with minor editorial modifications, appear in this volume as they were presented at the Symposium. To provide readers with a more cohesive and integrated book, the order of the chapters as presented here does not preserve the format of the conference, and this volume contains an introductory chapter by Allen Newell and an overview by John R. Hayes. The former of these contributions is intended as an orientation chapter, and the latter as a critique. Both are included here as compensations for two omissions. In one case, the chapter which was to have included a discussion of R. B. Cattell's paper and my own, the discussant was unable to meet the publisher's deadline date. However, neither Cattell's nor my paper escapes criticism in this book (see Chapter 9). In the second instance, the Simon and the Lederberg and Feigenbaum papers were discussed by Allen Newell. But the latter's remarks, at my request, were made sufficiently broad to be included in an introductory chapter to this volume.

Like the two volumes before it, the publication of this book has been made possible by grants from the Carnegie Corporation, the National Science Foundation, and lately from royalties accruing from the sales of *Problem Solving*: *Research*, *Method and Theory*. A portion of the time I spent preparing this volume has been supported by a grant from the Maurice Falk Medical Foundation. Again, I am indebted to these foundations, and to the symposium participants and my department colleagues for their generous assistance. The total cooperation of the Administration of Carnegie-Mellon University also made this symposium possible, and in this regard Dean Richard M.

Cyert deserves special mention for his part in this undertaking.

And for the third year running, plaudits are in order for Mrs. Betty H. Boal for her patient and gentle handling of the myriad administrative and editorial details that made this symposium and volume possible.

In dedicating this book to Dalia, my wife, and to our three boys, Don, Ira and Oren, I wish to acknowledge, at least in some minor way, the debt I owe them for having freed me of family obligations in order to give my time elsewhere.

January 1968   BENJAMIN KLEINMUNTZ
Pittsburgh, Pennsylvania

Contents

xi

xii   Contents

Formal Representation of
Human Judgment

CHAPTER 1

Allen Newell

Carnegie-Mellon University

JUDGMENT AND ITS REPRESENTATION: AN INTRODUCTION*

Like the two symposia before it, this one centers on an area of cognition. The first two had to do with problem solving and with concepts. This one has to do with judgment. Since the contributors use the term only as an umbrella under which to present specific research, it is perhaps not only appropriate, but nonredundant, to attempt in this introduction to delineate the area of judgment and the nature of the research problems that lie therein.

"Judgment" is an umbrella term, like "perception," "thinking," "learning," and "cognition." Its purpose, like that of the others, is to designate a class of phenomena well enough so that one knows where to start in the development and evaluation of scientific theory. It is a mistake to believe it can (or should) be a technical term or precisely defined. A moment's consideration of the nature of science shows why. Science deals with phenomena. It does so by proposing theories (models, descriptions, ...) about the phenomena. Within these theories precise definition is possible (and desirable). But terms are needed to refer to the phenomena, independently of any proposed theory. We wish to ask if theory T explains phenomena P. But if T is taken as defining P, although there could still be ways of talking about errors of commission (T could be wrong), there would be no way of talking about errors of omission (P has aspects never mentioned in T).

Thus terms such as judgment are never well defined. They are not necessarily ill defined, either. They belong to

*The research in this paper was supported by Research Grant MH-07722-01 from the National Institutes of Health.

1

the pretheoretical language, indicating a phenomenological focus, which is fuzzy around the edges. One discovers this focus by an analysis, more or less acute, of the prior use and mention of the term.

On What Is Judgment

If one goes back to the nineteenth century one finds judgment taken as the psychological side of a proposition. Actually, the matter was turned around. Judgment came first, and a proposition (what we would now call a statement) was the written expression of a judgment. A rather subtle shift in the status of ideas and subjective truth modified this to be: A judgment is the psychological act of affirming a proposition. Now the proposition comes first, or at least has some sort of logical priority, and judgment follows after.

In both of these the scope of judgment-cum-proposition is extremely broad; it becomes, practically, the unit of thought. Indeed, at the time when experimental psychology comes on the scene at the turn of the century this apparently was taken as its literal meaning. Humphrey (1951) provides a rather detailed picture of the dismayed reaction of the early German psychologists to the completely negative results of one of the early efforts (by Marbe) to apply the introspective technique and find out exactly what it is that made a mental act a judgment. Content there was in abundance, but no specific "judgmental" tag.

The muddy waters of both psychology and logic have cleared considerably in fifty years. "Judgment" has disappeared from logic entirely. And it has changed its role in psychology. Not too long ago, Donald Johnson attempted a straight-forward definition. Dividing thought processes into three functions, he first defined *preparation*, then *production*, and finally *judgment*:

> The third process, judgment, may be identified as the evaluation or categorizing of an object of thought. This is logically differentiated from productive thought in that typically nothing is produced. The material is merely judged; i.e., put into one category or another. Many of the subjective analyses of thinking have included a concluding phase of hypothesis testing or verifica-

tion during which the thoughts previously produced are judged. In experimental psychology, judgment is a well-developed topic, studied chiefly under the headings of psychophysics, aesthetics, attitudes, and rating of personnel. (Johnson, 1955, p. 51)

Thus judgment is characterized as one kind of process, a component of total cognitive operation. There appears the notion that its inputs—the items that that are to be judged—are already available. The link with the early definitions is clearly apparent. The result of judgment is a selection or categorization; any attempt to state this would be a proposition. Since this proposition is about what is already there, it seems permissible to assert that judgments produce nothing. And in any event, there is no necessary implication that any direct representation of a proposition is produced. Any response that indicates that the stimuli have been evaluated or categorized permits the inference (by an external observer) that a judgmental process has occurred.

Judgment is also seen as a terminating or concluding phase of a larger process. This can be emphasized by another quotation, this one a remark by John Cohen in his *Behavior and Uncertainty*:

The expression "decision making" is, indeed, frequently employed to include the making of a choice, the expressing of a preference, the arriving at a judgment, and many other "operations" which bring a process, so to speak, to a close. (Cohen, 1964, p. 13)

That explicit definitions of judgment are difficult to find in the literature is not surprising, since the term is used as a label for the phenomena—as a way of making contact between what the reader is assumed to know and technical terms that are being introduced. Note that in Cohen's remark above he is not interested in defining judgment, but rather in defining decision making. Similarly, neither in Restle's *Psychology of Judgment and Choice* (1961) nor in an edited series of contributions on *Human Judgment and Optimality* (Shelly and Bryan, 1964a), two somewhat recent volumes that have "judgment" in their titles, do we find much in the way of explicit definition of "judgment." The latter volume, however, does have a comment or two that clarify further the term's current scope.

If we need to limit it [the term "judgment"] in some way beyond its intuitive content, we can say that roughly a "judgment" refers to any verbal reaction (or its equivalent) that is the "direct" product of the individual's processing his sensory inputs in combination with his memories of "stored experiences." This would exclude reactions such as reading a number off a dial. (Shelley and Bryan, 1964, p. 9 fn.)

There is a temptation to assert that the logical vacuum to which the decision maker was brought in the last few sentences [namely, there is still choice to be exercised after all information has been used] constitutes the invitation to him to use his judgment. This would characterize judgment as a last resort, acceptable only after more rational processes are exhausted. A bit more generously, perhaps, one might claim that to exercise one's judgment is to utilize his intuition properly. Neither of these concepts appears to do justice to the notion of judgment, and an effort is made to identiy those parts of the decision process in which judgment is an appropriate component. There are some decision situations in which a decision must be made so rapidly that there is not time for analytical evaluation; these occur quite often while driving an automobile, for example, and judgment would seem to be a good name for the skill that a decision maker must have developed to be effective. Decisions in these situations are made so quickly that they are almost automatic reflex actions. If judgment is a proper name for this kind of thing. . . (Rigby, 1964, 41)*

From the first of these we take the notion that the judge contributes something to the reaction, rather than being simply the means of transducing information. In earlier times this same concern was expressed by saying that an association was not a judgment, some affirmation was required. (We can overlook the extreme breadth of the definition in this first quotation. This is an affliction of definitions that seek for generality of phenomenological terms which have clear foci but fuzzy boundaries.)

The second quotation agrees with the first in asserting that judgment is "going beyond the information given," to use Bruner's phrase. It adds to this a flavor of immediacy, and somewhat surprisingly, nonrationality. Thus judgment fills the gaps in rational calculation. If the calculation could do it all, then no judgment is required. This latter flavor is in fact characteristic of many of the articles in the book. It appears to arise in attempting to apply modern decision theory. That framework provides for the calculation of a decision if certain input information is given. These inputs tend to be the

*Quoted, but with abbreviations used by Rigby replaced by the full expressions; for example, "decision maker" for DM.

probability of events occurring (perhaps conditionally) and the preference for various events or states of the world. In any real application these events and situations are highly complex, and not completely defined. That is, their occurrence or non-occurrence may be operationally clear, but no formal description of their structure exists. Thus, the tendency is to create a division of labor: The human provides these inputs (i.e., judgments) and the formal apparatus combines them into the final decision. A certain parity of agent-like status is often obtained by thinking of these formal rules as embedded in the program for a computer. In recognition of this division of labor one of the chapters in the book is entitled *Subjective Programming* (Aumann, 1964).

The upshot is that whatever can be analyzed, becomes part of the formal apparatus, and the remainder is left to be subjective judgment. Thus, although one may still assert that there is good judgment and bad—that a man can somehow arrive at his inputs to the system appropriately or not—judgment occurs in precisely those situations where the scientist is least able to attribute rationality to them.

Let us pull together the definitional strands we have accummulated. Judgment (the act of judging) is a cognitive process with the following characteristics:

1. The main inputs to the process, that which is to be judged, are given and available; obtaining, discovering, or formulating them is not part of judgment.
2. The domain of the output—the set of admissible responses—is simple and well defined prior to the judgment. The response itself is variously called a selection, estimation, assertion, evaluation or classification (in the sense of identification of class membership, not of creating the classes), depending on the nature of the domain.
3. The process is not a simple transduction of information; judgment adds information to the output.
4. The process is not simply a calculation, or the application of a given rule.
5. The process concludes, or occurs at the conclusion of, a more extended process (the causal role is not completely clear).
6. The process is rather immediate, not being extended in time with phases, stages, subprocesses, etc. (If such occur, they tend to be referred to as preparation for judgment.)

7. The process is to be distinguished from searching, discovering, or creating, on the one hand; and from musing, browsing, or idly observing, on the other.

We have ourselves gone beyond the information given in constructing this list of particulars. However, we can test them to some extent by looking more closely at the structure of the situations in which the term judgment is used.

If one scans the psychological literature (haphazardly, to be sure) one finds certain situations in which "judgment" occurs with high frequency. Paramount among these are psychophysical experiments. One judges which of two weights are heavier, or tones louder. The items to be judged are given. The domain of the judgment (i.e., the possibilities of response) is both given and simple. The response is nonrational, in that there is no calculational rule (known to the experimenter?) that can be applied to get the answer. Thus, however immediate the response ("the left one is heavier"), it is not "simply" a transduction of information. There is an ambiguity about this, of course. Judgment is required only when the weights are close together. To judge a one pound weight heavier than a one ounce weight does not require judgment. If it does (or if we decide so to use the term to achieve consistency over the range of an experimental situation), then Shelley and Bryan's "reading a number off a dial" would not be excluded.

Another common situation in which "judgment" occurs is where humans are employed as measuring instruments. They are often called judges. Typically, they may judge the degree of hostility evidenced in a written paragraph, or the amount of leadership shown in group task. Again, the situation is structured as in the psychophysical experiment, with the items to be judged clearly stated and the response space clearly delimited. The response is an ill-defined function of the situation, in that no calculational rule seems apparent. Indeed, it is precisely the lack of such a rule that leads to the use of judges as a hopefully adequate surrogate for a simpler measuring instrument. Finally, the situation is one that occurs in a short period of time, from seconds to minutes.

There is a flavor to these latter situations that is absent from the psychophysical ones. Perhaps it is complexity, perhaps nonquantifiability, perhaps even noncomparability. In psychophysics there are corresponding physical measurements, which are essentially simple, quantitative and definite; and provide the starting point of all investigation. But there is no measurement of hostility other than that provided by the judges (although to be sure we can seek for interjudge consistency). This does not make the situation less judgmental. If anything, the opposite is true.

An interesting confirmation of the gap-filling character of judgment comes from work that culminated in a book called *Risk Taking* by Kogan and Wallach (1964). In trying to understand the relation of personality to decision making in uncertain and risky situations, these authors defined a type of variable they called "cognitive-judgmental." An example is "category width" (defined by Pettigrew) in which the person must estimate the extremes of a variable, given the mean:

> The average length of whales in the Atlantic has been estimated by zoologists to be roughly 65 feet. What do you think
>> is the length of the longest whale in the Atlantic Ocean: 120 ft., 190 ft., 86 ft., 75 ft.
>> is the length of the shortest whale in the Atlantic Ocean: 6 ft., 43 ft., 52 ft., 21 ft.

Note that no information is available at all on the item to be estimated. Humans tend to be consistent in making such estimation; that is, either setting wide bounds or narrow bounds given the alternatives available. Thus, the underlying notion is that humans add to the information available in the situation in order to make their judgments, even when they have no internal information relevant to the situation. Thus the mechanisms of judgment, whatever they are, are not necessarily rational.

Scientific Questions about Judgment

With all this informal phenomenological analysis in hand, we can now turn to the examination of what scientific questions are to be asked of judgment, and what role representation might play in forming or answering these questions.

At a sufficiently superficial level, the relevant scientific tasks are the same everywhere: to categorize and classify; to measure; to extract aspects capable of theoretical treatment; and to discern aspects whose explanations seem critical for an understanding of the whole. But one level down, each area takes on a distinctive flavor. For the area of judgment these questions would seem to be the following:

Upon What Information Is the Judgment Based? In the case of psychophysics we assume that the information given is the associated physical measurement. But in most other cases we do not know the information that is used. For example, in judging the expressed emotion of faces, the concern is precisely over what clues are used [see Woodworth and Schlosberg (1954, pp. 111-120) for an account of such work]. Similarly, when we turn to the judging of personality characteristics, not as an instrument but as an object of scientific investigation, we never know the information that is being selected for use.

What Is the Judgmental Law? Given that we know the input information, and can measure the output—namely, the resulting judgment—the immediate question is to understand how the judgment depends on the input information. By and large this is the main program of psychophysics, which seeks the psychometric function.

By What Process Is the Law Accomplished? This is the theoretical step, in which some decomposition of the function between input and output is proposed that purports to explain why the judgment is the way it is. It can be as elementary a decomposition as dividing the total judgment into a perceptual process concerned with acquiring individual items of information, and a combinatory process that puts these together; not specifying further any mechanisms internal to either component, but trying to devise experimental means of assigning features of the judgmental law to one or the other. It can be as elaborate as an entire computer program to simulate the judgment.

What Affects the Judgment? A judgment may be a function of many variables. There is usually a natural division between those that are viewed as its proper inputs—essentially, information about the items being judged—and other inputs, which are viewed as parameters. The attempt to show that there is a temperature affect on the judgment of time intervals provides an example, since the temperature of the environment is not seen as information about the time interval, but as something that affects the mechanism of judgment. Similarly, the attempt to find personality correlates of judgments, as in the work of Kogan and Wallach already mentioned, comes under this head.

By What Process Are the Effects on Judgment Accomplished? This is the problem of explanation for effects, corresponding to the one already stated for the main functional dependence.

These five questions provide a way of classifying much of the research on judgment. It is a simple-minded classification, corresponding to a translation into the area of interest of the tasks of discovering relevant variables, obtaining descriptive empirical generalizations, and developing explanatory theories. But at least something more can be said about them, flowing from the reasons why work is done on one question rather than another. These reasons come, by and large, from outside the scientific domain. The more important of these motivations seem to be:

Why Does Not a Human Make Optimal Judgments? That there is an optimal judgment to be made already suggests an underlying concern with human performance in the service of human goals. Thus, except in the psychophysical laboratory, weights get judged because one wants to know which weighs more for some larger purpose. Almost every chapter of the already mentioned book on *Human Judgments and Optimality* takes as its concern how to make better decisions and how to make use of judgments to that end.

Can a Machine (Algorithm) Make as Good Judgments? A derivative of the same concern with larger applied goals, this has a distinct flavor of its own, arising from the development of the computer. A variant (sometimes put forth as being more sophisticated or rational) is to ask about the proper division of labor between human and mechanized judgment.

How Do Humans Do Simply What Seems Complex? It is manifest that humans frequently (often routinely) make judgments rapidly in complex situations. A chess master glances at a board and judges "instantly" who is ahead. The automobile driver, we were reminded earlier, makes an almost continuous series of rapid judgments. Our admiration and wonder are called forth about how such judgments can be made. In most cases we do not know the information used by the judge, the assertion of complexity being based on the information available *a priori* to the judge. Thus, the truth may be that the processing accomplished is not astounding. However, the sense of wonder is not misplaced until the hidden simplicity has been demonstrated.

These motivations clearly affect which of the five questions of judgment are attended to. The first two generally focus concern on the first two questions: the information used and the judgmental law. Often, an attempt to measure how humans fall short of optimality does not require an exhaustive discovery of the information used by the human, as long as it is objectively known what information relevant to the judgment is available. The last of the three motivations, the wonder of it all, does focus interest precisely on the process used by the human.

Representation

In attempting any study of judgment except the rather casual phenomenology exhibited in the first part of this introduction, it is necessary to adopt some representation—some scheme which identifies a set of aspects and their relationships to each other, in terms of which explanations can be given and tested. Which scheme one adopts depends on the question asked, and the motivation for asking it. It also has consequences for the kinds of answers that will be proposed. Even if, in some long run, the empirical domain forces convergence toward theories which, if not identical, are behaviorally isomorphic, still the initial explanations proposed and the dead ends encountered will vary.

Let me describe four different possibilities for the representation of judgment. They cover, it seems to me, the representations used in the contributions to this volume. They can be of help, in conjunction with the questions and motivations already discussed, to see the volume whole.

Model with Maximum Formal Generality. I could almost as well have described this as the decision theoretic representation.   It would have come to about the same thing. We can simply borrow a version from the volume on *Human Judgments and Optimality*:

> The decision maker is faced with
> 1. a set A of alternative actions a;
> 2. a set X of alternative states x of the environment;
> 3. a set R of alternative outcomes r or results of his actions;
> 4. A function ρ, the outcome function, associating with each action-environment pair (a, x) and outcome $r = \rho(x, a)$.
>
> The problem confronting the decision maker is the choice of an action a that is optimal in some sense. I should emphasize at this point the possibly complicated nature of A, X, R, and ρ. In particular, an action in the foregoing sense may in fact be what is more commonly called a strategy, that is, a rule for taking action on the basis of some information about the environment. The description of the state of the environment is to be thought of as including all relevant factors that are beyond the control of the decision maker. The division of the determinants of the outcome r into two "variables," one controlled by the decision maker and the other uncontrolled, is in a sense an assumption, but experience in the formulation of decision problems suggests that this assumption can be satisfied by suitably definining the variables a and x. (Radner, 1964, p. 178)

This basic definition is then augmented first by a *preference ordering* on the set of alternative actions; then by a *utility function*, ν, which is a numerical function that represents the preference ordering on the outcome set R and finally by the payoff function, π, defined as the utility of the outcome of a given action and state of the environment, $\pi(x, a) = \nu[\rho(x, a)]$.

The main feature of this representation is its abstract formal nature and its generality. The author of the quotation is at pains to emphasize the latter. Its usefulness derives from the fact that whatever you can say about the problem at this level applies to all or almost all judgmental situations. The main difficulty is that it is hard to fill in the specifications for any realistic situation. The functions are messy in the extreme. The effect of this is a shift to the study of situations that are easily represented in these terms. A good example is the work on experimental games that has followed the development of game theory. There the normal form of the game plays a role that is equivalent to the scheme above. Most experimental games are direct translations of the normal form game into a real situation. This simplified class of games is in fact not paradigmatic of all games (as the normal form is, taken in generality), but has very special properties, such as being nonsequential and involving only certain special styles of reasoning. The amount that can be learned from them about, say, how people play chess, is almost nil.

None of this denies the usefulness of the representation or of the experimental work to which it gives rise. It does emphasize that a representation focusses attention and effort on those aspects of the total phenomena that are simply expressed in its terms. This is true, no matter what the ultimate theoretical reach of the representation. In the case at hand, effort focusses primarily on questions of the judgmental law. The question of the information used tends to be subordinated; the representation leading instead to identifying the states of the environment as those seen and analyzed by the external observer. Similarly the representation leads away from the consideration of the processes that might accomplish a given judgmental law. Motivationally, this representation is intimately connected with the concern for optimal decisions, and for the ways in which humans fall short of optimality. Optimality, properly considered, demands a careful statement of what is being optimized, and within what domain. The mathematical formalism of decision theory was created in large measure to permit adequate answers to such questions.

The work of Ward Edwards is very much within the decision theoretic framework. His finding in prior work that humans behave consistently, but not optimally, in a situation which admits of a complete decision-theoretic analysis, poses the problem for his paper in this volume.

Wherever in research on judgment we see a concern on the judgmental law, the situation can rather easily map into decision theory. Thus the psychophysical situation has received a good deal of treatment in these terms. The area of detection is another, where the application of the theory of mathematical signal detection, another close relative of the general framework given above, provides a clear and fruitful case.

The present paper by Paul Hoffman provides another case in point. He starts with a representation of judgments by regression equations. Working with artificially created environments (various scoring profiles) he does not face any major issue about the set of possible clues. The decision-theoretic language is not used, but there would be little difficulty in making the translation.   His concern is not, as with Ward Edwards, whether humans judge optimally. Rather, the underlying concern is with whether algorithms can do better than humans.   Or, even if they can in the area of clinical judgments (for which there seems to be some evidence), might there not be various aspects or the environment that the human can detect especially well.

Model of the Task Environment.   In complex situations, such as business judgments or personality judgments, there is great uncertainty over what information is entering into judgmental law. One may go even further and feel that if only the task environment were appropriately described, the nature of the judgment would be clear.   That is, the judgmental law is quite secondary, and amounts to doing the obvious with the information finally selected.

Thus, one is led to construct models of the task environment.   Unlike the decision theoretic representation, there is no single dominating model.   Indeed, what distinguishes this type of representation from the prior one is that the representation is developed in terms of the particular task environment of interest, and may have little generality beyond it.   A simple   example   is   the   already   mentioned   work   on   judging faces.   The unique contribution of that stream of work—the part one remembers—is its decomposition of a face into a set of components (forehead, eye region, nose region, mouth, and jaw) each of which had a set of possible values such that different   total   expressions   could   be   composed   by   combining values.   The analysis was not very deep, since the sets of values   were   simply   created   artistically   and   ad hoc.   But this is of no concern here.

A more complex example is provided by the work on chess playing programs.   One starts with a complex and difficult task, and the fact that some humans can make rapid and excellent   judgments   with   respect   to   it   (in   comparison   with   the rest of us).   Perhaps an adequate task analysis will reveal a set of relationships and items of information, such that if one takes   them   into   account   one   plays   good   chess,   and   if not (whether through ignorance or whatnot) one does not. Then the situation would be little different from that in which the peasant was considered to be a good judge of distances by his illiterate brethren   because   he   could   read   the   road   signs.   The development of chess programs, as examples of artificial intelligence with little concern for simulating human processing, is seeking for just such an analysis.

In the present volume the paper by Raymond Cattell is perhaps the purest example of worrying first about modeling the task environment. He is ultimately concerned with personality types, and judgments thereon. But, reflecting the remarks made earlier in contrasting personality judgments with those of psychophysics, he seeks first some way of structuring the environment. Only then will it be fruitful to ask how personality judgments are made.

Model of the Information Processes. If we are concerned not just with what information is used in a judgment and what relationship obtains between that information and the resulting judgment, but with how that relationship is brought about, then we need a process model. One might anticipate some side benefits as well in discovering and understanding other parameters that affect judgment, since many of these "unanticipated" effects arise because of features of the particular processes that realize judgment. That such a representation can differ from the first two—from a mathematical statement of the judgmental law or from a model of the task environment—reflects the familiar argument that structure is not determined by function.

At the level of complex decision, where issues of selection of information and its combination in ways dependent upon the nature of the task environment are paramount, the most well developed examples of process models are those that have grown up under the rubric of computer simulation of cognitive processes. One done some time ago by Clarkson will serve as an illustration (1962). The task was for a trust officer of a bank to determine what investments—that is, which stocks and how many shares—should be made for a newly formed trust amounting to a specified sum of money. This task, although it has elements of search and selection, would appear to have a large judgmental component: a stock, once it has become a candidate for attention, requires that a judgment be made as to its suitability for the account. Clarkson developed a program to simulate the behavior of the trust officer, based on detailed study of his actual decision making behavior. The resulting program is in effect a proposal not only for what information is used, but for what representations are developed and how they are processed. This is so because the program is not simply a calculating scheme to realize a judgmental law already adequately formulated in a precise notation. On the contrary, the program with its proposed information structures and processes for manipulating them comes first, and generates the judgmental law. If there were to exist another expression of this law, say stated in conventional mathematical terms, then this would stand as a discovered, simplified statement of the judgmental law generated by the proposed processes.

Ben Kleinmuntz's paper is an example of constructing process models with the underlying motivation of seeing whether machines can make the judgments better than humans. In his work on the MMPI, summarized and brought up to date here, this motivation is clear. In the new work on neurological diagnosis the goal of automation is somewhat repressed in the interests of getting an adequate process model. At least part of the reason for the difficulty of analysis of this latter task is that the features of the task environment that the neurologist responds to are unknown. In the MMPI, as in the environments used by Paul Hoffman, the task environment is clean and known.

The work on music by Herb Simon and Richard Sumner might seem to the reader an example of pure task analysis, as in the work of Cattell. But this would be a mistake. There already exists a complete representation of music (or almost so). The reorganization proposed by Simon and Sumner into a hierarchy of patterns is the first step in a proposal for how a human organizes his information about the musical environment so that he can make the various judgments required, both elementary as well as esthetic. It does assert, and this in common not only with the task environment model but also with the general Gestaltist view, that the first and biggest step is understanding how the environment is perceived—is represented internally. Most behavior flows naturally from this. Thus, this work is an example of a process model.

Model of the Embedding Process.   The natural strategy in science is to isolate the object of interest. This extends to the formulation of theories about it. In all of the above representations we focussed on the judgmental act. What else? It might be that only if you know the larger task and process in which the judgment is embedded would you finally obtain the information from which an adequate explanation would be forthcoming. That this may be more than just an abstruse scientific caution can be seen from the list of characteristics accumulated at the beginning of this introduction. There judgment had the flavor of the concluding edge of a larger process. Furthermore it was squeezed between the immediate response to a stimulus and a well defined calculation. Thus, it is a possible hypothesis that judgment as a distinct process will not be there, so to speak, when we finally understand it well enough. To put it in a somewhat more plausible form, there will exist an elementary comparison of some sort, in terms of which the behavior is differential and which serves as an identifiable locus of judgment. (The conditional transfer instruction in a computer program is an analog.) But, as in the magician's act, all the interesting properties were determined before this "judgment proper" began. And these determinations will extend a goodly ways back into the embedding process—far enough to be outside any reasonable boundary of a "judgment process." In our own work on human chess playing, for instance, there are indications that the judgment of the worth of a chess position is a much more trivial process than *a priori* informed opinion would have it (Newell and Simon, 1965).

The work by Joshua Lederberg and Edward Feigenbaum on the indentification of organic chemical molecules provides an example of this fourth model. It tackles a total problem, which is more then judgmental in nature. This can be seen from the central role played by a process for generating candidate molecules. Thus the judgmental tasks are distributed throughout the program and interwoven with other processes, which they serve. It offers an opportunity to the reader, not just to be fascinated by the project in its own right, but to ask whether in complex situations judgmental functions must always be considered in intimate relation to other nonjudgmental processes. Abstracted from the total process they may not look profound enough to carry the heavy responsibilities we often attribute to them.

There you have it: a small exercise in preparing the ground, which has led to a list of particulars that seem to characterize the phenomena under study; a list of the main types of questions to be asked of the phenomena; an external motivation or two; and some different types of representations. It is not meant to provide substantive alternatives to the pieces of scientific research that you will find in the remainder of the book. On the contrary, it is intended as a way of helping you to see how, in fact, the diversity of work here all pertains to the science of judgment.

CHAPTER 2

Ward Edwards

University of Michigan

CONSERVATISM IN
HUMAN INFORMATION PROCESSING*

EDWARDS: The purpose of this paper is to present the current status of research and theorizing about a phenomenon of human information processing that has come to be called conservatism. In order to highlight three major views about this phenomenon, I have chosen to cast this paper as an imaginary debate. The participants are Dr. Lee Roy Beach, Assistant Professor of Psychology at the University of Washington, Dr. Cameron Peterson, Assistant Professor of Psychology at the University of Michigan, and myself. I have chosen to use Lee Beach and Cam Peterson as straw men in part because they are major contributors to the research and thinking I will report, in part because they in fact hold much more sophisticated versions of the positions I will attribute to them here, and in part because I enjoy misrepresenting my friends in public. Since the versions of Lee's and Cam's positions that I will report here are somewhat fictional, while my own position is no more fictional than my positions usually are, I will probably do the real Lee Beach and Cam Peterson more than one injustice.

We start with brief statements of our three positions, followed by fuller expositions of the research on which these positions are based. The rules of this imaginary debate are very loose: each participant will speak up whenever he has something pertinent—or impertinent—to say.

My own position is very simple. An abundance of research has shown that human beings are conservative processors of fallible information. Such experiments compare human behavior with the outputs of Bayes's theorem, the formally

The research reported was supported by the Air Force Office of Scientific Research under Contract AF 49(638)-1731.

optimal rule about how opinions (that is, probabilities) should be revised on the basis of new information. It turns out that opinion change is very orderly, and usually proportional to numbers calculated from Bayes's theorem—but it is insufficient in amount. A convenient first approximation to the data would say that it takes anywhere from two to five observations to do one observation's worth of work in inducing a subject to change his opinions. A number of experiments have been aimed at an explanation for this phenomenon. They show that a major, probably the major, cause of conservatism is human misaggregation of the data. That is, men perceive each datum accurately and are well aware of its individual diagnostic meaning, but are unable to combine its diagnostic meaning well with the diagnostic meaning of other data when revising their opinions.

BEACH: I entirely agree with Ward that the conservatism phenomenon exists. But I don't agree that men are conservative processors of information. I disagree with Ward's misaggregation hypothesis. What actually happens is that men misperceive the diagnostic impact of each datum. Human information processing behavior obeys the formal rules of probability theory, and in particular Bayes's theorem. The only problem is, men fail to make the inputs to those rules correctly, and that failure produces conservative behavior. In my language, men are consistent, but not accurate. The hypothesis I am proposing could be called the misperception hypothesis.

PETERSON: I disagree with both Ward and Lee. While I agree that a large number of experiments have produced conservative behavior, many of those experiments have been so elaborate that the subjects couldn't be expected to have any idea what on earth their task was. It is easy to see why, with a clear starting position and a confusing task, subjects should not revise their opinions very much. Not all experiments have been that confusing. The simple ones, without exception till recently, have been what Ward calls bookbag and poker chip experiments. These are very special, very artificial situations; only in them can conservatism in simple tasks be found. Recently I have tried simple tasks using other kinds of situations and other kinds of data-generating processes, and have found that Bayes's theorem is a very good descriptive model of the behavior of my subjects. So I contend that the conservative behavior obtained in those experiments that obtain it, is essentially an artifact. Thus I agree with Lee that Bayes's theorem is a good descriptive model of human thought processes in information processing, and in addition argue that men perceive data-generating processes accurately, except in the very artificial bookbag and poker chip situation.

EDWARDS: There you have it. I think conservatism is caused by misaggregation, Lee thinks it is caused by misperception, and Cam thinks it is an artifact. Now let us examine the story of conservatism in some detail.

Probabilities quantify uncertainty. A probability, according to Bayesians like ourselves, is simply a number between zero and one that represents the extent to which a somewhat idealized person believes a statement to be true. The reason the person is somewhat idealized is that the sum of his probabilities for two mutually exclusive events must equal his probability that either of the events will occur. The additivity property has such demanding consequences that few real persons are able to conform to all of them. Since such probabilities describe the person who holds the opinion more than the event the opinion is about, they are called personal probabilities (see Savage, 1954).

Bayes's theorem is a trivial consequence of the additivity property, uncontroversial and agreed to by all probabilists, Bayesian and other. One way of writing it is as follows. If $P(H_A \mid D)$ is the posterior probability that hypothesis A has after datum D has been observed, $P(H_A)$ is its prior probability before datum D is observed, $P(D \mid H_A)$ is the probability that datum D will be observed if H_A is true, and $P(D)$ is the unconditional probability of datum D, then

$$P(H_A \mid D) = \frac{P(D \mid H_A)\ P(H_A)}{P(D)}.$$ (1)

$P(D)$ is best thought of as a normalizing constant, intended to make the posterior probabilities add up to one over the exhaustive set of mutually exclusive hypotheses being considered. If it must be calculated, it can be as follows:

$$P(D) = \sum_i P(D \mid H_i)\ P(H_i).$$

But more often $P(D)$ is eliminated rather than calculated. One convenient way of eliminating it is to tranform Bayes's theorem into its odds-likelihood ratio form. Consider another hypothesis, H_B, mutually exclusive of H_A, and modify your opinion about it on the basis of the same datum that changed your opinion about H_A. Bayes's theorem says

$$P(H_B \mid D) = \frac{P(D \mid H_B) \, P(H_B)}{P(D)}. \tag{2}$$

Now divide Equation 1 by Equation 2; the result is

$$\frac{P(H_A \mid D)}{P(H_B \mid D)} = \frac{P(D \mid H_A)}{P(D \mid H_B)} \cdot \frac{P(H_A)}{P(H_B)}$$

or $\qquad\qquad \Omega_1 = L \cdot \Omega_0, \tag{3}$

where Ω_1 is the posterior odds in favor of H_A over H_B, Ω_0 is the prior odds, and L is a quantity familiar to statisticians as a likelihood ratio. Equation 3 is as appropriate a version of Bayes's theorem as Equation 1, and often considerably more useful especially for experiments involving two hypotheses.

Bayesian statisticians argue that Bayes's theorem is a formally optimal rule about how to revise opinions in the light of evidence, that revision of opinion in the light of evidence is exactly what statistical inference consists of, and that therefore statistical inference should be structured around Bayes's theorem—with many consequent differences from classical statistical practice. For an elementary exposition of these ideas written for experimenting psychologists, see Edwards, Lindman, and Savage (1963). But we are not statisticians, or at any rate none of us are wearing our statistician's dunce caps today. Instead, as psychologists, we are interested in comparing the ideal behavior specified by Bayes's theorem with actual human performance.

To give you some feeling for what follows, let us try an experiment with you as subject. This bookbag contains 1000 poker chips. I started out with two such bags, one containing 700 red and 300 blue chips, the other containing 300 red and 700 blue. I flipped a fair coin to determine which one to use. Thus, if your opinions are like mine, your probability at the moment that this is the predominantly red bookbag is 0.5. Now, you sample, randomly, with replacement after each chip. In

12 samples, you get 8 reds and 4 blues. Now, on the basis of everything you know, what is the probability that this is the predominantly red bag? Clearly it is higher than 0.5. Please don't continue reading till you have written down your estimate.

If you are like a typical subject, your estimate fell in the range from 0.7 to 0.8—though the statement frequently made in the preceding paragraphs that men are conservative information processors may have biased your answer upward. If we went through the appropriate calculation, though, the answer would be 0.97. Very seldom indeed does a person not previously exposed to the conservatism finding come up with an estimate that high, even if he is relatively familiar with Bayes's theorem.

In about 1960, William L. Hays, a graduate student named Lawrence D. Phillips, and I were interested in finding discrepancies between human performance and that specified by Bayes's theorem. The simple example of the previous paragraph didn't occur to us; instead we were sure that we would need to use a fairly complex situation in order to get non-Bayesian behavior. So we used a hypothetical computerized radar system. There were 12 possible observations, 4 possible hypotheses, and so subjects had to understand and use a display of 48 different values of $P(D|H)$. Subjects worked under two conditions. In one, the subject saw a single stimulus, a dot in a sector of a radar scope; he then revised his prior probabilities over the four hypotheses on the basis of the datum by setting four levers to his posterior probability estimates, then reset the levers to 0 in preparation for the next stimulus. The second stimulus consisted of the old dot plus a new one; the subject set his levers to report the cumulative impact of both dots. And so on, until 15 dots had accumulated. In the second condition, the stimuli were shuffled, and the subject in effect started afresh with each new stimulus. To the surprise of the experimenters the prediction of Bayes's theorem that this difference in conditions should make no difference to behavior was borne out. Moreover, there was yet another condition in which each new dot was displayed alone, but the subjects were allowed to preserve their estimates from one stimulus to the next rather than resetting levers to zero after each estimate. Again, the variation in conditions made little difference to behavior.

The positive findings of the Phillips-Hays-Edwards

experiment were three in number. First, subjects were over-whelmingly conservative. Secondly, they were least conservative on the first dot, becoming more so with more dots. Finally, the sums of their probability estimates, which were not constrained, in general added up to more than 1, and increased as the subjects progressed through successive stimuli in an ordered sequence. Apparently the subjects found it easier to determine which hypothesis was favored by a stimulus, and so to increase the probability of that hypothesis, than to decide from which other hypotheses probability should be withdrawn in order to give it to the favored one.

We were notably dilatory in publishing this original conservatism experiment. Though the data were complete by 1962, the Phillips-Hays-Edwards paper didn't make it into print until 1966.

The magnitude and consistency of the conservatism finding startled us. It seemed appropriate to try much simpler tasks. So, without much faith, Phillips and I tried a pretest similar in character to the bookbag and poker chip example you tried above. To our surprise, it worked very well. Most of the current research comparing human behavior with Bayes's theorem can be traced to that pretest and the subsequent experiment.

If the proportion of red chips in the bookbag is p, then the probability of getting r red chips and $(n - r)$ blue chips in n samples with replacement in a particular order is $p^r (1 - p)^{n-r}$. So in a typical bookbag and poker chip experiment, if H_A is that the proportion of red chips is p_A and H_B is that that proportion is p_B, then the likelihood ratio is

$$L = \frac{p_A{}^r (1 - p_A)^{n-r}}{p_B{}^r (1 - p_B)^{n-r}} \tag{4}$$

Note that while Equation 4 was derived from considering the actual sequence of reds and blues in the sample, it could equally well have been derived from considering r reds and $(n - r)$ blues in any order; the binomial coefficient that represents the number of different ways one can obtain r reds in n draws appears in both numerator and denominator and thus cancels out of the likelihood ratio. This is an illustration of the likelihood principle of Bayesian statistics (see Edwards, Lindman, & Savage, 1963), which in effect says that a Bayesian need consider only the probability of the actual observation he has made, not the probabilities of other observations that he might have made but did not. This principle has sweeping impact on all statistical and nonstatistical applications of Bayes's theorem; it is the most important technical tool of Bayesian thinking.

In the special case in which $p_A = 1 - p_B$ (the symmetric binomial case), the likelihood ratio reduces to

$$L = \left(\frac{p_A}{1 - p_A} \right)^{2r-n} \tag{5}$$

Note that $2r - n = r - (n - r)$ is the difference between the number of reds and the number of blues in the sample; only that difference, and not the total number of observations, is relevant to inference in this symmetric case. Statistical tradition labels that difference successes minus failures, or $s - f$; $s - f$ is the usual independent variable of bookbag and poker chip experiments. To understand the rationale for the usual dependent variables, substitute Equation 5 into Equation 3, take logarithms and rearrange terms. The result is

$$\log L = (2r - n) \log \frac{p_A}{1 - p_A} = \log \Omega_1 - \log \Omega_0 .$$

If the subject is perfectly Bayesian, the log likelihood ratio that can be inferred by subtracting the log of the prior odds from the log of the posterior odds should be proportional to $s - f$, the independent variable. It is appropriate to plot the subject's inferred log likelihood ratio, thus calculated from his posterior odds (which in turn were calculated from his posterior probabilities if he was estimating probabilities) and the objectively appropriate prior odds, against $s - f$.

Most of the bookbag and poker chip experiments in the Michigan laboratory have used a display consisting of 48 numbered locations each containing a pushbutton, a red light, and a green light. When the button at a location is pushed, one of the lights goes on and stays on; subjects are told that this is equivalent to a sample with replacement of a chip of the corresponding color from the bookbag. The subjects are told that the program that controls the lights was prepared by sampling from a bookbag. Actually, for most experiments that program is rather carefully prepared so that the displayed sequence is appropriately representative of the bookbag, and in particular so that in each experiment samples of size n favor the untrue hypothesis appropriately often for the value of p_A being used, for all values of n.

Phillips and I (1966) investigated the effect of p_A, using sequences of 20 chips and p_A values of 0.55, 0.7, and 0.85. Subjects estimated posterior probabilities by distributing 100 white wooden discs over two troughs. Typical results of such experiments are presented in Fig. 2.1, for the 0.7 bag with various prior probabilities. Three findings, illustrated in Fig. 2.1, appeared for all subjects. First, the inferred log likelihood ratios were roughly proportional to $s - f$. Second, the prior probabilities were appropriately used; that is, the best fitting line through the data points passes through the origin. Third, subjects were conservative; the best fitting line was flatter than the line representing optimal Bayesian perform-

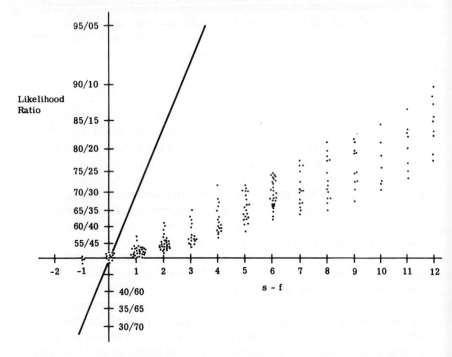

Fig. 2.1   A single subject's estimates for p_A of 0.7, expressed in inferred log likelihood ratios as a function of the difference between the number of successes and the number of failures in the sample.

ance. The finding of near-linearity of inferred log likelihood ratios with $s - f$ (or, equivalently, with Bayesian log likelihood ratios) suggests yet another dependent variable: the ratio of the slope of the best-fitting line through the subject's estimates to the slope of the Bayesian line. Peterson, Schneider, and Miller (1965) have named that ratio the accuracy ratio; they also found it more or less constant with $s - f$.

Figure 2.2 shows accuracy ratios for the Phillips-Edwards data for the three values of p_A . For the least diagnostic information, the subjects were more extreme than Bayes's theorem. (Dale has found the same thing; see Edwards, 1965.)

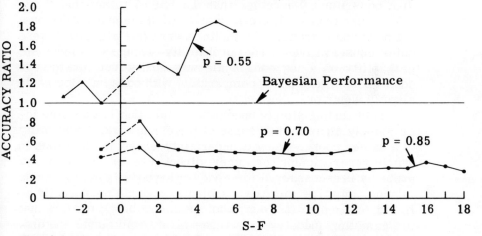

Fig. 2.2   Accuracy ratios for three values of p_A over various sample compositions.

But for information having reasonably high diagnostic value, subjects were conservative, and the accuracy ratio was nicely constant with $s - f$. Note that as diagnosticity increases, conservatism increases also. This is a standard finding of such experiments; any procedure that increases diagnosticity of the individual observation (of one chip or several) also increases conservatism. (See for example Peterson, Schneider, and Miller, 1965.)

Phillips and I, after obtaining these results, speculated that one reason for conservatism might be that subjects, knowing that the probability scale is bounded and observing that evidence might go on mounting up and up, were holding their estimates down. The obvious remedy, if so, is to use an unbounded response mode, like odds. So we ran a four-group

study.   The control group estimated probabilities by distributing 100 discs over two troughs, as before.   The verbal
odds group simply made verbal estimates of odds; we always
take odds as numbers equal to or greater than one, and therefore always accompany odds statements by statements of which
hypothesis is favored by the odds.   The odds on a log scale
group made their estimates by moving a pointer along an odds
scale which contained four log cycles, so that odds anywhere
from 1 : 1 to 10,000 : 1 could be estimated.   The fourth group
used the odds on a log scale device also, but the numbers
entered opposite the scale markings were probabilities rather
than odds (thus 0.5 rather than 1 : 1, 0.67 rather than 2 : 1,
0.80 rather than 4 : 1, etc.).   It was called the probability on a
log odds scale group.   The findings were that all groups were
quite conservative.   The probability group was most so,
probability on a log odds scale was next worst, and the two
odds groups were about comparable, with odds on a log scale
slightly superior.

This finding simply underlines a fact that has become increasingly clear in the course of Bayesian work.   Probability
is a rather poor measure of uncertainty, except in situations in
which repartitioning or other direct use of the additivity
property is necessary. Either odds or log odds is better.   Odds
is most intuitive for naive subjects, and can most easily be
linked to simple acts (e.g., choices among bets); the fact that
the gambling industry structures all its statements and displays around odds rather than probability is both recognition of
and perhaps cause of the greater intuitive value of odds.   Log
odds, uniquely among the more-or-less common metrics for
uncertainty, has the property that in that metric evidence is
additive. If opinion is measured in log odds, the amount of
change in opinion produced by a piece of evidence is independent of where the opinion was to start with. This elegant
property makes log odds uniquely convenient for Bayesian experiments.

The Phillips-Edwards data can be well fit by a simple
modification of Bayes's theorem:

$$\Omega_1 = L^c \, \Omega_0.$$

The constant c, the power to which each likelihood ratio is
raised before processing it by means of Bayes's theorem, is

the accuracy ratio. Unfortunately, it is dependent on important independent variables, including diagnosticity of the data and response metric. Still, the fact that so simple a descriptive model fits so well must be explained by any theory of conservatism.

Those are the basic experimental facts about conservatism. Now, Lee Beach will present some evidence for the misperception hypothesis. He will be followed by Cam Peterson, arguing that conservatism is mostly an artifact. I will conclude by presenting evidence for the misaggregation hypothesis. Lee?

BEACH: Thank you, Ward. Ward's presentation so far has been theoretically neutral. He has shown that people behave conservatively and that the accuracy ratio is constant as a function of $s - f$, but he has said nothing about why (except to discredit the idea that conservatism is unique to the probability response mode). The model which says that people raise each likelihood ratio to a power less than one before multiplying prior odds by it to obtain posterior odds can be interpreted in at least two ways. One is that people in fact process likelihood ratios this way; if so, they obviously misaggregate the data. But the other is that they perceive the data to start with in a way that leads to a likelihood ratio that is only the cth power of what it should be. I believe the latter to be the case, and my argument for it is relatively indirect. I will show by means of several experiments that Bayes's theorem in fact describes how people revise their prior opinions into posterior ones. If they use Bayes's theorem properly and yet are conservative, it must follow that they misperceive the diagnosticity of the data.

For years now I have been interested in probabilistic concept formation. A typical experiment goes as follows. The apparatus consists of decks of cards. Each card in the 60-card training deck has written on its back one of two words: yellow or orange. Each card has on its face a capital letter (selected from ten possibilities) and a number (selected from six possibilities). The stimuli on the face are called cues; those on the back are the concepts. No two cards contain the same combination of cues. Each subject works through the deck of cards twice, observing both faces. Then he is presented with cards from another deck. Each card contains either a single cue (e.g., capital letter) or a pair of cues. The subject estimates the probability that the card belongs to each of the classes by sliding markers along a 25-inch unmarked black metal bar. Independent variables in such experiments include the number of cues and number of possible values of each, number of concepts, number of times through the training deck, delay between training and test, nature of stimuli in the test deck, response mode, and the like.

In one series of such experiments (Beach, 1966), I made three kinds of analyses of the data. The simplest is concerned with reliability. Some test cards were presented twice: I calculated correlations between probability estimates on first and second presentations, and found them satisfyingly high, in the 0.80's and 0.90's. The next analysis is concerned with accuracy, that is, degree of resemblance between subjects' estimates and the right answer. (To calculate the right answer, I treated all cue-concept relationships as independent, even though in fact the cues were uniquely correlated, since no pattern of cues was presented twice. But the independence assumption clearly corresponded with the assumption the subjects make, and which the instructions were designed to encourage.) I calculated correlations between the right answers, calculated from Bayes's theorem, and subject's estimates. For single cues, these correlations are in the 0.30 to 0.50 range. For pairs of cues, they range from 0 to as high as 0.45, but are usually about 0.10 below the corresponding single-cue accuracies. All of these correlations are, of course, quite low. Moreover, the deviations from Bayesian values are overwhelmingly conservative.

The final and crucial data analysis is concerned with consistency. It is based on the following equation

$$\Omega\ (H_A/H_B\,|\,D_1 D_2) \propto \Omega\ (H_A/H_B\,|\,D_1)\ \Omega\ (H_A/H_B\,|\,D_2). \qquad (7)$$

To use this equation, I formed the indicated products of the single-cue posterior odds estimates and calculated the correlation between those products and the paired-cue posterior odds estimates. Such correlations are a function of the number of hypotheses being considered; they are typically in the 0.90's, but range down much lower when six hypotheses are used. (Actually the published paper (Beach, 1966) reporting this study contains an incorrect version of Equation 7 and of the analysis based on it. I have since then corrected the error, and am reporting the corrected version to you.)

These high consistencies indicate that subjects "possess a rule for revising subjective probabilities which they apply to whatever subjective probabilities they have at the moment;... whether they are accurate or inaccurate. ...The (subjects') revision rule is essentially Bayes's theorem." (Beach, 1966, p. 36). The low accuracies and conservative behavior, however, indicate that something has gone astray; of course the experiments were designed to produce low accuracy by using very scanty training. Presumably what has gone astray is subjects' perceptions of $P(D|H)$.

These high consistency coefficients say nothing whatever about misperception vs. misaggregation. What they show is that two different kinds of outputs of human information processing have the kind of relationship to one another that they should have. If Equation 6 holds, this should be true, regardless of whether conservatism is caused by misaggregation, misperception, or both.

The conclusion that men use probabilities in an internally consistent fashion is not by any means unique to me. Some unpublished experiments by Shuford indicate it. Peterson, Ulehla, Miller, Bourne, and Stilson (1965) performed three experiments, one of them Bayesian, all pointing to that conclusion.

Now, let us turn to experiments that bear more directly on the misperception hypothesis. Just to show you that what my adversaries here say is grist for my mill, I will next describe an experiment by Peterson, DuCharme, and Edwards (in press). Peterson, DuCharme, and Edwards were interested in subjective sampling distributions, that is, in subjective values of $P(D|H)$. If people are Bayesian but misperceive the diagnosticity of individual data, they will necessarily have inappropriate subjective sampling distributions. Specifically, those distributions will be flatter than they should be, if use of them in Bayes's theorem is to produce conservatism. So, in a first experiment, Peterson, DuCharme, and Edwards asked subjects to estimate sampling distributions for 0.6, 0.7, 0.8 bookbags and for all possible samples of sizes 3, 5, and 8—nine sampling distributions in all. Subjects indicated their distributions roughly at first by making marks on an appropriate set of bar graphs. After a rough estimate was completed, they applied some tests. For instance, they made sure that the modal value was on the appropriate sample, and they checked ratios between adjacent samples to make sure they seemed appropriate. After these checks, they revised their estimates if necessary until they were satisfied.

Figure 2.3 shows the results, averaged over 41 subjects. Two conclusions emerge from the figure. The first is that the performance is rather good. The second is that where it deviates from optimal performance, it deviates in the direction of conservatism; that is, low probabilities are overestimated and high ones underestimated.

But were the deviations from optimal estimation of $P(D|H)$ sufficient to explain conservatism? To find out, Peterson, DuCharme, and Edwards ran a second experiment using two tasks. First the subjects performed a probability revision task of the usual bookbag and poker chip variety, presenting the data for a given sample and bookbag all at once, rather than one chip at a time, and requiring only one revision per sample and bookbag. Second, subjects estimated subjective sampling distributions, this time by distributing 100 markers over as many troughs as there were chips in the sample being considered. (This did not require them to estimate at least 0.01; if they wanted to estimate less, they could simply write the estimate down. But above 0.01 estimates had to increase in steps of at least 0.01.) Third, subjects were taught theoretical sampling distributions, by observing sampling from a bookbag, rigged so that the eventual sampling distribution came out exactly right. Finally, they repeated the probability revision task.

The first probability revision was conservative, and the subjective sampling distribution estimates were like those in Fig. 2.3. To calculate Bayes's theorem on the basis of the subjective sampling distributions, Peterson, DuCharme, and Edwards assumed that there was no color bias, and that consequently $p(3 \text{ reds and } 5 \text{ blues} | p = 0.7) = p(3 \text{ blues and } 5 \text{ reds} | p = 0.3)$. This assumption permits calculation of the necessary likelihood ratios. Figure 2.4 shows the result. The accuracy ratios calculated with the theoretical binomial values in the denominator and subjects' inferred log likelihood ratios in the numerator show the usual increase of conservatism with increasing sample size and increasing diagnosticity of each datum. When values from the subjects' estimated sampling distributions were substituted for the theoretical binomial values, accuracy ratios showed no conservatism. The effect of diagnosticity of the individual datum is much reduced, and the effect of sample size is reversed. Peterson, DuCharme, and Edwards speculate that the over-Bayesian performance at

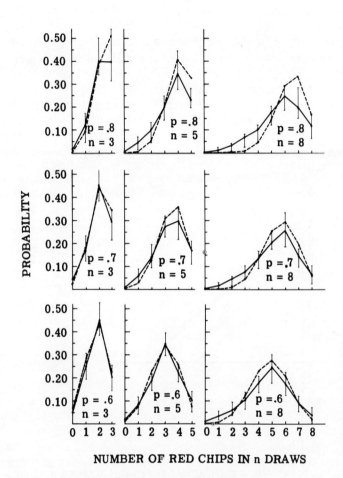

NUMBER OF RED CHIPS IN n DRAWS

Fig. 2.3 Sampling distributions estimated by subjects compared with corresponding theoretical values. Dashed lines connect theoretical points, solid lines connect medians of estimates, and vertical lines show the interquartile range of the estimates. The values of p and n refer to the probability of drawing a single red chip and the total number of chips in the sample, respectively.

31

larger sample sizes is artifactual, caused by the difficulty, with the response mode used, of estimating probabilities between 0.01 and 0.02. (Of course, the larger the sample size, the smaller the probabilities of unlikely samples.) In short, the subjective sampling distributions nicely account for the conservative posterior probabilities, and would do even better except for the artifact.

One feature of the Peterson, DuCharme, and Edwards experiment didn't work out so well. The training on optimal subjective sampling distributions in phase 3 of the experiment was supposed to reduce the conservatism of subjective sampling distributions and so to reduce the conservatism of posterior probabilities collected in phase 4. Unfortunately, the phase 4 posterior probability estimates were almost as conservative as the phase 1 estimates had been. For that reason, Gloria

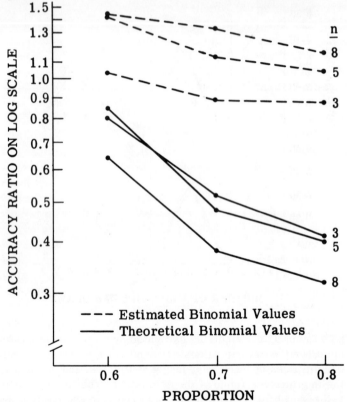

Fig. 2.4   Median accuracy ratio as a function of population proportion (p_A) and sample size (n).

Wheeler and I, in an as-yet-unpublished experiment, set out to repeat and improve on the Peterson, DuCharme, and Edwards experiment. Uniquely in the bookbag and poker chip literature (except for an early experiment by Peterson and Miller) we used asymmetric hypotheses; one bookbag had 80% red chips and the other had 40% red chips. Only samples of size 8 were used. Subjects estimated subjective sampling distributions by distributing 100 markers over 9 troughs (we also permitted written estimates of less than 0.01, but few were made). After they had made their initial sampling distribution estimates, they were trained by a betting procedure. They were told that they would be shown a series of samples that the experimenter had randomly drawn from the urns after flipping a coin each time. After seeing a sample they were to bet on which urn it was drawn from by selecting a pair of payoffs from a list provided to them. This list was prepared using Toda's (1963) quadratic payoff scheme, which is so designed that for each probability a different bet is optimal. Thus choice of a bet can be interpreted as corresponding to a probability estimate. If the urn that they bet on actually was the source of the sample they would receive the high payoff in the pair, otherwise they would receive the low payoff. After they made their bets the experimenter told them which urn was correct. The sequence of urns and of samples from each urn was carefully prearranged to display the correct sampling distributions over the 200 samples used. At intervals during this training process, the subject reestimated subjective sampling distributions.

The results are easily summarized. Before training, the posterior probabilities inferred from the flat estimated sampling distributions are consistent with the conservative revised posterior probabilities inferred from the choices among bets. Training decreased conservatism. After training, the more veridical estimated sampling distributions for those subjects who were more veridical were consistent with the less conservative revised probabilities.

These results supplement those of Peterson, DuCharme, and Edwards by showing that subjective sampling distributions are consistent with subjective probability revisions before and also after training, and that training changed both toward increased accuracy.

I contend that the flattened subjective sampling distributions found by both Peterson, DuCharme, and Edwards and

Wheeler and myself clearly indicate that subjects misperceive the diagnostic impact of the data, while the consistencies among various kinds of probability estimates found in all three studies I have reported show that men, operating as intuitive statisticians, are able to conform quite well to the various internal consistency requirements of probability theory, including Bayes's theorem.

EDWARDS: Thank you, Lee. Before we go on to Cam Peterson, I would like to make a couple of comments about these experiments. I quite agree with Lee Beach that the experiments he reviewed show that men conform well to the internal consistency requirements of probability theory, including Bayes's theorem. Of course, this conformity is not unlimited. I note that Lee did not ask his subjects to estimate the probability that a single chip, sampled from a bookbag with 70% red chips, would be red. I assume his reason for not doing so is that he expects, as I do, that the subject would look at him pityingly and answer 0.7.[1] And yet in such experiments, subjects are conservative. Consistency cannot be unlimited; something is slipping somewhere.

A more important comment from the point of view of the misaggregation hypothesis is that both the Peterson, Du-Charme, and Edwards experiment and the Wheeler and Beach experiment deal with already-aggregated data. The subjects are given a 50-50 prior, see a single sample consisting of three or five or eight chips, revise their opinions once, and then start over again. All that these two experiments show, then, is that subjective sampling distributions based on already-aggregated data are conservative, sufficiently so to be consistent with conservative posterior probabilities based on those data. They say nothing about whether the conservatism is caused by misperception of the diagnostic impact of the data, or by misaggregation. They simply show that whichever of these processes (or both) may be causing the conservatism, it causes it equally substantially for both kinds of distributions.

These findings do present a problem for the simple model of conservatism specified by Equation 6, which says that subjects raise each likelihood ratio to a power less than 1 before

---

[1]Slovic and Lichtenstein (unpublished) have recently tried exactly this experiment. This prediction about its result turns out to be quite wrong.

processing it.   In these experiments, subjects estimated $P(D|H)$, not likelihood ratios.   It would be tempting to suppose that they flatten their $P(D|H)$distribution by raising each Bayesian $P(D|H)$ to a power less than 1. Simply raising each $P(D|H)$ value to power less than 1 would not, however, produce a proper sampling distribution; it would be necessary to renormalize.   And the "likelihood" ratio formed by taking the ratio of these renormalized $P(D|H)^c$ values will not except by coincidence be equal to the number obtained by raising the original likelihood ratio to the power c for the Wheeler-Beach situation, though it will for the Peterson-DuCharme-Edwards situation.   Thus that model predicts that subjective sampling distributions should not be able to predict conservative posterior probability revisions, though subjective likelihood ratios might.   But since the prediction from subjective sampling distributions is far from perfect, a more detailed data analysis could still vindicate the model.   No such analysis has yet been performed.   It should be.

To do an experiment that really speaks to the misaggregation vs. misperception question, it would be necessary to obtain subjective sampling distributions (or subjective likelihood ratios, or both) for single data—to do something the equivalent of asking a subject how likely he is to get a red chip from a 70% red bookbag.   Cam, you planned just such an experiment.   Will you tell us about it?

PETERSON: Thank you, Ward.   I did indeed plan such an experiment—but never carried it out. And neither you nor Lee will like the reason why.

Binomial experiments are inappropriate for studying subjective sampling distributions, for the reasons Ward has explained.   So the obvious thing to do is to use a different data-generating process, and the obvious one to turn to is the normal distribution. So Wes DuCharme and I designed an experiment based on two normal distributions having the same variance but different means. First, we set out to exhibit conservatism in this situation.

In order to communicate well with our subjects, we used heights of men and women as our data.   In our first experiment, we displayed two overlapping normal distributions for heights of men and of women, using essentially the correct information.   We had two conditions.   In one, we would select a sex, with 1 : 1 prior odds, sample one height from it, and then ask the subjects to revise their odds (*not* probability) about whether males or females had been sampled from. In the other condition, we did the same thing except that we sampled four heights, rather than one, from the chosen population; the subjects revised their odds after each height. Figure 2.5 shows the results for the independent trials. The line is perfect Bayesian performance; it is rare indeed to see so good a fit of model to data, even for descriptive models. A plot of the results for trial 1 of the four-trial condition looks exactly the same. A plot for trials 2, 3, and 4 is contained in Fig. 2.6. While quality of performance has obviously gone way down, the problem is not one of conservatism; it is just variance.

This finding distressed us. There seemed little point in trying to explain conservatism by means of conservative subjective sampling distributions if we could find no conservatism. But on reflection, it occurred to us that maybe the difficulty was that we displayed the sampling distributions continuously to the subjects. Their optimal response is to estimate the ratio of the heights of the ordinates at the point of the datum, for single data, and this is apparently what they did. The obvious cure, if they have simply turned the task into a graph-reading task, is to take away the graph. So we repeated the experiment without

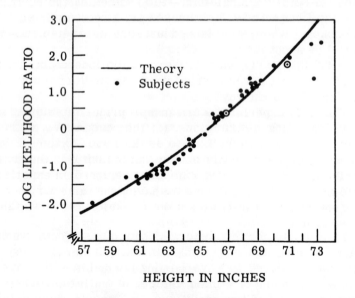

HEIGHT IN INCHES

Fig. 2.5   Theoretical and inferred log likelihood ratios for independent, single trial estimates as a function of the sampled heights.

the display; only the height equally likely to belong to a man or a woman was displayed. Figure 2.7 shows the results for the independent trials. The curve through the data was a running average. Here at last is some conservatism—but not very much. The first trial of the four-trial sequences fits the same running average equally well. The second, third, and fourth trials also fit that function, but with a great deal more variance. The amount of conservatism found is not nearly enough to justify using this situation for an experiment on subjective sampling distributions.

This experiment climaxed a series of studies that have found relatively small amounts of conservatism. I cannot report on them all. But one of especially substantial interest was concerned with beta distributions, and was done by Edwards, Tom Scopp, and I. The beta distribution is conjugate to binomial observations. That is, if your prior opinions about the proportion of blue chips in a bookbag are described by a beta distribution, which is a smooth and (except for one special case) single-peaked distribution over the interval from 0 to 1, then your posterior opinions should also be described by a beta

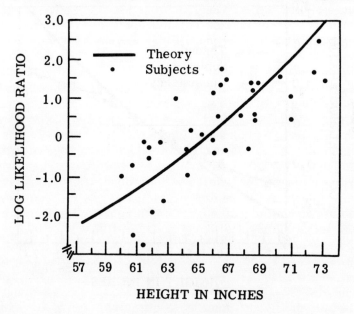

Fig. 2.6   Theoretical and inferred log likelihood ratios for trials 2, 3, and 4 as a function of the sampled heights.

distribution. The beta distribution is described by two parameters, which I shall call b and y. (I use these symbols because
the chips used in this experiment were blue and yellow.) When
both b and y are one, the distribution is uniform over the 0-to-
1 interval. A formally optimal Bayesian would simply add 1 to
b each time a blue chip was sampled and 1 to y each time a
yellow chip was sampled. The resulting beta would become increasingly peaked, with the peak located very near to $b/(b + y)$.

In our experiment, we displayed a beta distribution on a
cathode ray tube attached to a PDP-1 computer. The subject
controlled two springloaded three-position toggle switches.
Normally they were in the middle position and the display did
not change. Pressing the left key up increased b at the rate of
2 units per second; pressing it down decreased it at that same
rate until it hit its minimum of 1. The right key did the same
thing for y. Of course the subject knew nothing about beta-
distributions or b or y; he simply observed the display changing in the height and location of its peak as he operated the
keys.   He observed successive samples from a bookbag,

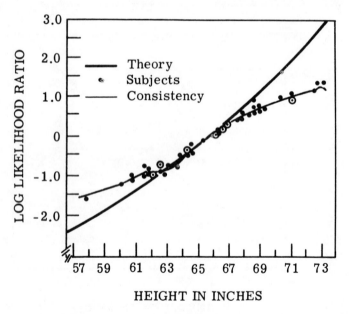

Fig. 2.7   Theoretical and inferred log likelihood ratios for independent trial estimates without the display as a function of the sampled
heights.

changing the display after each sample until it represented his current opinion about how likely each possible percentage of yellow in the bookbag was to be the true one. The main idea used in instructing him about this is that the ratio of any two ordinates of the beta should be the betting odds as between those two possible percentages of yellow. When he was satisfied with the revised beta, he pressed a button, whereupon the computer recorded his values of b and y, changed the displayed trial number, and changed the slide on which all samples to date were displayed for a new one containing one more sample.

The data analysis for this experiment cannot be as simple as for the two-hypothesis binomial experiments. One concept useful in expressing the total diagnostic impact of the data is that of inferred sample size. If the subject were perfectly Bayesian, then it should be true that $b_s + y_s - 2 = n$, where b_s and y_s are the subjects' current estimates of b and y, and n is the actual number of chips in the sample. The ratio of inferred sample size to actual sample size is somewhat similar to an accuracy ratio. Figure 2.8 shows that ratio for one of the sequences used, one for which the eventual proportion of yellow chips in the bag was 0.52. The results for the sequence in which that proportion was 0.24 look almost identical, except for a little less early conservatism. Clearly the subject starts out conservative, but is essentially optimal by the end of the 48-sample sequence. Figure 2.9 shows the same thing for the third sequence, where the eventual proportion of yellow chips was 0.94. Here there was no conservatism at all. Another way of looking at the data is to plot b_s and $b_s + y_s$ as a function of samples; Figure 2.10 does so for the 0.52 sequence. The data are conservative, but not very. And they are still less so for the other two sequences of samples. Still another data analysis compares the subjects' means, given by $b_s \mid (b_s + y_s)$, with the Bayesian means. The means for the 0.52 sequence are exactly Bayesian; the means for the 0.24 and 0.94 sequences are nearer the 0.50 value than they should be. But the discrepancy is seldom as large as 0.05, and it gets smaller as the experiment progresses.

This is impressively good performance—conservative, but not very. Ward is dissatisfied with this conclusion, and points out that the effect of the controls on the display varies depending on what beta parameters are in use at the moment. When b and y are small, the display changes very rapidly; when

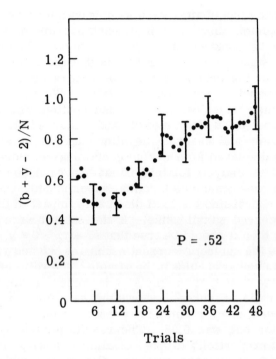

Fig. 2.8   Ratio of inferred sample size to actual sample size as a function of trials for the sequence with final p of 0.52.

both are large, it changes quite slowly. To produce a perceptible change at all at large values of b and y, the subject must operate his switch for a comparatively long time, thus behaving less conservatively. The obvious solution is to put the rate at which the display parameters and therefore the display change under the subject's control. We are revising the controls and computer program to make this possible. But it seems quite clear to me that the conservatism found here is much smaller in extent than the results of the typical bookbag and poker chip experiment would lead one to expect.

A number of other experiments have also found little or no conservatism. In their very extensive program of research on Bayesian information processing systems at Ohio State University, Schum and his collaborators, using a very highly trained crew of subjects, have found little or no conservatism in complex multinomial situations. (For a typical report, see Schum, Goldstein, and Southard, 1966.) Unpublished studies by

Gordon Pitz and Sarah Lichtenstein have found little conservatism.

A good many other studies have found conservatism only in estimates based on the second and subsequent data in a sequence. Swensson and I did an experiment in which we allowed the subjects to infer the composition of one bookbag by observing samples before asking them whether that bookbag or its complement was generating another set of samples. Subjects were essentially Bayesian on the first probability estimate of each sequence of samples; only for later samples in the sequence were they conservative. Phillips, Hays, and Edwards (1966) found the same thing. There is some suggestion of the same finding in the original Phillips-Edwards data that Ward has reported to you.

Peterson and Phillips (1966) did an experiment on human estimation of credible intervals (the Bayesian version of confidence intervals.) Their results were inconclusive; the

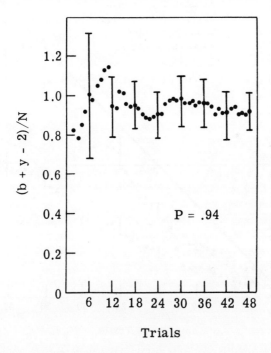

Fig. 2.9   Ratio of inferred sample size to actual sample size as a function of trials for the sequence with final p of 0.94.

estimated credible intervals were very close to the corresponding Bayesian ones, but intervals estimated by a theoretical Bayesian subject who requires two data to do one datum's worth of work are also very close to the optimal Bayesian values.

One way of interpreting these findings would be to question verbal estimates of odds or probabilities as a way of reporting on subjective uncertainty. Almost all experiments in this tradition use such verbal estimates. Yet subjects typically feel

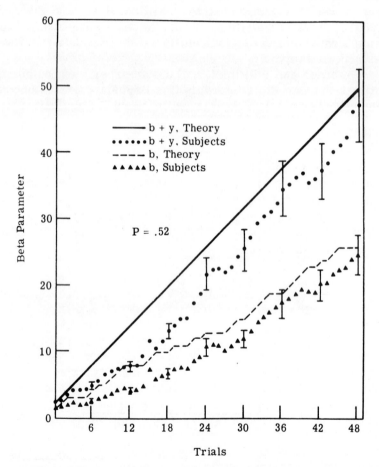

Fig. 2.10 Subject's estimates of the beta parameters b and $b + y$ and the theoretical values as a function of trials for the sequence with final p of 0.52.

very uncomfortable when asked to translate their uncertainty into numbers. Schum, Goldstein, and Southard (1966) have shown that when people accumulate experience with probability estimates, their performance improves; unfortunately, it is difficult to separate the effect of experience with probability estimation from the effect of experience with the data-generating process. Beach and Phillips (in press) have done an experiment in which subjects indicated judgments of probability based on experienced relative frequencies. Direct numerical judgments and probabilities inferred from choices among bets were compared with the relative frequencies; all three agreed very well. This study is in conflict with the idea that verbal estimates are unsatisfactory responses. But the frequent finding in inference experiments that the first estimate is Bayesian, while subsequent estimates are less so, suggests that troubles may arise in related sequences of verbal estimates, especially when the relation is specified by Bayes's theorem; the Beach and Phillips experiment is irrelevant to this possibility.

All in all, the picture is confusing. That conservatism can be found in simple symmetric binomial experiments is clear. That it can be found in fairly complicated multinomial experiments is somewhat less clear, but the Phillips-Hays-Edwards data make me believe it, in spite of the Ohio State results. But no one has established that it can be obtained on the first trial with unaggregated data. And in a lot of experiments where conservative performance is obtained, there is much less of it than the Phillips-Edwards data would lead us to expect.

Tentatively, I conclude that conservatism is an artifact. It occurs in very complex situations like the Phillips-Hays-Edwards experiment and the Beach (1966) experiment, unless the subjects are so well trained that they no longer find the situation complex, as in the experiment by Schum, Goldstein, and Southard (1966). But when things are simple, it never occurs at all. When things are made complicated by compelling the subject to deal with more than one datum, whether simultaneously or sequentially, it appears in some studies, especially the symmetric binomial studies, but not in others.

If this argument is right, the misaggregation and misperception hypotheses are both beside the point, though some color of meaning remains in the misaggregation hypothesis; I agree that things become more difficult after the first datum.

And if this hypothesis is right, fancy information processing systems designed to correct for human conservatism are also beside the point. I imagine Ward will want to comment on that.

EDWARDS: I am somewhat confused by Cam's contention that people become conservative when things get complicated. The whole point of the symmetric bookbag and poker chip experiment is that it is as simple as an experiment can get and still embody Bayes's theorem in a meaningful way. And although a number of experiments do show that conservatism is worse after many samples than after one, it is also true that most bookbag and poker chip experiments produce markedly conservative behavior on the very first draw.

I am puzzled by the absence of conservatism in the normal distribution experiment, and by the finding of less conservatism than might have been expected in the beta distribution experiment. The normal experiment may have included an artifact. Only one separation between means was studied, and the data were explicitly numerical. The subjects may simply have been judging the ratio of distances from the means, which would lead to rather optimal behavior for the region between the two means and not too close to either. At any rate....

PETERSON: Just a moment, Ward. One of my spies reported that idea to me, so I plotted that model against the normal data. Your distance judgment model disagrees with Bayes's theorem at all points but one, of course. And every data point lies closer to Bayes's theorem than it does to that distance judgment model.

EDWARDS: Ouch! Well, I still distrust those heights as stimuli. We plan to replicate the normal experiment using nonnumerical stimuli and various separations of the means. Cam already mentioned that I believe the increase in optimality as a function of trials in the beta experiment is artifactual, caused by the fact that the display responds only sluggishly to changes in the beta parameters at high values of those parameters.

As for your objection to verbal probability or odds estimates as a response mode, Cam, I am curious about what response mode you would prefer. Suppose, for example, that the experiment by Beach and Phillips comparing verbal estimates with choice among bets had not revealed good agreement between the two response modes. Which would you have preferred?

PETERSON: The one that came closer to the objectively correct answer.

EDWARDS: That seems reasonable. And yet why do you suppose that the answer that is objectively more nearly correct is also a better representation of what is going on inside the subject's head?

Some decision theorists feel that economic behavior is the focus of decision theory, and so would always prefer choice among bets to other response modes. Yet the inference of personal probabilities from choices among bets requires a long, tortuous chain of reasoning based on the assumption that men maximize expected value—an assumption well known to be false. The interpretation of personal probabilities from verbal estimates requires only the assumption, time-honored in psychophysics, that men can and will tell the truth about their experiences.

PETERSON: It also requires the assumption that men know what their experience of uncertainty is like sufficiently well to be able to tell the truth about it.

EDWARDS: I doubt that the experience of uncertainty is any more vague than the experience, for example, of the loudness of a multicomponent tone.

PETERSON: If all response modes agreed with one another and with Bayes's theorem, then there would be no problem. If response modes disagreed with one another and with Bayes's theorem, and were internally inconsistent to boot, again there would be no problem; we would simply conclude that people are no good and go study something else. But the available evidence indicates that at least one response mode, verbal estimation, is internally consistent, and is sometimes also consistent with Bayes's theorem. The occasions when it is not consistent with Bayes's theorem could be explained as failures of Bayes's theorem to describe the internal processes, as you and Lee in different ways believe, or as failures of the response mode to report accurately on the internal processes, as I believe. Eventually, I hope to show that the situations in which Bayes's theorem fails to predict responses are also the situations in which different response modes disagree, and that the situations in which people are Bayesian are the situations in which the response modes agree also. Since I don't have the data to back this claim as yet, I must fall back on the assertion that nothing in the data as yet available forces the conclusion that this view is false. I might add that unpublished research by you and Jay Russo shows that in information purchase situations people behave very reasonably in their decisions about whether or not to buy information, while making conservative probability estimates that, if one took them seriously, would lead to the prediction that they would buy much more information than they do.

EDWARDS: I can't offer any evidence against your position, Cam, though I don't share it. But I do have some evidence to offer against Lee's misperception hypothesis. As you know, the crucial experiment to discriminate between the misperception and misaggregation hypotheses would be one in which judgments of the diagnostic impact of a single datum are compared with judgments of the posterior probability distribution produced by a sequence of data, and the difficulty has been that of finding a data-generating process that produces data whose diagnostic impacts are sufficiently ambiguous to be worth judging, and yet in which conservative posterior probabilities can be obtained. Two such experiments have been done, and I will conclude this debate by reporting them.

The first experiment is a very large one, intended to demonstrate the merit of a Probabilistic Information Processing system, or *PIP*. This is the "fancy information processing system designed to correct for human conservatism" that Cam mentioned. *PIP* is an idea about how to design man-machine systems that must process information for the purpose of reaching a conclusion about what state the world is in. Examples of settings in which such information processing must be done include medical diagnosis, military command (in which a commander may need to determine whether or not he is under attack, and if so, what his opponent's plan is), and business management (for example, in the case of a businessman deciding whether or not to manufacture a new product). The idea of *PIP* is much too complicated to explain in detail here. For recent expositions of it, see Edwards, Lindman, and Phillips (1965), or Edwards (1966). The essence of it is that the task of diagnostic information processing can be divided into two classes of subtasks. One class of subtasks consists of the judgment of the diagnostic impact of an individual datum on a single hypothesis or pair of hypotheses. For the verbal, qualitative kinds of data and hypotheses that characterize many real diagnostic settings, this seems to be a task necessarily done by men, the more expert the better. But the second class of subtasks is the aggregation of these separate diagnostic impacts across data and across hypotheses into a picture of how all the hypotheses currently stand in the light of all available data. This aggregation task is readily mechanized by means of Bayes's theorem, if the diagnostic impacts of the individual data are judged in the form of $P(D|H)$ values or likelihood ratios. (In most situations, though not all, judgments of likelihood ratios are clearly preferable, for formal reasons, to judgment of $P(D|H)$.)

About fifteen collaborators and I were interested in finding out whether PIP works or not. So we designed an imaginary but elaborate world of 1975. In that world we listed six hypotheses that subjects were to consider, specified three data sources (the Ballistic Missile Early Warning System, a reconnaissance satellite system, and the intelligence system) that provided data bearing on these hypotheses, and designed four information processing systems to process the data. The four systems were named PIP, POP, PEP, and PUP. In PIP, the subjects estimated five likelihood ratios per datum. One of the six hypotheses was "Peace will continue to prevail" and the other five were various possible wars; the five pairings of a war with peace specified the five likelihood ratios to be estimated. The other three information processing systems all had in common that the subject estimated posterior odds or probabilities or similar posterior quantities; thus in PIP the computer aggregated the data by means of Bayes's theorem, while in all three other systems the subjects had to aggregate the data in their heads. To help them do this, the subjects in POP, PEP, and PUP had their estimates after the nth datum available when they considered the $(n + 1)$th datum, so they only needed to modify those estimates affected by the datum.

There were a total of 18 scenarios, with 60 data items per scenario. All data items except for those from the Ballistic Missile Early Warning System were in the form of short paragraphs. The 34 subjects were exhaustively trained in the characteristics of the world, the hypotheses, the three data sources, and the information processing system each was to operate.

Since PIP was clearly best and POP was next best, I shall present only the comparison between them. (PUP was third best, and PEP, the nearest we could get to how such information processing is done now, was worst.) Figure 2.11 shows the final odds, after the 60th datum in each scenario, in favor of each war as compared with peace for PIP and for POP. The two most important things to note about the figure are that the two groups agree very well qualitatively (the correlation between them is 0.895), but they disagree quantitatively. PIP is much more sensitive to data than POP; the same scenario that will lead PIP to be very sure of peace or of some war will lead POP to be much less sure. To put it another way, PIP is much less conservative than POP—presumably because in POP, the subjects must aggregate the data, while in PIP, the subjects judge the diagnostic impact of each datum separately and Bayes's theorem does the aggregating.

You should note also that both axes on Fig. 2.11 are logarithmically spaced. If you translate the difference in efficiency back into odds, the dramatic difference between PIP and POP becomes apparent. For example, calculating from the regression line, if a scenario led PIP to give 99 : 1 odds in favor of

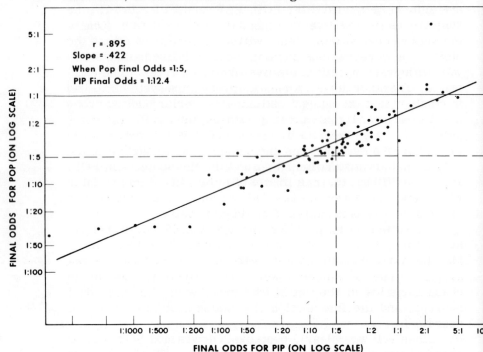

Fig. 2.11   Final odds in favor of war for POP vs. PIP plotted on log scales.

some war over peace, POP would give only 4 : 1 odds in favor of that war over peace.

The misperception hypothesis cannot possibly explain this discrepancy between PIP and POP. The PIP subjects estimate the diagnostic impact of each datum separately; the POP subjects must aggregate in their heads—and do so quite conservatively. Since no model of the data-generating process is available, it is impossible to say what the right posterior odds are. But the difference between PIP and POP is clearly caused by a difference in the aggregation process.

Larry Phillips, one of the collaborators in this experiment, was concerned about the fact that no model of the data-generating process was available and so it was not possible to say with certainty whether PIP or POP was more nearly right. So for his Ph. D. thesis he compared PIP with POP in a situation in which a model of the data-generating process was available, it was meaningful to ask for a likelihood ratio estimate for a single datum, and the POP procedure produced conservative estimates. His subjects were the editors of the University of Michigan student newspaper. He took each editor's editorials for a semester, counted the first two letters and the last two letters of each word of each editorial, and thus for each editor prepared a bookbag full of beginning bigrams and a bookbag full of ending bigrams. For the PIP task, he took certain bigrams, and asked an editor to estimate (for his own bookbags only) the likelihood ratio, taken with the beginning-bag hypothesis in the numerator and the ending-bag hypothesis in the denominator, associated with each bigram. For the POP task, he prepared a sequence of bigrams sampled from one of the bookbags, and asked the editor, as he worked through the sequence, to estimate the posterior odds that it was the beginning, not the ending, bag being sampled from. Much care was devoted to preliminary training of the editors, and likelihood ratio estimates were collected twice, once before and once after posterior odds estimates.

A problem in data analysis arose because all judgments, for both PIP and POP, were biased in favor of the beginning bag. This is probably because it is much easier, for example, to think of words that begin with re than to think of words that end in re, even though re is more common as an ending than as a beginning; we are accustomed to tagging words by their beginnings, not endings, when we, for example, look them up in a dictionary. However, it is possible to correct for such biases. Figure 2.12 shows the results after such a correction. The veridical odds, calculated from the actual bigram counts, are most extreme. Next come the odds calculated from the second set of likelihood ratio estimates. Next come the odds calculated from the first set of likelihood ratio estimates. And, closest to the middle and therefore most conservative, are the directly estimated posterior odds. If we believe these data (and I do), though PIP is considerably less conservative than POP, it is still too conservative—but PIP estimates improve with practice.

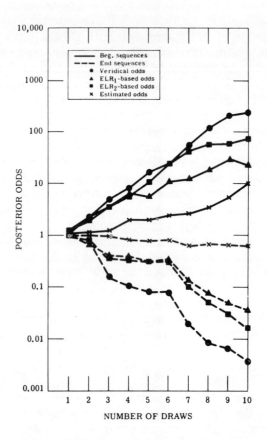

Fig. 2.12   Median posterior odds, across subjects, in favor of the beginning bookbag as a function of number of draws.

In both of these experiments, if subjects estimate likelihood ratios and Bayes's theorem does the aggregating, the result is much less conservative than if subjects aggregate the
data in their heads. So whether or not subjects underestimate
the diagnostic impact of the data, it seems clear that they aggregate data conservatively. The spirit of parsimony would in-
vite us to accept the misaggregation hypothesis and to reject
the misperception hypothesis until more evidence is found for
it.

BEACH: Ward, doesn't the fact that in Fig. 2.12 both PIP-
based posterior odds were conservative indicate that subjects
were also underestimating the diagnostic value of each datum?

EDWARDS: Yes, that is right. But the situation is complicated somewhat by the bias correction. The data aren't quite
that pretty before the bias is removed. Still, I agree with the
spirit of your comment. I would give long posterior odds that
we will end up concluding that both the misperception and the
misaggregation hypotheses are true. I do believe, though, that
misaggregation contributes considerably more to conservatism than does misperception.

I wish that I could conclude this paper with the comfortable
feeling that I understand the issues discussed in it. But I don't,
and I have no option but to confess my confusion. Misaggregation seems well-established. Misperception is less well-
established, but is probably there. But I have no clear
demonstration of the relative contribution each makes to
conservatism, and no idea what the extent of each contribution
depends on. And I can give only the sketchiest exploration of
when subjects will be quite conservative, when they will be
slightly conservative, and when they won't be conservative at
all.

Of course my confusion is your opportunity. Poker chips
are cheap, and the surface of this kind of research has barely
been scratched. Why don't you settle these questions?

Note: An error in the computer program used in analyzing the data
from the normal   distribution experiment described on pp. 36-37
was discovered too late to correct the discussion or the figure on p. 37.
The corrected data analysis shows that all results from Trials 2, 3,

and 4 of that experiment, regardless of display, show substantial conservatism, but less than what is found in typical symmetric binomial experiments. The conclusion is that men are conservative information aggregators is thus further strengthened.

CHAPTER 3

Paul J. Hoffman

Oregon Research Institute

CUE-CONSISTENCY AND CONFIGURALITY
IN HUMAN JUDGMENT*

INTRODUCTION

In its most general sense the judgment problem is the problem of arriving at an adequate characterization of a presumed cognitive process by which the identifiable characteristics of objects become synthesized, eventuating in an observable response. In a more formal sense, the judgment problem can be described as the problem of finding an adequate transformation which will map multidimensional stimuli onto a response dimension. The adequacy of a given transformation rule may be evaluated according to the usual and well-established scientific criteria for the testing and evaluation of a theory. The transformation rule may never be said conclusively to exemplify the cognitive process it is supposed to represent (cf. Hoffman 1960), but may be assessed in terms of parsimony, predictive accuracy, construct validity, etc., and revised or embellished as broader degrees of generality of the phenomena are included within the theoretical framework.

The establishment of general laws seems to require, at the outset, the development of valid and parsimonious principles of very limited scope, and under carefully controlled conditions. The need for controls necessarily limits the generality of the phenomena under investigation. Often, the experimental procedures required for the establishment of first principles are such as to demand the collection of data under quite artificial circumstances. Progress in the advancement of knowledge is then measured in terms of the extent to which principles

This research was supported by National Institute of Mental Health Grant MH-04439-08.

established within the controlled and artificial framework can be shown to have validity in a broader context. Frequently this form of generalization can be accomplished only after extending the theoretical system. For example, a control condition may be relaxed, introducing an additional source of variation. This may be compensated for if the predictive system is made to include functions which describe the effects of the new variable.

Judgmental research at Oregon Research Institute has followed this type of evolutionary pattern. The original studies were conducted within a carefully controlled framework. Of primary interest was the establishment of first principles concerning the covariation of judgmental responses with selected cue-characteristics of objects. These early studies therefore adopted a standard set of stimulus materials—a set of uniformly constructed profiles containing uniformly scaled values on a uniform set of dimensions or scales. Further, the response required was a rating along a standardized scale, and the testing was carried out under rigorously controlled conditions.

Typical of this approach are studies described by Hammond and Summers (1965); Hoffman (1960); Knox and Hoffman (1962); Martin (1957); Todd (1954); Uhl and Hoffman (1961). These investigations of the human judgment process utilize linear regression techniques, for the most part, and the general paradigm or model is considered by Hammond (1955) to be an analogue or derivative of probabilistic functionalism as described by Brunswik (1949). The general procedure in these studies has been to provide subjects with quantified multivariate information to which they respond by designating a category or value along a judgmental scale or dimension. In early studies at ORI, for example, subjects were asked to judge *Intelligence* from plotted values on nine predictor variables: High School Rating, Status Scale, Percent Self-support, English Effectiveness, Responsibility, Mother's Education, Study Habits, Emotional Anxiety, and Credit Hours Attempted; or to judge *Sociability* from values on eight of the scales from the Edwards Personal Preference Schedule: Deference, Exhibition, Affiliation, Succorance, Dominance, Abasement, Change, and Heterosexuality. Figure 3.1 illustrates a typical stimulus for this task.

On the basis of judgments made in response to 100 or so profiles presented during an experiment, a regression equation

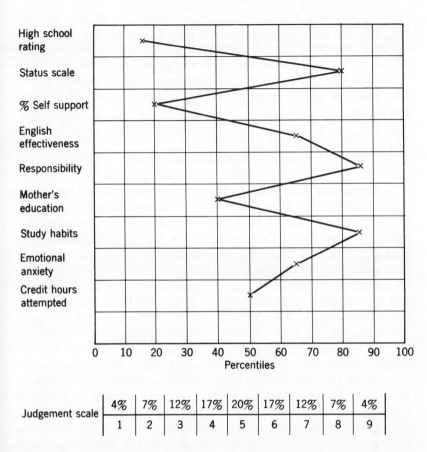

Fig. 3.1 A sample profile from which judgments of diagnosticians are made.

can be computed for each subject or "judge." Thus the set of profiles constitutes a set of multidimensional stimuli or predictor variables, and the subject's own judgments constitute the dependent variable. With certain technical limitations, which we shall not consider here, the regression equation describes the judgment process and provides a good first approximation to the judge's weighting of each of the predictors. The square of the multiple correlation (R^2) is a measure of the precision by which a linear combination of the variables, weighted by parameters that have been uniquely estimated for each judge, can account for the variance of his own judgments. The multidimensional stimuli were initially randomly selected sets of scale scores of actual students or

mental patients, and were administered in the same sequence
to each subject (judge) performing in our experiments. The
specific multidimensional structure of the data was considered
of importance only in two senses: (a) that it be "representative" of some denotable and familiar population, and (b) that it
be invariant from judge to judge and from experiment to experiment.

ILLUSTRATIVE RESULTS

There are many things which can be said about regression
approaches to the study of judgment, some critical, some con-
structive, and some practical. Time does not permit a detailed discussion of this topic, which is, after all, beyond the
major purpose of this paper. But, it should be said that these
procedures do offer much that is of immediate practical value
to the diagnostician or clinician who finds himself in an in-
stitutional setting or in private practice. For regardless of
the theoretically interesting and important basic research
questions concerning the nature of the judgmental process and
the methodology which must be employed to give it more adequate characterizaton, the systematic collection of judgmental
responses from objective data, and the employment of the most
simple linear regression techniques culminates in a set of
regression coefficients which are both enlightening and useful.
Consider, for example, the usefulness of knowing, in some
sense, how Minnesota clinicians utilize the MMPI scales in
diagnosing psychoticism. Figure 3.2 displays the regression
coefficients for the eleven MMPI scales utilized in the extensive studies reported by Meehl (1959), from data collected by
Meehl and Dahlstrom (1960).
These data were made available to the ORI staff through
the courtesy of Professor Meehl, following which the regression coefficients for the scales were determined for each
clinician and averaged. Of course, these coefficients are arti-
facts of averaging, but it is important to note that the majority
of individual clinicians yielded configurations of regression coefficients that did not depart significantly from the pattern
displayed in Fig. 3.2. Furthermore, the consistency of these
results from one hospital sample to the next is readily seen
in the figure.

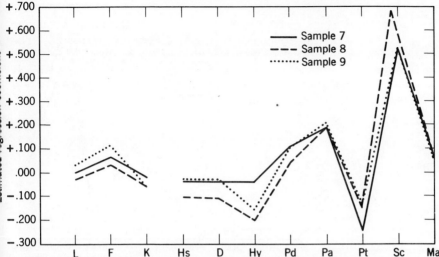

Fig. 3.2 A regression coefficient of each of the 11 MMPI variables. The criterion used was the pooled judgment of 29 clinicians and trainees along a neurotic-psychotic continuum.

Of equal interest is the extent to which trainees differ from experienced clinicians in their utilization of MMPI information. Of the 29 clinicians pooled in Fig. 3.2, 13 were experienced Ph.D.'s and the remaining 16 were trainees. Figure 3.3 provides a comparison of these two groups. One need hardly comment on the similarity.

Finally, a very important practical application of such methods has to do with the resolution of differences in judgment or diagnosis when two or more clinicians disagree. In everyday life, disagreements about opinions, judgments, or alternative courses of action provide continual friction and animosity between people who represent opposing points of view. Efforts to resolve such differences through verbal exchanges seldom achieve their objective, for each protagonist is busy rationalizing his own point of view, defending his stature, or degrading his opponent. It is undoubtedly a weakness of *Homo sapiens* that such behavior is so frequently addressed to the ego, and so seldom to the underlying differences in the values which are placed on the various elements which have led to the opinion or judgment. In clinical psychology, differences in judgment are traceable not only to differences in perceptions, but also to differences in the values that clinicians place upon their perceptions of various attributes of the patient, in relation to the dimension being judged or evaluated.

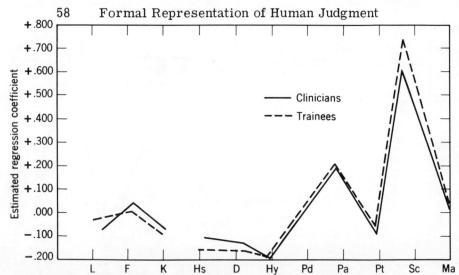

Fig. 3.3 Comparison of clinicians and trainees by means of regression models. The regression coefficients are the averages of the clinicians and trainees, respectively—i.e., derived from the individual regression models.

Though regression models may not be wholly adequate in providing characterizations of the relative importance placed upon objective data in judgment studies, they appear remarkably useful in this regard. Thus, Fig. 3.4 presents the

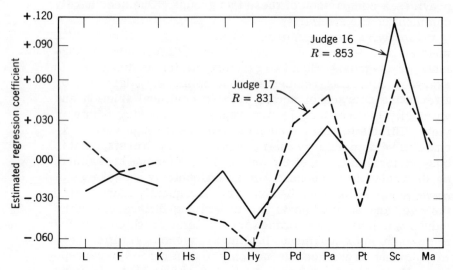

Fig. 3.4 Two judges who differ markedly in their utilization of MMPI data.

configurations of coefficients for two clinicians who were in rather consistent disagreement when judging psychoticism. It would seem that both clinicians might profit by seeing themselves described in this way. If they were then to engage in discussions concerning the optimal utilization of the MMPI, such discussion should focus upon the specific points at issue: namely, differences in the values placed upon the various MMPI scales. The research possibility suggested by this excursion are exciting. Professor Hammond's laboratory will be pursuing this promising line of research at the University of Colorado.

THE LINEARITY PRINCIPLE

The early "models" of the judgment process were chosen both for their parsimony and for feasibility of calculation of the necessary parameters. Thus, to recapitulate, the simplest model of human judgment conceptualizes a constant set of m dimensions, cues, or defining characteristics of objects, and seeks to approximate the judgmental responses by a least-squares best-fitting hyperplane defined by the regression of responses upon the stimulus space. The slope of the hyperplane with respect to each of the dimensions is an estimate of the "importance" of that dimension, and the set of these slopes, the regression coefficients, may be considered as indices of the pattern of relative importance of the stimulus dimensions.

The concept of a best-fitting hyperplane implies a sort of averaging of the effects of all points in the multidimensional space, and, since linearity is assumed, the regression coefficients are invariant over the entire stimulus space. If this model were adopted as an adequate description of judgmental processes, it would therefore imply that individuals do not alter their mode of "weighting" the dimensions of information, regardless of the pattern or configuration of values inherent in the object being judged.

What is the evidence which favors acceptance of the linearity principle? On the surface, the evidence seems over-powering. For example, in at least three separate studies at ORI involving judgments of intelligence from profiles like those in Fig. 3.1, or involving the judgment of sociability from profiles of personality scale scores, the multiple correlations range between .80 and .90, while the retest reliabilities of the same judges range from .80 to .90 also. This is to say that from 64% to 81% of the variance in judgments of the profiles can be attributed to a linear combination of the attributes of the profiles, while 19% to 32% of the remaining variance can be attributed to unreliability. These studies have consistently shown that virtually no improvement in predictive accuracy can be expected beyond that achieved by a linear model.

Hammond and Summers (1965) cite more than a dozen studies of clinical or quasi-clinical judgment in which the accuracy of prediction derived from linear regression analysis was sufficiently great as to suggest that judges are primarily linear in their mode of combining cues. An additional study published the same year (Naylor and Wherry, 1965) serves to illustrate the point. The authors had 50 Air Force supervisors rate hypothetical specialists from scores on 23 traits considered relevant to job success. Linear regression analysis produced a median R of .89 for these 50 subjects, and the authors report little difference between the 50 individual regression models. In summary, large amounts of empirical data support the hypothesis of linear cue-utilization. Little or no residual variance remains following the determination of the composite linear effects of the variables, other than that which should be accounted for by unreliability or error. Furthermore, these findings have been found to hold for a variety of judgmental domains, utilizing different sets of objective information; and the findings appear valid for experienced decision-makers as well as for naïve subjects.

In spite of these seemingly overpowering data, a conceptualization of human judgment as a simple linear weighted composite of a small number of variables is nevertheless debatable, and I am willing to join many of my so-called fuzzy-headed colleagues in refusing to accept it. Just why I choose not to accept the linearity principle in spite of its being established, presumably beyond all question, can only be made clear after the problem of configurality is addressed and fully explicated. This is the subject to which we now turn.

THE PROBLEM OF CONFIGURALITY

Several factors mitigate against acceptance of the linearity principle in human judgment, in spite of these well-established results. I shall discuss three which seem especially important to consider: for convenience, these might be labeled (1) the intuitional feelings of clinicians, (2) the paramorphic problem, and (3) the statistical problem.

When we say that the intuitive feelings of clinicians must be considered before accepting the linearity principle, we mean to imply not that intuition be substituted for fact, but rather that intuition continue to serve as the well-spring of hypotheses for the advancement of knowledge. I personally find it very compelling that the most skilled and knowledgeable clinicians and diagnosticians, whose professional lives are in large part concerned with diagnosis, decision-making, and judgment, universally reject the linearity principle out of hand. These people report in fairly emphatic terms that judgment involves a sequential consideration of many dimensions (symptoms, signs, or cues), and that the interpretation of a given dimension is conditional upon the values of other dimensions. Nothing so clearly suggests the possibilities of quantizing or modeling nonlinearly as does the foregoing type of statement of subjective experience. For, if, in predicting Z the interpretation of X is conditional upon Y, the best-fitting regression surface of Z on (X, Y) should be some sort of curved surface, perhaps, but certainly not planar. And the regression equation must be modified to accommodate the hypothesis that the coefficient of X is a function of Y.

More precisely, beginning with the linear equation

$$Z' = A_0 + A_1 X + A_2 Y \tag{1}$$

we assume first that A_1 changes *linearly* with Y. Then,

$$A_1 = B_0 + B_1 Y \tag{2}$$

and, by substitution in (1) we obtain

$$Z' = A_0 + B_0 X + B_1 XY + A_2 Y \tag{3}$$

Or, assuming that the importance of X changes as a second degree function of Y, we might write

$$A_1 = B_0 + B_1 Y + B_2 Y^2 \tag{4}$$

from which, by substitution in (1), we might have

$$Z' = A_0 + B_0 X + B_1 XY + B_2 XY^2 + A_2 Y \qquad (5)$$

as a general model of judgment.

These kinds of exercises illustrate the algebraic characterization of moderator effects. They can be generalized to incorporate hypotheses of a more complex sort concerning the dependency relationships among a set of predictors. This results in polynomial equations of higher degree, and with terms which increase geometrically in number with increases in the order of complexity of the relationship of the moderator variables to the primary variables. The illustrations do not themselves challenge the validity of the linearity principle, but they do reveal a gaping weakness in the wall of empirical evidence on the question: namely, that there exist widely held beliefs about the nature of clinical judgment which are at variance with the linearity principle; that these beliefs are capable of explicit operational formulation; and that in spite of the existence of such seemingly readily testable hypotheses, there are virtually no published studies either to support or refute such hypotheses.

I turn next to the second problem area, which I have labeled the paramorphic problem (Hoffman, 1960). Briefly stated, there are two subproblems here. First, two or more models of judgment may be algebraic equivalents of one another, yet suggest radically different underlying processes. This point is self-evident and requires no further explication. Second, two or more models of judgment may be algebraically different, yet be equally predictive, given fallible data. Thus, there are sets of data for which the function

$$Z' = A_1 X + A_2 Y$$

and the function

$$Z'' = B_1 X^2 + B_2 Y$$

lead to exactly the same residual variance. Such examples serve to emphasize that in judgmental research, as in science in general, models can be little more than descriptive of the phenomena of nature; they cannot be fully explanatory. Hence, the achievement of a high level of predictive accuracy for a linear model does not negate the possibility of configural relationships; but it does place the additional burden upon the experimenter to find a more adequate test, a different experiment, or a special type of data structure that would be more likely to reveal a degree of superiority for his hypothesized configurations.

Finally, we turn to problems of a statistical sort which have impeded the search for configural relationships. It is inviting to begin this search after having divested oneself completely from suppositions or intuitions concerning the nature of the prediction function, and to devise a sufficiently general model, or a sufficiently adaptive computer program that would come to reveal the "true" relationships by itself. After all, we are simply after better-fitting response surfaces to the multidimensional stimulus space, and modern computers are capable of handling large numbers of complex terms, if these be needed.

However, an undirected search for configural relationships within a finite set of data is fraught with difficulties, and virtually doomed to disappointment. Without having literally tens of thousands of cases available, predictive schemes which randomly search for configurated terms can seldom be reliably replicated, for a very large number of such terms must be investigated, and the problem of parameter estimation becomes increasingly acute as the number of dimensions or terms is increased. Furthermore, the error in estimating the parameters of such models is adversely affected even more as the complexity of the individual terms is increased. This is so because the concept of configuration, implying, as it does, the *interdependence* of variables, demands the inclusion, in a general model, of terms which are functions of several variables, and which are therefore highly intercorrelated. Under such circumstances, the rare but significant configural parameter lies embedded in a sea of chance relationships, from which it cannot reliably be distinguished. Thus, the failure to discover configural models which maintain their superiority over linear models under adequate cross-validation may be due to the fallibility of statistical methods rather than due to inherent lack of configurality in behavior.

To remain hopeful under such circumstances is to recognize the challenge facing statisticians and to be confident that these problems will yield. I say this in spite of some seemingly discouraging theoretical findings by Horst (1964). Horst has proved that if a set of predictors can be transformed to a set of mutually orthogonal variables, multinormal with the dependent variable, *no* configural variables can add to the linear multiple correlation. Obviously, to be wedded to configural models means abandonment of the assumption of multivariate normality!

EVIDENCE FOR CONFIGURALITY

Since there is overwhelming evidence to support the linearity principle, is there a developing body of evidence to support a configurality principle? Can we hang our hopes upon something more than the knowledge that past failures may have been due to methodological difficulties? The answer to both of these questions is "yes." There *are* data to indicate nonlinear cue-utilization. These data have invariably developed, not out of the methodology described in the foregoing sections of this paper, but out of uniquely different approaches.

One such exemplary approach is that which involves the correlation of residuals, and owes its development to Dr. Kenneth Hammond and his colleagues. This approach may be represented schematically by a lens model, as was suggested originally by Brunswik (1947). In this model (Fig. 3.5), the X's represent the cues (e.g., MMPI scale scores). The true state (e.g., diagnosis) is represented by Y_e, and the judged state by Y_s. Correlations among attributes of the object are also shown. This model characterizes a cognitive process for a single judge.

Overall response accuracy, the correlation between the criterion diagnosis and the judged diagnosis is designated by r_a. The correlation, $r_{i,s}$, between the judgments and an individual cue would be a good index of cue-utilization if the cues were independent and the criterion linerarly predictable. However, in the case of MMPI scales, as in many other cases, the cues are not independent. Some other index of cue-utilization is therefore required.

Consider, therefore, two multiple regression equations, the first relating the cues to the true state, the second relating the cues to the judgments.

$$\hat{Y}_e = \beta_{e,1} X_1 + \dots + \beta_{e,n} X_n$$

$$\hat{Y}_s = \beta_{s,1} X_1 + \dots + \beta_{s,n} X_n \tag{6}$$

Now, the correlations, R_s and R_e, between the values predicted by the regression equation and the actual values, provide a measure of the linear predictability of the judge and the environment, respectively. If that variance which cannot be linearly predicted is labeled Z_e for the true state and Z_s for the judged state, then the following relationships hold:

$$Y_e = \hat{Y}_e + Z_e$$

$$Y_s = \hat{Y}_s + Z_s \tag{7}$$

Let G be the correlation between the linearly predictable

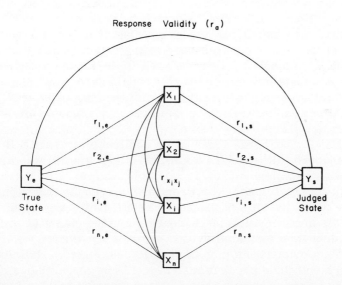

Fig. 3.5 The lens model. The symbols represent environmental cue-weighting ($r_{i,e}$); diagnostician's cue-weighting ($r_{i,s}$); cues (X_i); cue-intercorrelations ($r_{x_i x_j}$); R_e = multiple correlation between cues and true state; R_s = multiple correlation between cues and judged state.

components, and C the correlation between the residual components. Then the overall response accuracy may be represented as

$$r_a = GR_e R_s + C \sqrt{1 - R_e^2} \sqrt{1 - R_s^2} \qquad (8)$$

as was shown by Tucker (1964). An alternative form of this equation was earlier presented by Hursh, Hammond, and Hursch (1964) as

$$r_a = \frac{1}{2}(R_e^2 + R_s^2 - \Sigma d) + C \sqrt{1 - R_e^2}\sqrt{1 - R_s^2} \qquad (9)$$

In either case, the right-hand side of the equation is composed of two parts, the first having to do with linear accuracy, and the second having to do with configural accuracy.

Consider, first, linear accuracy. R_s and R_e indicate the linear predictability of the judge and the criterion, respectively. But, given that a criterion and a judge are both highly linearly predictable, it does not follow that the judge must necessarily be accurate. Whether he is or not depends upon the extent to which his model matches that of the ecological side of the lens. One measure of the extent of this matching is indicated by Σd. As can be seen in the foregoing equation, when the matching is perfect, Σd equals zero. The judge can never achieve a higher linear accuracy than that given by R_e^2; to the extent that the weights he uses are inappropriate, his linear accuracy will be lower than R_e^2.

Now, what of the residual or nonlinear variance? It may be random on either one or both sides of the lens, in which case no incremental accuracy is possible. However, if there are nonlinear relationships between the cues and the criterion, and if the judge is able to use these relationships appropriately, then his accuracy will be increased, and the extent of that increase will be indicated by $C\sqrt{1 - R_e^2} \sqrt{1 - R_s^2}$.

The evidence for configurality is mixed. Hammond, Hursch and Todd present analyses of 15 judges used in a study by Grebstein (1963). These judges, ranging from naïvete to clinical sophistication, made predictions of Wechsler-Bellevue IQ's of 30 patients, based upon 10 cues from their Rorschach (Beck) psychograms. The correlations between residuals (C) for these judges ranged between -.06 and .39. The values are

not at all exciting, and of rather dubious statistical significance, based as they are upon an N of 30; but they are just
large enough to dissuade one from outright rejection of the
configurality hypothesis. To further obscure matters, it must
be said that C indicates the presence of only one specific *kind*
of nonlinearity—that which matches the residuals from linearity
of the judge with residuals from linearity in regressing the
criterion upon the predictor space. A nonsignificant value of
C *may* indicate that the judge is utilizing data configurally but
inappropriately!

Rorer and Slovic (1966) conclude, following exhaustive
analysis of their clinical training data, that there is indeed
clear evidence of configural cue-utilization, as exemplified by
Hammond's C, though the configural component of judgment was
not helpful in improving predictive accuracy, either for the
clinicians or the naïve subjects used in their study.

AN ANALYSIS-OF-VARIANCE APPROACH

Though the structural models underlying the fixed effects
and random effects analysis-of-variance (ANOVA) designs are
quite similar to the multiple regression model, these models
have not previously been used to represent the judgment process. It seems desirable to take advantage of this similarity
between models so as to be able to apply the elegant inferential
and descriptive capabilities of the ANOVA techniques to the
study of judgment. This can be done by regarding the cues
X_1, X_2, ..., X_n in a judgment experiment as categorical treatment factors in the ANOVA design, rather than as continuous
random variables. Judgment stimuli should be constructed so
that the cues are orthogonal (uncorrelated). One way of doing
this is to construct all possible combinations (patterns) of the
cue levels in a completely crossed factorial design. The judgments made to the configurations of cues serve as the dependent variables. The model assumes that the judgments may be
represented by an additive combination of the terms in the
model.

When judgments are analyzed in terms of an ANOVA model,
a significant main effect for cue X_1 implies that the judge's
responses varied systematically with X_1 as the levels of the
other cues were held constant. Provided sufficient levels of the

factor were included in the design, the main effect may be divided into effects due to linear, quadratic, cubic, etc., trends. Similarly, a significant interaction between cues X_1 and X_2 implies that the judge was responding to particular patterns of those cues; that is, the effect of variation of cue X_1 upon judgment differed as a function of the corresponding level taken by cue X_2.

Significance tests can provide an idea of whether the judge is using a particular cue individually and/or in combination with one or more other cues. If one is interested in generalizing his results only to the particular set of cues and the particular levels of those cues from which the stimuli were constructed, then a fixed effects ANOVA model applies and F ratios may be constructed accordingly.

The ANOVA model has potential for describing both the linear and the nonlinear aspects of the judgment process. Within the framework of the model, it is possible to calculate an index of the importance of individual or patterned use of a cue, relative to the importance of other cues. The index ω^2, described by Hays (1963; pp. 324, 382, 407), provides an estimate of the proportion of the total variation in a person's judgments that can be predicted from a knowledge of the particular levels of a given cue or a pattern of cues. Its interpretation is analogous to the interpretation of the squared product moment correlation as a proportion of variance explained, and it is therefore a percentage reduction in uncertainty. This being the case, its advantage is that it provides a measure of relationship or degree for effects where normally only a measure of significance is considered.

The possibilities provided by ANOVA procedures in the determination of configural cue-utilization have led a group of us at ORI to carry out a study in medical diagnosis (Hoffman, Slovic, and Rorer, 1967). The domain selected was that of the differential diagnosis of malignant vs. benign gastric ulcers. Consultation with a gastroenterologist revealed that this differential is seldom made without a radiological examination. Further, it became possible to select seven cues or signs, objectively definable from inspection of the X-rays, some of which are presumed by experts to combine in a configural manner for this diagnostic task. These signs were:

1. Ulcer is extraluminal.   (Yes or No)
2. Associated filling defect is present.   (Yes or No)

3. Ulcer contour is regular. (Yes or No)
4. Rugal pattern is preserved around ulcer. (Yes or No)
5. Evidence of associated duodenal ulcer is present. (Yes or No)
6. Ulcer is located on the greater curvature. (Yes or No)
7. Ulcer crater is small. (Yes or No)

Hypothetical ulcer patients were constructed by forming all possible combinations of the seven signs. Since each sign could take one of two levels (present or absent), this produced 2^7 or 128 cases. A typical case is shown in Fig. 3.6.

Case #037

	Yes	No
1. Extraluminal	x	
2. Filling Defect		x
3. Regular Contour	x	
4. Rugal Pattern		x
5. Duodenal Symptoms	x	
6. On Greater Curvature		x
7. Small Crater	x	

Benign	Malignant
1 2 3 4 5 6 7	

Fig. 3.6 A sample profile used in a study of judgment processes of radiologists in the diagnosis of malignant and benign gastric ulcers. The seven signs are those frequently noted on the radiologist's report.

Because the plausibility of the cue patterns was a matter of some importance, all of the 128 possible patterns were reviewed by a competent gastroenterologist, who was asked to indicate whether any of them were sufficiently implausible as to cast doubt upon the meaningfulness of the study. This gastroenterologist eliminated exactly 32 of the patterns, all because they paired "Ulcer is extraluminal (No)" with "Associated filling defect (No)." Apparently an intraluminal ulcer is by definition one with an associated filling defect. However, all of the remaining 96 profiles, or cases, were considered plausible. Sign 1 and Sign 2 were, therefore, combined into a single variable treated at three levels:

Level 1: Ulcer is extraluminal (No) and associated filling defect (Yes).

Level 2: Ulcer is extraluminal (Yes) and associated filling defect (No).
Level 3: Ulcer is extraluminal (Yes) and associated filling defect (Yes).

This resulted in a 3×2^5 complete factorial arrangement of case patterns. Each of the resulting 96 cases was presented twice during the experiment; thus, each subject had 192 cases to judge. The profiles for the second replication were partially interspersed within the first administration, though a profile for the first replication always preceded its exact counterpart in the second replication. This method offered two advantages. First, the interspersion of duplicate profiles within a single administration of the task minimizes order effects. Second, it reduces temporal effects, since identical profiles are in closer proximity than would be the case if the two replications were completely separated. It was not the purpose of the experiment to assess the stability of judgments over time, but rather to assess the reliability of the behavior at a given period in time.

The judgments were made on a seven-point scale ranging from 1 (definitely benign) to 7 (definitely malignant). The subjects were six practicing radiologists and three radiologists-in-training at the University of Oregon Medical School. The reliabilities of the judges are generally high, indicating that, whatever the underlying judgmental process, it was applied in a reasonably consistent manner. Furthermore, the disagreement between judges is real and not due to inconsistencies or unreliability. Intercorrelations among the ratings of judges make this point clear. Twenty-one of the 36 interjudge coefficients are .40 or less, and 15 of them are .25 or less. Even if corrected for attenuation due to unreliability, these coefficients are closer to .0 than to 1.0. The differences between judges appear real, and they demand an interpretation in terms of differences in underlying judgmental processes. In order to determine the significance of these differences, one large ANOVA was run using the data from all nine radiologists. Radiologists were considered to be a random sample from a larger population of expert judges, and replications were considered nested within radiologists. Since the symptoms were considered to be fixed effects (nonsampled), the appropriate error terms for the F tests in this analysis were governed by a mixed model (Hays, 1963; pp. 439-449). The results for the main effects and significant interactions are listed in Table 3.1. The first source of variance listed in the table, that due to radiologists, was statistically significant. This indicates that the radiologists differed in their mean judgments across the 192 stimuli. The significant main effects for symptoms 1 and 3 indicate that, when data were averaged over radiologists, the mean judgments varied systematically with the levels of these cues. The significant interactions between radiologists and individual symptoms indicates that the radiologists differed from one another in the extent to which they relied on this symptom. This could be a difference in direction as well as in degree; for example, some may have thought a symptom to be a positive indicator of malignancy, while others may have considered it a contraindicator. The significance of individual differences in the use of each of the six individual symptoms is of more than passing interest.

TABLE 3.1   Analysis of Variance Performed
on the Combined Data from All Radiologists

Source of Variation	df	Mean Squares	F	P
Radiologists (R)	8	25.8	46.1	＜0.01
Symptom 1	2	576.7	11.5	＜0.01
Symptom 2	1	163.2	4.5	NS
Symptom 3	1	411.2	10.2	＜0.05
Symptom 4	1	62.6	2.8	NS
Symptom 5	1	9.3	1.2	NS
Symptom 6	1	3.1	0.2	NS
R × 1	16	49.8	82.7	＜0.01
R × 2	8	36.6	61.0	＜0.01
R × 3	8	40.4	67.3	＜0.01
R × 4	8	22.3	37.2	＜0.01
R × 5	8	7.7	12.8	＜0.01
R × 6	8	18.8	31.3	＜0.01
1 × 4	2	3.6	4.2	＜0.05
2 × 4	1	4.6	5.6	＜0.05
R × 1 × 3	16	2.1	3.6	＜0.01
R × 2 × 3	8	2.6	4.3	＜0.01
R × 3 × 4	8	3.2	5.3	＜0.01
1 × 2 × 5	2	1.4	2.3	＜0.05
1 × 5 × 6	2	3.1	3.8	＜0.05
3 × 4 × 5	1	2.4	4.0	＜0.05
4 × 5 × 6	1	2.3	3.8	＜0.05
R × 1 × 2 × 3	16	1.8	3.0	＜0.01
R × 1 × 3 × 4	16	1.5	2.5	＜0.01
R × 1 × 4 × 6	16	1.4	2.3	＜0.01

In similar fashion, the two-way interactions between cues indicate whether or not a particular pair of cues was employed configurally by the group as a whole; the three-way interactions with radiologists as one of the factors tell whether there were individual differences in the configural use of a pair of cues, etc. All in all, there were some pairs of cues and some three-symptom patterns that were used configurally by the group as a whole, and other two- and three-element patterns whose use differed among radiologists. No configurations involving more than three cues reached significance in this analysis.

These analyses indicate a substantial number of statistically significant interactive terms, particularly where radiologists are factors in the interaction terms. The study therefore reveals as much about individual differences in cue-utilization as it does about the configurality principle. Previous studies have demonstrated individual differences in linear cue-utilization, but this study demonstrates that *the particular patterned or interactive utilization of cues also varies from one individual to the next.* In fact, the lack of agreement among diagnosticians who are presumably experts in the task is both striking and disconcerting. The ANOVA technique proved to be quite capable of tracing disagreement among judges to underlying differences in cue-utilization. Such analyses could lead to marked improvement in the quality of many kinds of complex inferences.

It should be emphasized that while this study provides a source of evidence favoring configural cue-utilization, the effects are small in relation to the sources of variation attributable to main effects or to linear components.

I have elaborated upon this experiment not because its findings are typical, but because it is so rare. One does not, characteristically, find significant configural relations in fallible psychological data, yet here they are. Why?

First of all, it should be said that the choice of task was deliberately engineered so as to maximize the probability of significant findings. There is something inherent in the medical conceptualization of ulcers that virtually demands configural employment of the clinical signs. Second, the experimental design employed was that of ANOVA rather than regression analysis, as a result of which parameter estimation of the many interaction terms could be accomplished with satisfactory reliability. Third, there were two replications of each of the 96 possible patterns, yielding error estimates which were themselves free from interactive effects.

Considering these conditions, it is not surprising that significant configural effects were found. What is surprising is that those effects were nevertheless so small!

Other studies could be cited, for example, Anderson and Jacobson (1965), Dudycha and Naylor (1966), and Wiggins and Hoffman (1967a), but the conclusions are about the same. It is possible to establish configural relationships in judgmental data, but to do so requires careful attention to experimental design and to content of the task. When such effects are found they are slight.

Let us ask now whether the research strategy for discovering configural effects can be improved upon. Earlier in this paper it was suggested that the search for configural terms is likely to be self-defeating when no *a priori* decisions are made concerning the *particular* terms one is looking for. The infinitude of possible terms and models poses great obstacles for the undirected approach.

The earlier work of Kleinmuntz (1963) is valuable in its attempt to simulate the cognitive processes of diagnosticians; and careful work in this direction can indeed provide a useful set of hypotheses concerning patterned or sequential relations to which the clinician is responsive. Of course, in depending upon the clinician as a source of hypotheses, one hangs his faith upon the insight of the clinician into his cognitions and upon his ability to articulate the process sufficiently to allow objective description. On these matters, no sound evidence is available, to my knowledge. What alternatives are left in the *a priori* specification of configural elements or terms?

A STUDY IN CUE-CONSISTENCY, AND AN
A PRIORI NOTION

Slovic (1966) examined the influence of a particular kind of patterning among cues upon the use of cues. Subjects were asked to judge the intelligence of a person on the basis of nine cues presented in profile form, the level of each cue being displayed as a percentile. Previous research with this task had determined that judgments of intelligence could, for the most part, be accounted for by a linear combination on only two of these cues—High School Grade Rating (HSR) and English Effectiveness (EE). The consistency of a profile was defined in terms of the degree of agreement between the levels of these two cues. Each subject judged fifteen "consistent" profiles in which the percentile difference between HRS and EE was rather small and fifteen "inconsistent" profiles in which the percentile difference was quite large. Cue-utilization was analyzed separately for consistent and inconsistent sets of profiles by means of a multiple correlation technique. The results indicated that a person's judgments were dependent upon both HSR and EE when these cues agreed with one another. However, when these cues had contradictory implications, the subject seemed to rely upon only one of them. Variation of the other cue did not influence the judgments for this inconsistent set. A recent study by Dudycha and Naylor (1966) has also found that consistent (highly correlated) cues are weighted more uniformly than inconsistent ones.

The importance of these data stems from the fact that they contradict the linearity principle. The linear model assumes that the weight given any cue is constant over the entire set of judgments—that is, that it is not influenced by any patterns formed by this and other cues for a particular stimulus. The observed changes in cue-weights due to consistency patterns would seem to call for a modification of this notion.

A second experiment was designed to further examine Slovic's finding that subjects used both critical cues when they were consistent but only one of them when they were inconsistent. Two important modifications in the experimental design of the original study were instituted here. By defining consistency in terms of the relationship between just two out of the nine cues, the original study ignored possible inconsistency or consistency due to the other cues. The study therefore used only two cues.

The second modification was introduced because the two cues (HSR and EE) used in the original experiment were expected by subjects to be highly congruent with one another. When inconsistency occurred, the disconfirmation of this strong expectancy may have led them to doubt the validity of one or both of the reported scores. The two cues used in the *second* study, one an aptitude measure, English Effectiveness (EE), the other a motivational index, Need Achievement (NA), can more easily be viewed as independent in nature. Thus stimuli having discrepant implications should not seem so incongruous here as in the earlier study. This might be expected to result in less of a tendency to discount one of the discrepant cues.

Subjects were asked to predict the Grade Point Average (GPA) that some former University of Oregon students obtained during their freshman year in college. They were provided with the two cues on which to base their judgments of each student. The two cues were displayed in profile form, the levels of each cue representing the student's percentile standing on that cue with respect to the rest of his freshman class. Subjects were asked to predict each student's percentile standing on GPA as compared to the rest of his freshman class.

The total set of stimuli was composed of five subsets, each containing 16 profiles. Figure 3.7 shows the location, in two-dimensional space, of each profile in each subset. Note that the profiles in sets 1 and 5 contained inconsistent cues. These stimuli were high on EE and low on NA or vice-versa. Sets 2, 3, and 4 contained consistent cues. Stimuli which had identical values for the two cues were omitted. The two cue variables were orthogonal across the 16 profiles within every set. Furthermore, the standard deviations of the levels of both cues were equal within a set and across sets. These constraints were introduced to facilitate the unambiguous determination of cue-utilization weights. The five sets were randomly intermixed and 26 warm-up and filler stimuli were added, making a total of 106 profiles for each subject to judge. The subjects were 17 undergraduates from the University of Oregon. Regression analysis of these data is direct and unambiguous. Regression of the judgment upon the two-dimensional orthogonal cue-space provides slope estimates for each of the cues. If the linearity principle holds, these slopes should be invariant throughout the cue-space. Consequently, the regression coefficients estimated within subsets should be the same. On the other hand, if the consistency or inconsistency of cues affects the judgment process, the regression coefficients will depend upon the subset of cues utilized for estimation purposes.

Table 3.2 shows the effects of consistency for each of the 17 judges. The drop in the regression coefficient of NA is so obvious as not to require a statistical test. Every one of the 17

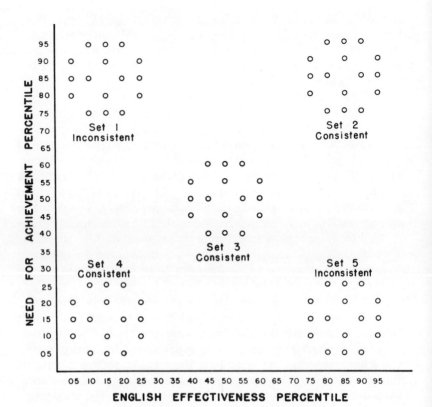

Fig. 3.7 Schematization of the two-dimensional domain (English effectiveness and need achievement), also used in constructing subsets of profiles. Judgments were of grade point average.

judges displayed a reduction in the coefficient associated with NA! The study therefore confirms Slovic's earlier finding rather dramatically, and provides support for configural, rather than linear, cue-utilization.

We have said previously that the configurality principle in judgment implies that the response surface of judgments upon the cue-space is nonlinear. Now suppose we make the very plausible assumption that whatever the judgmental process is, it can nevertheless by represented as some kind of weighted sum of the cues. If clinicians do what they say they do, and if Slovic's findings have generality, the weight they place upon a particular cue changes, depending upon the values of other

TABLE 3.2 Effect of Cue-Consistency upon Cue-
Utilization Coefficiencies r_{EE} r_{NA}

Subject	Set 1 Inconsistent Profiles			Set 2 Consistent Profiles		
	R^2_J	r_{EE}	r_{NA}	R^2_J	r_{EE}	r_{NA}
1	1.000	1.00	.00	.749	.83	.24
2	.355	.58	.12	.796	.59	.67
3	.339	.55	.19	.893	.70	.64
4	.352	.44	.39	.653	.18	.79
5	.868	.78	.52	.938	.62	.74
6	.608	.77	.10	.918	.60	.74
7	.408	.60	.23	.812	.66	.62
8	.722	.79	.30	.803	.18	.88
9	.789	.77	.45	.762	.50	.71
10	.716	.69	.49	.696	.40	.74
11	.246	.18	.46	.748	.64	.58
12	.346	.46	.37	.775	.62	.62
13	.453	.48	.47	.497	.28	.65
14	.327	.57	.00	.892	.65	.68
15	.800	.74	.50	.848	.56	.73
16	.051	.17	.15	.838	.45	.80
17	.861	.93	-.06	.792	.48	.75

cues. Why should the value of a particular cue change? Why
should the cue become more important as a member of one set
of information and less important as a member of another?
Surely a given cue carries an implication, for the judge, with
respect to the attribute being judged; why should the implication be different for different profiles or objects being judged?
I can think of no explanation that does not involve the notion of
cue-consistency. It seems perfectly reasonable to suppose that
people come into judgment situations with certain expectations
or implicit notions concerning the interrelatedness of cues or
characteristics which define other people, objects, or events.
In addition, people possess subjective notions concerning the
validity of individual cues or characteristics in relation to the
criterion or attribute being judged. A cue should be strongly
weighted if it has high subjective validity, but its weight should
be "adjusted," depending upon the congruence or incongruity of
the cue-value with the values of the other cues which describe
the object or person being judged. And to say that the judge is
responsive to congruity (or consistency) among cues implies
that he is attending to discrepancies or differences between
cues.

If these notions have validity, one can hope to explain configural cue-utilization by postulating functional relationships between the parameters of individual cues and discrepancies among them. This is psychologically more satisfying than assuming that the judge functions as an intuitive polynomial—computing power and product of terms, and applying constant weights to the resultant values.

These considerations make it possible to entertain psychologically meaningful speculations concerning the organization of perceptions, the expectations of ordered relations in multivariate information displays, and other similar constructs, and to evolve theoretical notions and formal models concerning judgmental behavior. All such models will, however, be special forms of a discrepancy model, which considers that the patterning of cues of any multidimensional object judged is viewed by the subject as congruous or incongruent, and that this perception affects the utilization of the information contained in the object judged. Discrepant values of cues will invoke a different judgmental process than that employed when the cues are nondiscrepant. By this hypothesis, a discrepancy between ecologically valid cues which have similar implications for the observer becomes the occasion for the adjustment of the weight of one or more of the cues, leading to what are found to be configural or interactive effects, and the problem of human judgment becomes the problem of determining lawful relationships between structural characteristics of stimuli, on the one hand, and judgmental responses on the other. An understanding of configural responses to judgmental tasks therefore appears to require a direct concern with the problem of structure.

THE INDIVIDUAL DIFFERENCES PROBLEM

A priori rules or hypotheses based upon considerations such as described above carry with them an implication which is dubious, at best, and which must be carefully tested before full credence can be given to the particular configural models said to exemplify the judgment process. The implication is that the structural characteristics of the data are both uniformly and accurately perceived by the judge. Thus, to say that a discrepancy between Need Achievement and English

Effectiveness scores leads the judge to invoke a particular model is to say that *most* judges, and perhaps *all* judges, infer or anticipate a significant positive correlation between these two cues in the environment, therefore reacting to the discrepancy on a given profile as though it were atypical. The fact is that this implication fails to be upheld in a number of experimental studies, the most relevant of which can be characterized as factor analytic approaches to the study of individual viewpoints in judgment.

Messick and Jackson (1961), writing with reference to the area of person perception, generalized the judgment problem to take individual differences into account. Their statement of the problem is in terms of ". . . rigorously representing ordered schemata and realistically allowing for multiple ordering both in the characteristics of the people being judged and in the points of view of the judges about these characteristics." Tucker and Messick (1963) provided one variant of a multi-dimensional scaling model which allows the determination of the number of stimulus dimensions separately for distinct, homogeneous subgroups of judges. This model has been utilized to identify individual differences in perceptual dimensions in such areas as color vision (Helm and Tucker, 1962); social desirability judgments (Wiggins, 1966); Rep test constructs (Messick and Kogan, 1966); and personality traits (Walters and Jackson, 1966).

In a paper by Wiggins and Hoffman (1967b), direct insight into the problem of individual differences comes from inspection of the correlations of idealized individuals with cues and cue-combinations. Of particular interest was the finding that, for at least two individuals of that study, similarity judgments could be best explained as being based upon perceived discrepancies between pairs of cues, whereas, for other individuals similarity judgments appeared directly related to particular single cues or to their sum. Such individual differences as these strongly suggest the need to search for explanations of configural judgmental behavior on the basis of individual points of view. The work cited earlier in this chapter, concerned with the diagnosis of gastric ulcers, also offers strong support for this thesis.

Let us review the thread of discussion up to the present point. First, it was shown that the linearity principle should not be considered as sufficient. Second, it was suggested that if judgmental behavior involves configural cue-utilization, the search for configural models should proceed from *a priori* assumptions of some kind. Third, it was noted that one particular assumption, the assumption of uniformly perceived discrepancies between relevant cues is upheld in some recent experiments, and that such experiments imply a sequential utilization of cues, the second stage process being governed by the presence or absence of such discrepancies. Fourth, it was shown that, in spite of positive experimental confirmation of the assumption of uniformly perceived discrepancies, data exist which emphasize the importance of individual differences in point of view. Finally, reference was made to multidimensional scaling data which support the hypothesis of individual differences in the utilization of discrepancies between cues in judgments of similarity. It was stressed that a complete understanding of judgmental process require that attention be given to the multidimensional structure of data and its differential perception.

DEFINITIONS OF CONSISTENCY

Since it is our purpose to evolve an increasingly comprehensive theory, we wish to focus attention upon particular structural characteristics of stimuli and to develop measures of such characteristics, where feasible. It should be recognized that implicit in any intuitive approach to this question is the notion that certain patterns or configurations of cues ought, collectively, to "go together," to "be congruent," or to "be consistent" in order for them to identify meaningful objects or persons. Conversely, objects or people who exhibit cues or characteristics which appear incongruous, disparate, or inconsistent are greeted with bewilderment and doubt. One need not be a Gestalt psychologist to appreciate the possibility that it is the congruence of cues or characteristics which may be responsible for giving events in the environment their object-like quality.

We shall settle upon the term *consistency-inconsistency* to denote the qualities under discussion, and consider some possible operational definitions in terms of the explanatory power of such a concept. A number of specific definitions might be advanced, among which are the following:

1. The consistency of a stimulus is the extent to which the distinguishing cues or characteristics of the stimulus match those of the population (of objects or persons) of which the stimulus is a member. If I hand you a fruit, and it is soft, round, and juicy, it is consistent, for the world of all objects of the class of fruit is so arranged that this pattern is frequently occurring. But, if I hand you a fruit which is soft, tetrahedron-shaped, and juicy, the object is inconsistent.

This is essentially Slovic's concept of cue-discrepancy. It is a concept easily identifiable, in many instances, as a structural characteristic. Especially where a population of objects can be sampled, the relevant cues can be quickly identified (as would be done by inspection of the intercorrelations among the cues of the objects which comprise the sample). Then particular objects which lie distant from the main cluster of objects in the multidimensional space can be identified as inconsistent.

However, such an operational definition of consistency-inconsistency ignores individual differences in point of view, as we have seen, and substitutes the assumption that the observer brings to the judgment situation valid implicit notions concerning the multidimensional structure of the object world.

Whether, in fact, observers differ in point of view, and whether their points of view are valid would seem to depend as much upon the objects being judged as upon the observer. Perceptions of the interrelationships among the defining characteristics of physical, inanimate objects should be highly veridical, for the most part, since the characteristics are most often unambiguous, and since the language structure of the culture usually brings about a high degree of conformity of opinion concerning such objects. However, where the objects judged are people, either hypothetical or real, no such uniformity exists, and the defining cues or characteristics are often abstract concepts which have no direct physical referents. Consequently, individual differences should be expected not only in the perception of the characteristics but also in the implications derived from perceptions and in the expectations concerning interrelationships among the characteristics. Even if all observers did have correct implicit notions of this multidimensional structure, they could not be considered to be equally tuned to the same cues or characteristics. Rather, the discrepancies between cues would be serious or not, depending upon the importance attached to the cues by the observer. This latter consideration leads to a second proposed measure of consistency.

2. The consistency of an object is a sum of the consistencies of the separate cues. The consistency of a cue varies directly with its relative importance to the observer, and inversely with its objective atypicality. Out of such a notion, we have derived a "believability index" which satisfies the above definition. For this purpose, "objective atypicality" is defined as the square of the residual of the regression of the cue on all other cues (standard scores). Designating this residual as P_i^2, let the relative importance of the ith cue for the jth observer be given by

$$\alpha_{ij} = \frac{\mid \beta_i{}^r{}_{oi} \mid}{\sum\limits_{h=1}^{m} \mid \beta_h{}^r{}_{on} \mid} \tag{10}$$

Then for the jth observer, we have the ratio α_{ij} / P_{ik}^2 as this cue's contribution to the "believability" of the kth multidimensional stimulus for the jth observer. The numerator of this fraction is an index of cue-utilization unique to the observer. The denominator is an index of the cue's typicality in the ecology of objective events.

Actually, P_i^2 is distributed as X^2, with $0 < P^2 < \infty$ and mean equal to $P^2 = 1$. Our believability index would be more meaningful if the contribution of each cue was finite for $P_i^2 = 0$, and if its contribution decreased rapidly to zero with increasing values of P_i^2. An exponential function seems appropriate. Hence, we rewrite the ratio for a given cue as α_{ij} / e^{Pik^2} and the believability index (of the kth stimulus) is then expressed as the sum, over the cues,

$$B_{jk} = \sum_{i=1}^{m} \frac{\alpha_{ij}}{e^{Pik^2}} \tag{11}$$

In this form, B will vanish to zero as the cues depart from their corresponding regression planes, and B will equal 1 as an upper limit, when each of the cues of the stimulus coincides exactly with the regression plane. This is an index which is mathematically precise, and one which takes into account individual differences in the relative importance of cues, when the stimuli are being judged with respect to a given attribute.

Figure 3.8 presents three MMPI profiles representing low, medium, and high believability indices as perceived by (the average of) 29 clinicians. Those familiar with the MMPI will be able to judge the face validity of B_{ij} from this illustration. However, the "objective atypicality"defined in the denominator of the index is a measure based upon ecologically valid relationships among cues, not perceived relationships. It would appear then that this definition of consistency gets us halfway to our goal.

   3. We define the *consistency* of a stimulus as the degree to which the defining cues or characteristics of the stimulus, when considered in their totality by the judge, are perceived by

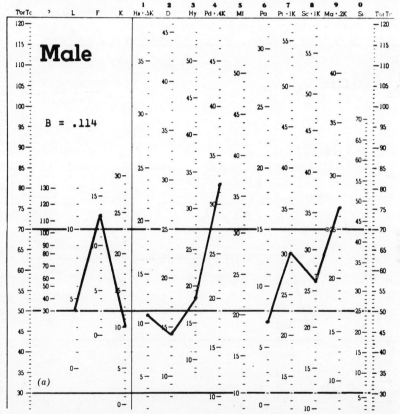

Fig. 3.8a An unusually "unbelievable" profile. The believability index ($B = .114$) suggests that most clinicians would have difficulty reconciling the information as indicative of the MMPI profile of a real person.

him to be representative of an actual, familiar, known or believable stimulus or object. Conversely, we define the *inconsistency* of a stimulus as the degree to which the defining
characteristics are perceived not to be representative of an
actual, familiar, known, or believable stimulus or object.

In operational terms, consistency-inconsistency might be
measured by first suggesting to the judge that a given set of
objects (profiles) contains some taken from a well-defined
population of some sort, and some, interspersed within the set,
which are purely fictitious, having been generated from a table
of random numbers. Then, the judge might be asked to try to
rate each profile on a scale marked at one end by "real

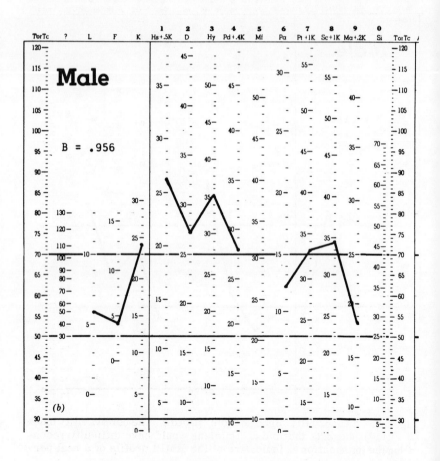

Fig. 3.8b An unusually "believable" profile.

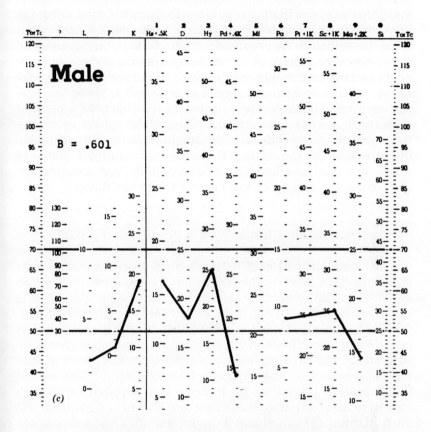

Fig. 3.8c A profile of "average believability."

people," and at the other end by "fictitious people." In actuality, such a measure will ordinarily fall short of our purposes, as will now be explained.

THE RELATIVITY OF CONSISTENCY

If individual differences exist for points of view of judges with respect to the perception of the structural features of stimuli, the consistency or inconsistency of a stimulus has no meaning. Consistency-inconsistency must be defined as a perceptual variable, and this in turn implies an interaction between perceiver and object. It is, therefore, an oversimplification to state that every stimulus may come to carry a rating along the consistency-inconsistency dimension as a result of the operations described in the previous section. In fact, the measure of consistency of stimuli will be in the form of a matrix, each row representing a stimulus, and each column representing an observer or a homogeneous subset of observers. Since the consistency of a stimulus is relative to the observer's point of view (or frame of reference), the values of the matrix cannot be filled in without first developing a method for the classification of individuals on the basis of the homogeneity in their points of view. We shall now adopt this third definition of consistency, and turn our attention to the measurement problem.

THE MEASUREMENT OF CUE-CONSISTENCY

An exemplification of the method of measurement of cue-consistency is more to the point than a formal set of abstract rules, since the procedure is complex. From a previous study, Knox and Hoffman (1962), data were available from 32 judges, each of whom rated a set of 75 profiles in an experiment concerned with the effects of T-$score$ versus percentile format on judgment. The profiles were alleged to be descriptions of college sophomores. They contained nine cues: (1) High School Grade Rating, (2) Status, (3) Percent Self-support, (4) English Effectiveness, (5) Responsibility, (6) Mother's Education, (7) Study Habits, (8) Emotional Anxiety, and (9) Credit Hours Attempted. One of the tasks in that study involved a judgment on a nine-point scale as to whether a given profile was "clear" or "muddy." A "clear" profile was defined as one in which the particular configuration of cues was such that they seemed to the judge to be describing a real person. A "muddy" profile was defined as describing an unreal or unbelievable person. These clear-muddy judgments of 75 profiles generated a 75 profile × 32 judge data matrix X. The sums of cross-products and squares matrix was generated between subjects $(X'X)$ and factor analyzed by the method of principal components. Seven factors were extracted as "significant" and these factors were rotated according to the orthogonal analytic Varimax criterion. Each judge was classified as belonging to only one of the seven groups on the basis of his projection on the seven rotated factors. It is noted that the highest projection relative to all the factors determined a subject's classification.

For each of the seven factorially defined subgroups of judges, the clear-muddy ratings comprise the basic data for the development of a scale value for each profile. Were a sufficiently large number of judges available, this treatment might have embraced any of a number of scaling techniques. However, since this study is primarily descriptive, we present only the means of the ratings for each judge, for a selected subset of the 75 profiles. Such a table serves to exemplify the nature of the consistency measures.

The matrix of consistency scores provides a basis for grouping profiles into consistent and inconsistent subsets for particular idealized individuals. Thus, from the point of view of idealized individual I, profiles 1 and 10 are regarded as

TABLE 3.3   Consistency Matrix (Mean Clear-Muddy Judgments of Idealized Individuals)*

Profile No.	Idealized Individuals						
	I	II	III	IV	V	VI	VII
1	7.00	6.20	6.33	2.67	9.00	7.67	9.00
2	6.83	6.60	7.33	3.67	6.00	5.67	4.50
3	6.50	5.20	7.00	7.00	7.50	4.33	5.00
4	3.17	5.00	6.00	4.00	5.00	4.33	3.50
5	5.00	3.80	3.67	4.33	4.50	5.00	5.00
6	5.00	5.00	4.67	8.00	5.50	6.67	5.50
7	5.83	5.80	2.33	5.00	3.00	6.33	6.00
8	6.00	5.20	4.67	4.33	5.50	4.00	6.50
9	3.67	3.20	4.33	4.00	2.50	1.67	2.00
10	6.67	4.80	7.00	3.67	3.00	5.00	6.50
11	5.00	4.60	1.67	4.67	4.00	3.67	7.00
12	6.33	6.60	5.33	3.00	4.50	7.00	7.00
13	3.50	5.40	6.67	6.33	3.50	5.67	3.00
14	4.50	5.20	4.33	4.67	6.00	2.00	6.00
15	4.67	3.60	4.67	3.33	5.00	4.33	3.00

*Only the first 15 of the 75 profiles are shown here.

consistent, while profiles 4 and 13 are inconsistent. A different grouping of profiles results for idealized individual II, and so on. It is of interest to note the disparity between individuals I and IV. The most consistent profile in group 1 (profile No. 1) is the most inconsistent profile in group 4. The second most inconsistent profile in group 1 is one of the most consistent of group 4. Other striking differences are apparent from the inspection of this table.

Whether a pattern of cues is seen as clear (consistent) or muddy (inconsistent) depends more on the relationship among the cues than on their absolute level considered singly. To say that one believes implicitly that height of forehead and intelligence are related is to say that if one sees a person with a high

TABLE 3.4   Intercorrelations of Cues for Selected Subsets
of Consistent (a) and Inconsistent (b) Profiles
Idealized Individual I

Var.	2	3	4	5	6	7	8	9	Mean	σ
1a	-.1161	-.1558	.4404	.0126	.5462	.4097	.1173	.7799	57.000	22.605
1b	-.0149	-.1517	-.7141	.1020	-.2547	-.1666	-.1192	.4863	33.000	34.511
2a		.4702	.1571	-.4986	-.3607	.0146	.1286	-.0054	55.500	27.060
2b		.2717	.0675	-.0847	-.0350	.1133	-.0648	-.1916	48.000	32.109
3a			-.2933	-.1895	-.3401	.1235	.0975	-.1547	52.500	28.395
3b			.1739	-.7658	.4867	.3256	.2935	.1887	57.000	30.265
4a				.4176	.2027	.5181	.1326	.7297	63.000	25.515
4b				-.2030	-.0294	-.1065	.4241	-.2868	50.000	40.373
5a					.3735	.4774	.2688	.2761	38.500	28.111
5b					-.4619	-.3737	-.6314	-.5202	43.500	26.837
6a						-.0223	.0877	.4559	62.500	23.691
6b						.3243	.0088	.0276	52.000	23.152
7a							.5465	.3468	54.500	26.024
7b							.1627	-.3122	64.000	25.573
8a								-.1441	44.000	25.278
8b								.4180	30.500	31.973
9a									63.000	27.313
9b									59.000	22.672

forehead he expects that the person is also intelligent. One's belief system concerning the structure of the environment includes implicit expectations of covariation among certain traits or cues in the objects perceived. In this example, high foreheads might be considered inconsistent with low intelligence. It is as though the observer expected these traits to have a positive covariance. If one is asked to make judgments of clear versus muddy profiles (i.e., to indicate how "real" or "consistent" an individual represented by a profile is) he would particularly note the cues that his implicit theory tells him are related in a particular way. Thus, an observer projects the pattern of cues against his implicit expectations concerning the multivariate cue-space. If the pattern of the profile is consistent with the individual's implicit theory, the profile would be judged consistent. Otherwise, and to the extent that the pattern of cues contradicts the implicit theory, the profile would be judged inconsistent.

Examination of the table of intercorrelations of cues (derived separately for consistent profiles and compared with a second table of correlations derived from inconsistent profiles) should provide enlightenment on the nature or basis of perceived incongruities. Table 3.5 is just such a table in intercorrelations, shown for Individual I. The upper entry in each cell is the correlation between cues within the consistent subset of profiles. It is suggested that the pairs of cues (e.g., 4 and 9) that show marked reversals in the magnitude of the correlation (comparing consistent and inconsistent profiles) reflect the implicit process underlying judgmental phenomena.

The consistency matrix provides an assignment of each profile to a group of idealized individuals and thereby defines the consistency of individual profiles for that person. Furthermore, the consistency matrix becomes a "key" for the scoring of subsequent subjects. It is possible to reliably classify a new subject on the basis of his clear-muddy responses to no more than perhaps twenty appropriately selected profiles. The significance of all of this is that once an individual can be classified relative to more than one subset of profiles, judgmental studies can be conducted to directly reveal the presence or absence of configural effects. In other words, by directly addressing oneself to the problem of relativity of consistency, one is able to build experimental tasks that in a sense imply *a priori* notions regarding differential cue-utilization. We said previously that configurality implies a differential weighting of cues in different portions of the stimulus space. The method advanced here allows the construction of sets of profiles in the subspaces between which the greatest changes in cue-utilization should occur. Further experimentation should illuminate both the degree to which such configural effects can be found and the extent of individual differences in such effects.

SUMMARY

This paper has sought to clarify some of the issues in configural judgment. It is held that, despite rather overwhelming evidence favoring the linearity principle, configural models will eventually come to have better descriptive and predictive power for the characterization of human cognitive processes.

Emphasis is given to the inadequacies of past approaches to the empirical verification of configural cue-utilization, and evidence is offered, illustrative of contemporary research in this area.

It is shown that the adequate characterization of judgment may indeed involve configural elements, but it is emphasized that the search demands recognition of the fact that configural representations are of necessity relative to the observer, and to the data-structure as perceived by the observer. Models which seek to explicate the process must, therefore, take individual differences into account.

CHAPTER 4   *Bert F. Green, Jr.*

Carnegie-Mellon University

DESCRIPTIONS AND EXPLANATIONS:
A Comment on Papers
by Hoffman and Edwards

The preceding excellent papers by Dr. Hoffman and Dr. Edwards summarize current issues in two related aspects of human judgment. Hoffman treats the situation in which several different kinds of information are to be combined in making a single judgment, whereas Edwards asks the judge to combine several items of information of the same kind. Each author presents a model that adequately describes the observed behavior, and then discusses extensions of, and challenges to, the model.

Implicit in the papers is a basic question about models. When shall the adequate fit of a model be taken as an explanation of a psychological process? Are there some models that have a strong chance of fitting a wide variety of data, including data that are in fact the result of processes not included in the model? I shall argue that there are, and that, indeed, each of the present papers provides such a model.

THE PERVERSE PERVASIVENESS OF LINEARITY

Hoffman recounts many experiments in which a judge is asked to estimate some criterion (dependent variable) on the basis of values of several predictors (independent variables). A linear regression model is found to fit the observed judgments very well. That is, the criterion estimates are very nearly a linear combination of the values of the predictor variables. Nevertheless, Hoffman believes that the judgment process is not that simple. He discusses ways of analyzing the data to discover nonlinear, configural components, but reports that such analyses are usually discouraging. The configural effects, if any, appear to be masked by the overwhelming linear effects.

Linear regressions are common in a great many areas besides human judgment. Most multivariate studies find that the linear regression of the dependent variable on the independent variables accounts for most of the accountable variance. Any configural technique that attempts to analyze departures from this regression plane has very little to work with. This is especially true if, for each independent variable separately, the relation between it and the criterion is monotonic. Educational psychologists have for years been trying unsuccessfully to add to the linear regression of college grades on high school grades and college entrance test scores. The monotonicity of the interrelationships, however, seems to preclude any utility from nonlinear, configural elements. Since monotonic relationships with the criterion characterize the MMPI scales and most of the other scales in the studies discussed by Dr. Hoffman, the discouraging fate of configural analyses is not surprising.

In an important sense, linearity is contributed by the analysis, rather than being an inherent property of the data. Consider a simple example from curve-fitting, as shown in Fig. 4.1 (p. 98). The "data" are described exactly by the parabola $y = 10 - (x - 4)^2$. From one point of view, this is purely a second-degree system with no linear component. And, if the data points indicated by the solid round dots are fit, using the standard technique of orthogonal polynomials, all of the variance will be described by the quadratic term, none by the linear term. If, however, a curve is fit to the data points indicated by x's, a different pattern emerges: the linear component accounts for 42% of the variance, leaving 58% for the quadratic. The usual interpretation of this result is that the data curve can be described by a weighted sum of a straight line and a parabola symmetric on the range of the data points. It is obvious in the present case that such a combination results in a curve that is a segment of a different parabola. What is usually overlooked is that this is *always* the case. *Any curve that is a weighted sum of a straight line and a parabola is a segment of another parabola.* Are the data partly linear and partly quadratic, or completely quadratic? The right answer is "Both." The analysis provides alternative descriptions of the data: a linear model describes 42% of the variance, a special symmetric quadratic model describes 58% of the variance, and a general quadratic model describes all the variance.

To carry this example one step further, consider an analysis of the four data points indicated by open circles in Fig. 4.1, which are monotonically related to the criterion. Here 92% of the variance is attributable to the linear component, only 8% to the quadratic component. For all practical purposes the data may be treated as linear, although theoretically they are quadratic.

This example dealt with a single variable, but similar effects can easily be shown for multivariate data. Many years ago Thurstone (1947) used his celebrated box problem to show, among other things, that linear multiple factor analysis could discover the dimensionality of a set of variables that were not linearly related to underlying parameters. Thurstone measured the length, width and height (x, y, and z) of a collection of boxes, and constructed about twenty variables from these measures. Most of the variables were nonlinear, e.g., $\sqrt{x^2+y^2}$, xyz, $\log x$. A factor analysis of the data showed that three factors accounted for most of the covariance as well as most of the variance—the communalities of the variables were uniformly high. Further, the rotated factors could readily be interpreted as length, width, and height. Thus, linear factor analysis provides a good approximation to the data even when the underlying structure is nonlinear.

Hoffman suggests that analysis of variance may help to uncover the nonlinearities. In fact, as Hoffman notes, analysis of variance is a kind of linear regression analysis, and can therefore be expected to favor linearity. The study cited by Hoffman that used analysis of variance is a case in point. The main effects account for most of the variance; individual differences in weighting account for most of the rest.

Yntema and Torgerson (1961), in their thoughtful account of machine simulation of human judgment, provide a clear example of the insensitivity of analysis of variance to nonlinear effects. They constructed some artificial data in which the criterion, y, was related to three independent variables in a "purely" interactive way. Letting i, j, and k be integers ranging from 1 to 7, they defined $y_{ijk} = ij + jk + ik$. A standard three-way anovar of the $7 \times 7 \times 7 = 343$ "observations" showed that the three main effects accounted for 94% of the variance, leaving only 6% for interactions. In this case, each variable separately, and each pair of variables jointly, is monotonically related to the criterion. Yntema and Torgerson go on to point out that the model need not match the y_{ijk} values precisely in order to match the human judgments. The model need only rank the y's in the same order as the observed values. In that case, the linear model would be even better than the 94% figure would indicate.

The new index proposed by Hoffman seems to me not to solve the problem. It will still be analyzing departures from linear regression, and thus doomed to work with small residuals.

The point, as Hoffman says, is that the judgment is unequivocal when the values of the independent variables agree, and a decision problem arises only when the values are contradictory. The observed linearity reflects the fact that only a small number of cases are decision problems, and in many of those the range of contradiction is small. To study the details of the decision process, it is necessary to focus on those cases containing conflicts, rather than averaging them with the unequivocal cases. Only by separating the critical cases can the overwhelming effect of linearity be avoided.

Another difficulty with standard configural techniques, analysis of variance, and the new index, is that they are essentially fishing expeditions. The experimenter will covet any configural effect, any interaction that he can find. He cannot begin to examine all the possible nonlinear effects, and is very likely to miss those that are present, unless he knows where to fish.

A better strategy is to form some hypothesis and seek support for it in the data, or to specify some model for human judgment, and examine the fit of the data to the model. This not only restricts the alternatives, but it helps in setting up a reasonable experiment. Indeed, carefully counterbalanced experiments may not be worthwhile if there is no model, no hypothesis, but only a hope of catching something interesting. Perhaps the experimenter might rather run a number of exploratory studies, trying this or that, until he forms some hypotheses or sees how a model should be constructed. An excellent example of this procedure, leading to an information processing model of decision-making, is given by Kleinmuntz in this volume.

ARE PEOPLE CONSERVATIVE BAYESIANS?

Edwards has presented some impressive data, and has

referred to many other studies that show a different linear effect. When subjects estimate the odds for a particular combination of "poker chips" in a "bookbag," there seems to be no question that log likelihood and log prior odds combine linearly to produce log posterior odds. The optimum combination is an unweighted sum, but people seem to overweight the prior odds and underweight the likelihood. Edwards calls this behavior conservative.

The behavior of subjects in the bookbag and poker chips experiments can certainly be described by a conservative Bayesian model. Yet the term "conservative" seems to prejudge the issue. Is this perhaps the same sort of situation as the overbearing linear effect observed by Hoffman? Could not the apparent regularity of the data be masking some more complex processing? To use a cognitive term, are the subjects *intending* to be conservative, or are they intending something much more complex that looks on the surface like a conservative Bayes strategy?

There are a few indications in the data reported by Edwards that the behavior might be more complicated. First, there is considerable intraindividual variability. Second, the extent of conservatism seems to depend on the experimental situation for no apparent reason. In some cases, the subjects behaved as if they were estimating the odds correctly.

It is interesting to note that in a real-life situation in which people are accustomed to estimating odds, namely horse-betting, it turns out that they do it well, on the average. The parimutuel odds, which are determined by the amounts bet on each horse, when corrected for the take of the track and the government, match very closely the actual odds for each horse, as determined by past performance (Griffith, 1949). There is a slight "conservative" underestimate of the short odds and a slight "liberal" overestimate of the long odds, but these effects are minor. Horse players claim that the accuracy of the odds estimates is related to many other variables (e.g., there are too many long-odds bets in the ninth race, by losers trying to recoup their losses), but here I am going beyond the data. My point is merely that whether people are conservative or liberal depends very much on the situation.

A case of overly liberal behavior occurs in many studies of clinical prediction. When clinicians (or anyone else, for that matter) predict college grades on the basis of college board test scores and high school grade averages, they typically overweight all predictors, consequently putting too much variance in their predictions. In this case it is the statistical theory that is conservative.

I suspect that laboratory situations can be contrived in which subjects would overreact to current information; (i.e., would be liberal rather than conservative). Some colleagues and I once tried to set up a probability tracking task, in which a red or a green light appeared on each trial, as in a typical binary choice experiment. The subject's task was not to predict which light would come on next but to set a dial to estimate the probability of the red light. In our tryout the subjects overreacted, changing the setting much more frequently than the theory would support.

Dr. Edwards has pointed out to me that Robinson (1964) did a similar experiment, carefully controlled and balanced, and found that his subjects were quite accurate. His subjects made settings continuously rather than indicating their estimates after every flash. His subjects were adjusting their estimates much more frequently than the objective probability was changing, but this could be interpreted as refining the estimate rather than indicating a presumed probability change. I would still guess that a variant of the task could be set up in which subjects overreact.

For the above reasons and prejudices, I object to the term "conservative." Until we know more about the conditions in which people overreact and those in which they underreact, I would prefer a noncommittal term like "suboptimum."

It is not news, as Edwards knows well (1964), that people often behave suboptimally in experiments involving probability processes. In binary choice experiments, in which subjects are asked to predict sequences of independent binary trials, the negative recency hypothesis is popular though wrong (after a run of reds, green is thought to be "due"), and people persist in "probability matching" although they would be better off always choosing the more likely alternative. Indeed, the binary choice experiment provides a good comparison with the bookbag and poker chips experiments. In binary choice, the overriding effect is probability matching (i.e., subjects choose red about as often as the light is likely to be red). Nevertheless, there is evidence that subjects are doing something much more complicated. The negative recency phenomenon was already mentioned. Close analysis of sequential behavior reveals other regularities that indicate active hypothesis testing by sub-jects. Feldman (1961) showed quite clearly that subjects were interpreting the situation as a problem to be solved and were engaging in hypothesis formation and testing, although when the data were averaged across trials they showed prob-ability matching. Feldman and Newell (1961) have shown that a wide variety of models exhibit probability matching. Spe-cifically, they showed that if the sequence is viewed as the interleaving of any number of subsequences, such that for each subsequence the probability that subject will predict "red" for the next item is a weighted average of the events of the pre-ceding trials in that subsequence, with any arbitrary nonnega-tive weights, then subjects will exhibit probability matching. This general model includes the mathematical learning theory approaches to the binary choice experiment, but can also, by suitable choice of subsequences and weights, include problem-solving approaches to the situation.

In binary choice experiments and in models of binary choices, then, it is very difficult to avoid probability match-ing, even though the processes governing subjects behavior are much more complicated. No comparable result is yet avail-able for the Bayesian experiments but I believe the *a priori* odds are high for the existence of such a result. It seems likely that a wide variety of mechanisms will yield a linear relation between log posterior odds and a weighted sum of log prior odds and log likelihood ratio. Further, it seems likely that the processes governing subjects' behavior in the situation are more complicated. Pitz and his co-workers (1967), for example, have found much stronger intertrial dependencies than Bayes law would predict. It would certainly seem worthwhile to explore the Bayesian situation in close detail to seek more evidence of complex, cognitive behavior.

DESCRIPTION vs. EXPLANATION

The question raised by both papers is the extent to which an adequate description of the data provides an adequate ex-planation of the process generating the data. For Hoffman this is the central problem; he acknowledges the descriptive power of linear regression but would like to reject the linear ex-planation of the decision process. Edwards and his alter-egos

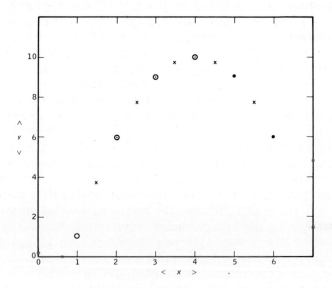

Fig. 4.1   Data fit by a quadratic function.

accept both the description and the explanation. I cannot deny the description, but I doubt the explanation.

There can be no resolution of the quarrel on theoretical grounds. More evidence is needed. Experiments should be designed to study some of the details of the process, focusing on a small subset of situations so that the main effects will not mask the more intricate regularities.

At a more general level we have seen that a simple general model can mask complexities. Nonlinear relationships and interactions are to a first approximation linear and additive. Hypothesis testing is to a first approximation probability matching in the binary choice experiment. We venture to guess that hypothesis testing is to a first approximation a conservative Bayes strategy in the bookbag and poker chips experiments. Whether one accepts the first approximations as good descriptions of reality or as fictions contributed by the method of analysis depends partly on one's purposes. If the goal is prediction in some practical situation, an adequate description will serve. But if the goal is to understand the process, then we must beware of analyses that mask complexities.

CHAPTER 5

Raymond B. Cattell

University of Illinois

TAXONOMIC PRINCIPLES FOR LOCATING AND USING TYPES (AND THE DERIVED TAXONOME COMPUTER PROGRAM)*

1. THE ROLES OF TYPES AND ATTRIBUTES

Concepts and procedures for dealing with types, in psychology and elsewhere, have remained questionable and crude compared with those developed for attributes, which operate in terms of factorial source traits and surface traits. It is the contention of this article that much of the tardiness has been due to a confusion of two distinct entities—a type as a group of highly *similar* people, and a type as a *separated* group of people—which we shall soon define and discuss as "stats" and "aits" respectively.

This, and some confusions inherited from certain rash uses of Q-technique, plague the sophisticated psychometrists; but the statistically unsophisticated clinical or "literary" psychologist is plagued by a legion of more elementary confusions. Elsewhere, the present writer (1957) has encompassed a whole museum of rank and riotous uses of "type" in the psychological literature of this generation, beginning with Jung (1923) and harking back to William James. One consistent use which emerges is that of speaking of the individuals at the extremes

*The present paper is a derived and extended version, by the senior author, of an earlier paper (Cattell and Coulter, 1966a), and contains expressly his own evaluations of the issues treated earlier. The investigation was supported in part by Public Health Service Research Grant No. MH10274-02 from the National Institutes of Mental Health.

The author wishes to thank the editor of the British Journal of Mathematical and Statistical Psychology, as well as The British Psychological Society for their kind permission to reproduce certain diagrams and tables here from his article in that journal, listed in the bibliography.

99

of some bipolar attribute as two "types." This is often inevitable as a mode of speech, but it is a redundant concept, since these are more aptly handled by assigning them notably high and low scores on a single dimension, continuous or dichotomized. If "type" is to add something new it must in addition imply something about distribution. Otherwise it degenerates into making as many types as there are human attributes, for example, the type of man who talks and the type who does not; the type of golfer who slices and the type that hooks, and so *ad nauseum* through the particular fixations of interest of every armchair "theorist."

To say that a type must have some distribution property—that of corresponding to a mode or a region of unusually high similarity of cases—is to place our usage squarely in the midst of what the biologist does with his species, genus, family, etc.; or the astronomer, with his black dwarf stars; and so on for most other sciences in which taxonomy has been properly developed. The question of whether one recognizes, beyond types *per se*, also hierarchies, textures, etc., as we eventually do here, is a matter for further definition.

In psychology one recognizes at a common sense level that types are instanced in occupational skill groupings, clinical syndrome pigeonholes, religious and political attitude constellations, and certain genetic patterns. So long as psychology dealt with very *broad* personality factors, for example, such source traits as general intelligence, surgency, ego strength, anxiety, etc., quantitative treatment was able to develop a high and effective level of prediction without much concern for types, and for the curvilinearity of relations implicit in them. There is indeed much evidence that, except for slight modifications in loading pattern, these source traits are universal across age and culture. But whenever one approaches the dynamic interest investment patterns, the cognitive skills, and specific abilities, the existence of discrete types forces itself upon one's attention.

2. TWO TYPES OF TYPES: HOMOSTATS AND SEGREGATES

Throughout this chapter the role of type description and of attribute description must alternate rapidly in the

perspective of thought, as in the face and obverse of a spinning coin. They must always be brought into a consistent whole, even though we momentarily concentrate on the abstraction from one direction only. Let us begin by considering a distribution of ids[1] in a space defined by attribute coordinates, as in Fig. 5.1.

This figure aims to bring out:

1. That nonnormal, modal groupings can easily exist in a multivariate distribution even when the distribution projected on any one of the dimensions is virtually normal;
2. That all modal condensations are relative as to density so that, as at A_1, A_2; B_1, B_2; C_1, C_2; and D_1, D_2 in Fig. 5.1, one can have "types within types," and
3. That *there are really two distinct possible definitions of type*, one hinging on: (a) high mutual similarity of members, i.e., all coming within a circumscribed distance of one another as illustrated by those lying in the dotted circles 1, 2, 3 and 4, and (b) forming part of a discrete mode, as shown by the types B and C. Discreteness, of course, implies a pattern of *relative* densities, instead of absolute densities, as in (a). Thus, A and C_1 plus B_3 persons belong to each of two types according to definition (a) whereas there are three types, A, C_1 and B_3, according to definition (b).

These two possible meanings of type I shall call respectively a *homostat* and a *segregate* (or later, *stat* and *ait*)—homostat defining operationally "standing in a similar (or same) position" and segregate having the usual meaning. It must be noted here, as will be commented upon in more technical terms later, that Fig. 5.1(b) has within it the possibilities of latent inconsistency present whenever we try to bring person-space and test-space into a single geometrical representation. If, as in later discussions, the coordinates X and Y are considered to be factors, their mutual obliqueness should accommodate to the changing correlations of the test vectors in ranges at different score levels, as affected by the changing

---

[1] In the *Handbook of Multivariate Experimental Psychology* (1966), I have suggested the generic term "id" for any replicated object of measurement—a person, a group, a biological specimen—bounding the data box in which we insert attribute measurements.

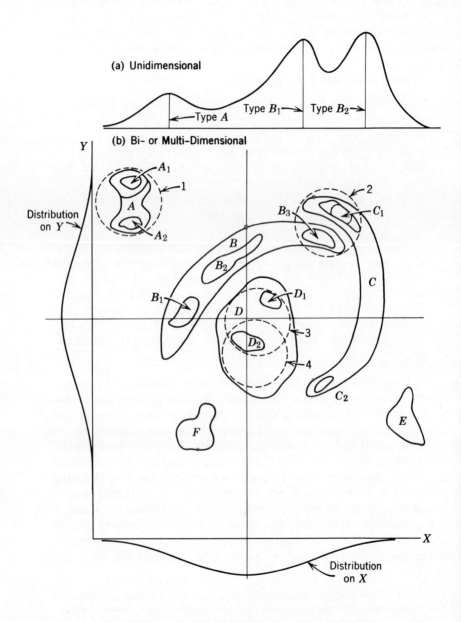

Fig. 5.1 The recognition of types as modal densities.

distributions of people. Thus even though the total distribution in Fig. 5.1(b) is bivariate normal, the coordinates of the space are a compromise among the changing angles that would be necessary among the factors in different parts of the distribution.

Before proceeding to our present treatment let us note retrospectively that practically all metric research on types to date, including, say, McQuitty's pattern analysis (1963) and our own work (Cattell, 1949) with the profile similarity coefficient, r_p, has aimed to recognize only homostats. The biologist's use of "taxon" for a group of very similar creatures has been used by Sokal and Sneath (1963) apparently with the same meaning though one could argue that the logical concepts of Linnaeus or Darwin fit equally the operational definition of a segregate. As we proceed it will become evident that a fatal ambiguity, or at least limitation of uniqueness, besets the homostat concept, but that not one researcher operationally employing it seems yet to have stumbled thereon. At any rate, a successful empirical approach to taxonomy needs both the segregate concept and an improved, qualified homostat definition—if only because the latter is a necessary stage in reaching the former. Probably one reason for the somewhat obstinate clinging to the stat concept and the continuing blindness to its defects is that a stat can be located by analytical methods whereas the ait requires topological concepts and procedures.

3. MORE PRECISE STATEMENT OF THE MODEL

A theoretical treatment of types requires reference both to methods for locating them and for using them—in descriptive and predictive undertakings. Accordingly we address ourselves to:

1. Developing a methodology for objectively, operationally locating and identifying (defining) (a) homostats and (b) segregates.
2. Describing the necessary mathematico-statistical formulae, based on these improved models for "typing," for using type information in taxonomy, prediction of criterion associations and the derivation of whatever further laws arise from studying types.

Briefly to indicate what this second step may comprise, one should point out that Aristotelian classification permits one to make predictions of the kind: "This is a dog; therefore it may bite"; "This is a schizophrenic; therefore the prospect of remissions is not high." In other words, a classification of objects by variables of one kind may permit prediction on others not at the time included. Parenthetically, despite the illustrations, these predictions need not be categorical, but can be parametric. What we then recognize as peculiar to type prediction is that the continuous measures may show a relation of "test" to "criterion" which is very different *within* the species from that *among* the species. That is to say, the relation of a feature of a type to the criterion could be nonlinear across the genus but linear within each species (or with different linear functions in the different settings). However, the use of types, instead of individuals uniformly distributed along a dimension extending across a genus, involves more computer interruption in that a visit to an encyclopedia is needed (to check the properties of the species) between the visits to the computer. The reward, however, is likely to be a more accurate prediction from any given individual's scores. It may lead to the discovery of clearer laws operating in each of the segregated types, than would be recognized if we dealt only with the genus as the population.

Both the discovery (aim (1) above) and the use (aim (2) above) of types require that we now make explicit the main features of the model we are to work with—beyond the above initial definition of a type as a multidimensional mode. Since these features could differ somewhat from area to area (e.g., zoology, psychology, mineralogy) a proper discussion of the arguments for the best *general* model could take us farther afield than present space permits. However, if the model and the statistical machinery we devise is to be adequate, no apology is needed here for entering an apparent digression into the natural origins of types, which will help us arrive at the best model.

If we glance over the biological, the human artefactual, and the inorganic worlds, in all three of which what are called types--modally replicated entities--are well represented, an argument can be made that they derive primarily from two sources: (a) adaptation of parts to a particular function, as in natural species and the objects manufactured by man, and (b) repetition of a particular coincidence of natural laws, as in rivers, planets, icicles and clouds. That wings go with feathers, and large aperture camera lenses with high speed shutters, constitutes illustration of the first. That river valleys are classified by the geographer into rias, etc., is an example of the latter. Obviously psychology has types of both kinds: the combinations of skill and personality patterns appearing in different occupations are examples of patterns developed as functional adaptations; on the other hand the repeating behavior patterns of delirium tremens or Huntington's chorea have no adaptation value and simply bring together behaviors which are examples of natural law operating on neurological properties.

Both origins result in some combination of certain parameters being represented by high (modal) frequency while other zones in the coordinate system, equally mathematically possible and theoretically occupiable, are blank. Ultimately, the theoretical taxonomist is likely to find some formal properties distinguishing these two kinds of types but we are concerned at present only with what is common. However, one cannot avoid observing that in functional adaptations, whether they arise from natural evolution or human invention, there will tend to be dendritic relations expressing the paths of evolution and there may be other differences of distribution. For example, the possibility must be considered that some zones are unoccupied not because they are nonfunctional, but because they cannot be, or have so far not been reached. In biology the intermediate mutational steps necessary to reaching some advantages of pattern may be lethal. The giraffe's neck had time to grow gradually as his forelegs grew, as did his special valves for the blood pressures reached, so that he achieved the advantages of height without either losing his capacity to drink or becoming giddy, but other biological combinations are more of a *tour de force*.

Where phylogenetic "steps" are involved in the genesis of types, as in biology, cultural anthropology, and the field of human mechanical invention, what we may call a dendritic pattern among the types may be expected, additional to the primary type segregation itself. That is to say, the familiar hierarchy of order, family, genus, species, and local variety, so engrossing to Linnaeus and Darwin, will in some form appear. Sokal and Sneath (1963) in their approach to the "numerical taxonomy" problem with which we here wrestle, have drawn the useful distinction between *phenetic* classification—

on purely phenomenal characteristics of the organisms— yielding *phenons*; and *phyletic* classification, yielding the biologist's *taxa*, into which information about historical derivation is allowed to enter. Our approach here is purely to phenons, in which we distinguish *stats* and *aits*, since we believe that it is desirable to keep the two sources of evidence—taxonomic and historical—independent up to the last step of mutual checking.

In many fields there may be other kinds of higher structuration than those known to the biologist in his dendrograms, and we shall reserve here the term *texture* for the general designation of whatever higher order structure exists in a domain of recognizable types. In any case, dendrogram and texture are features to be found out later, for they require as a research precondition the discovery of types as such.

The most probable model, therefore, is one in which:

1. Some particular range in parameter x will be found to be associated with some particular range in parameter y (in the sense that a high modal frequency will arise there in the bivariate distribution) because this is functionally useful, and is therefore multiplied. This does not prevent another pair of optimum ranges from also existing, but between such modal combinations, instances of individuals at other, intermediate combinations will be rare.

2. In the ids (specimens) found at these modes some entirely new dimensions may appear not present in the general "population" (and therefore on which a markedly "skewed-to-zero" distribution would appear for the general population), for example, among the types on the tea table only teapots have any distribution at all on the "length of spout" variable. Although, on the variables on which all types can be measured, we should expect that the existence of types would upset a strictly normal distribution, yet we should note (Fig. 5.1) that if types are sufficiently numerous, a discontinuous or multimodal distribution in multidimensional space is not incompatible with a continuous and normal distribution on each variable separately. Shortly we shall take up more explicitly the question of within and between (or "super-species") variables[2] and distributions—or "in-

---

[2] The terms within and between species are used here initially as in analysis of variance. However, by definition of types the null hypothesis

type" and "cross-type" dimensions. However, even if normal distributions of cross-type measures are obtained when all types are thrown into a single population, non-linearity of relations is inescapable in getting the best predictions from cross-type dimensions to the behavior of individuals, and has implications for the nature of our original coordinate system. The true across species (super-species) variables may then be almost normally distributed despite many type segregations. By contrast, the within species variables will be badly skewed if measured across the population, for most ids will have no score at all on some of the dimensions.

3. Beyond the segregation in types we may expect, in different fields of data, as indicated above, a different model of *higher order structure* and *texture.*

It will save some trouble if in addition to this look at the model, we take a glance at the model-seeker—the typical mathematical statistician. To explain what has happened—or mostly what has not happened—in this field we must recognize that the abstractive habit of mind of the mathematician and particularly his reliance upon analytic geometrical and algebraic repertoires when topological ones are needed, have stood in the way of any really effective grappling with the problem. The attempt to solve it by dimensional treatment, as in the misuse of Q-technique referred to above and elsewhere, is a typical example. The problem is one of describing essentially irregular masses; it is not even topology, but rather topography. It is precisely that of discovering the cloud structure in an n-dimensional sky. Almost everyone begins by thinking of discrete and similar cumulus clouds neatly arranged in a summer sky. But any realist is forced at the end to come to terms with the ultimate in irregular masses—an October storm-wrack. Geometrical models and statistical procedures have no alternative but to prepare to loosen their rigidity to cope with this degree of complexity. They have to acquire some of the mechanisms of the human perceptual apparatus.

is never sustained. Moreover, only one class of variables—the cross-type variables—meets the analysis of variance requirement of applying both to individuals and to means. The in-type variables can be used only to fix individuals in the given species and have no application across the means of species.

4. TWO MAIN APPROACHES TO LOCATING HOMOSTATS

As has been hinted repeatedly above, the majority of methods used over the past 20 years in locating types are fallacious. They fail either through rigidly following statisticians' and mathematical analysts' rules which do not fit what is really the most likely scientific model as indicated above, or, more commonly among tyros by ignoring comparatively elementary mathematical statistical requirements.

It will help simultaneously to clear the garbage from the site, and to illustrate certain principles, if we pause ever so briefly to mention some of the more conventionally respected procedures of which we are critical, such as: (1) Use of the correlation coefficient to express degree of similarity or nearness. This takes no heed of differences in *level* between two profiles, and thus invalidates certain findings frequently inferred from both Q- and $\bar{Q}$-techniques.[3] It seems to invalidate some inferences in the otherwise very thorough treatment of numerical taxonomy by Sokal and Sneath (1963). (2) Use of Q-sort, which only avoids the difference of level problem by ignoring it (by using a rank order correlation) and which, additionally, by ignoring also the problem of sampling variables, or substituting factors for variables, yields a numerical answer which is meaningless. McQuitty's pattern analysis, though less grossly vulnerable to the choice of items for comparison, still lacks adequate methodological defense against this subjectivity. (3) Use of Holzinger's (1941) B-coefficient, since the ultimate composition of the group depends upon the point at which one chooses to begin, and no distinction is made between what we call below phenomenal and nuclear clusters. (4) Use of latent class analysis (Gibson, 1956; Lazarsfeld, 1960), which, though elegant, does not adapt to the common requirement of a *continuum* of factor or variable scores, and (5) Use of the multiple discriminant function. This last is, of course, a method of obtaining weights to *emphasize* group

---

[3] Unless, of course, size happens to be unimportant. Incidentally, to avoid confusion "$\bar{Q}$-technique" is best applied to seeking *clusters* of people (or ids generally) in a Q-matrix, whereas "Q-technique" is applied to seeking factors in a Q-matrix, i.e., to the *transpose* of R-technique. Henceforth we shall refer to a square matrix of relationships (by any suitable index) among a set of ids. e.g., a matrix bounded by the same people top and side. as a Q-*matrix*.

segregation, not of *finding* natural segregations. Any use of it to "locate" types is therefore essentially no better than a rationalization of subjective prejudices.

Granted the fundamental definition of a *homostat type* as a group of ids which are unusually close together in an attribute space (homostat =similar position) our only concerns become (a) "How is the space in which we operate to be defined?" and (b) "How do we measure the closeness or distance apart of any two ids, in an absolute or relative expression?" For the moment we shall by-pass some of the ultimate subtleties needed in defining the space, and describe it as the space fixed by the coordinates represented by the factors obtained from factoring across the population of ids using a stratified sample of the population of variables (cross-type variables) needed to describe those ids.

In the Euclidean space thus provided, the finding of the distributions and modal masses hinges on beginning with a suitable expression for the distance apart of any two ids. Many investigators have used the generalized (n-dimensional) distance function:

$$d = \sqrt{(a_1 - a_2)^2 + (b_1 - b_2)^2 + \ldots + (n_1 - n_2)^2} \qquad (1)$$

commonly called Mahalanobis's D (1936). But the present writer (1949) has reasoned that this is unsuitable in its crude form because its magnitude gives—as a result of different scale metrics for different coordinates—no immediately meaningful value. Even when such a crude d is improved upon, by giving it the more constant meaning from transforming all n-distributions into standard scores, it is still an inadequate basis for expressing degree of similarity because: (1) as the function has typically been used it proceeds by making each *variable* an orthogonal coordinate, when in fact variables are substantially correlated—thus different sets of variables get uneven representation; (2) since we need to compare resemblances in different dimensionalities it is desirable to use an expression for the distance which cancels the effect of the number of dimensions involved, so that, other things being equal, the statement is independent of that dimensionality, and (3) it is desirable to give equal weight to each dimension and domain—this requires that we substitute orthogonal factors for variables, thus giving equal weight at least as far as domains have been investigated at the given stage of science. Such a space is no longer accidentally defined but reflects the correlational realities among variables and brings meaning to "equality of dimensions."

Granted that we can thus define a space and the degree of resemblance of any two ids within it, one approach—which we shall call the *inter-id relation method*—is available to us for describing the natural groupings. Before pursuing this, and the proposition of substituting the profile similarity coefficient, r_p, for the simple d function in this pursuit, let us notice, however, that there are really two distinct ways in which one can go about determining distributions in such a space. One, the above-designated inter-id method, starts with the points constituted by the ids and asks how they are related. The other, which we may call the *cartet count*, begins with the framework of dimensions and essentially counts as in making up a histogram, but in n space. Either approach will initially give a statement about stats and only later a statement about aits.

1. *The Inter-id Relation Method.* By this approach we begin with ids, finding how they relate to one another, regardless of their location in the total space. One begins with a Q-matrix—a square matrix bounded by the same set of people on top and side—with r_p or other indices of nearness (resemblance) of the two people in each cell. Matrix cluster search methods then operate, as described below, to find the subgroups of cohering ids. The positions of these sets in the coordinate framework are a matter for secondary calculation.

2. *The Cartet Count or n-Dimensional Histogram Method.* Here one begins with the coordinate system, instead of the individuals, as in (1) above. Certain "latitude and longitude" intervals on the coordinates having been fixed, the computer is asked simply to count the number of people in each "hypersquare" or, rather, "hypercube." No term having come into common use for such a cube in Cartesian space, perhaps we may temporarily refer to it conveniently as a *cartet*. Beginning with some arbitrary small size of cartet and programming the computer to count and set aside all those above some average density (i.e., number of ids per cube), one would arrive at a list of homostats—except that they would be cubes rather than

spheres as in the id relation procedures—from which further procedure to aits, or other groupings among the cartets themselves, would be possible.

This cartet count approach we shall not pursue further here, not because of any inherent defect, but because it is in some ways less attractive and threatens to become a large task even for a computer. For example, with only 16 dimensions, and intervals restricted to just 3 standard score unit intervals, plus and minus, on each (i.e., 6 per coordinate), the total number of cartets (hypercubes) to have their contents examined is $6^{16} = 2,830,000,000,000$ (approx.). On the other hand, it must be recognized that with increasingly large numbers of ids the task by the id-relation method accelerates rapidly also.

In concentrating on pursuit of the id-relation method, we propose initially that the resemblance or nearness not be measured by any of the simple distance functions, for the reasons given above, but by the pattern similarity coefficient which, for orthogonal coordinates is written (Cattell, 1949) as follows:

$$r_p = \frac{2k - \sum_1^k d^2}{2k + \sum_1^k d^2} \tag{2}$$

where k is the number of profile elements; any d is the difference of the two people concerned in standard scores, on any one profile element, and k is the median chi-square value for k degrees of freedom. At $k = 20$, $k = 19.337$. Indeed, above, say, 20 profile elements there is not much argument for using k rather than k. Since the former will *exactly* divide the possible r_p's into *equal* numbers of positive and negative values, whereas the former will give a zero *sum* of negative and positive r_p's, there is not a lot to choose between the two.

The advantages of this r_p over D have been indicated above but may be set out more specifically as follows:

1. That it gives, regardless of the different metrics and numbers of profile elements, a value which behaves very similarly to the familiar correlation coefficient, registering 0 where the relation between two ids is no better than chance, +1.0 when they are perfectly alike and -1.0 where they are as unlike as possible. By contrast, one never knows what the meaning of a particular D value is without

an elaborate additional supply of information and reference to further calculations.

2. In particular this freedom from dimensionality and metric permits comparison of the degree of resemblance of the people in two different pairs when one pair is measured in k dimensions and another in k + x dimensions. Since different experiments frequently use fewer or extra dimensions, this makes it valuable in integrative surveys.

3. A significance test has been worked out by Horn (1961) for r_p. This, and other equipment and properties, permits a superstructure of further methods and programs to be erected upon its use.

On the other hand, r_p values are not simple distances, and if we set out to use them as such—much as one would use resemblances in multidimensional scaling procedures—we do so only by requiring our original space to become non-Euclidean. Actually the distortion is not great, as will be seen from the relation of r_p to D (when the latter is brought to standard scores) plotted in Fig. 5.2. It will be seen that through the central range the relation is *approximately* linear. This approximation can be made still closer by using the r_p derivative, r_n (the coefficient of nearness), proposed for certain uses below. Of course, the upsetting of Euclidean properties, though by a function of minor degree, would be serious if those properties were needed for other calculations, but further discussion will show that there are few purposes for which the simple Euclidean properties are appropriate and many for which even more complex derivatives than this simplest form of r_p are needed.

Equipped with a definable space, an index for measuring closeness of ids therein, and a preliminary definition of a homostat, we are ready to tackle the technical problems of search. Before doing so, however, one should perhaps pause to point out to the psychologist and other scientists interested in the scientific model more than the statistics that nothing in the procedures and concepts so far introduced confines the utility to types among objects only. Introductorily, it is true we confined ourselves, implicitly, to the class of "objects," but let the reader reflect that the models and procedures here can be applied equally to the grouping of those phenomena we call "processes." A process, as a configuration (Cattell, 1966), can be reduced first to a succession of factorial scores, which can then be handled as an id profile. The methods here described can be applied to sets of patterns of any kind— spatial, temporal, and so on. It is probably important to point this out to the clinical psychologist who will otherwise justly object that his typing of patients rests on more than static measures as seem indicated here. It can depend in fact partly upon process observations (e.g., schizophrenia is partly defined by process). The total configuration of the id entry in our analysis can, indeed, be partly process and partly trait values.

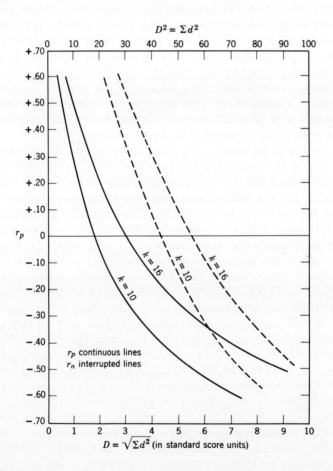

Fig. 5.2 Degree of preservation of simple euclidean space properties when r_p and r_n are treated as distances. (Plot of r_p and r_n against D values, for $k = 16$ and $k = 10$).

5. THE HOMOSTAT: ITS DEFINITION IN GENERAL
AND SPECIAL CRITERION TERMS

Let us now tighten our definitions of concepts and operations, beginning with a homostat as follows: *A stat* (for brevity, henceforth) *is a group of ids all pairs among which resemble one another beyond a certain fixed absolute value.* This value has to be fixed by various considerations but most frequently will meet the condition of being significantly higher than the average value obtaining among all *possible* pairs in the total population. It is remarkable that this notion, which has been central to almost all type-seeking formulations, for example, the biologist's definition of a taxon, McQuitty's (1963) pattern analysis programs, etc., has in general been used without perception of the almost absurd lack of objectivity which still besets it. This limitation consists of the fact that a homostat may have all members meeting the requirement and yet leave its center and boundaries entirely dependent on the place (the id) at which one happens to start the search. The nature of the difficulty will be seen most readily by looking at circles 3 and 4 in Fig. 5.1. Accepting for the moment (the assumptions are not relevant) the close approximation of r_p to the distance function, d, and taking this two-space example, we see that a set of ids meeting the above definition of a stat is contained in a circle of a diameter corresponding to the r_p (or other distance function) value fixed upon (e.g., an r_p of +0.8). It will be seen that in the segregate D, two circles are placed within the segregate which are in fact but two among a large number of overlapping circles which could be placed within it. (Just how many different circles would be a function of the number of ids, in that neighborhood.) A segregate has an objectively recognizable boundary, but the boundary of a stat is in part subjectively determined by where the experimenter happens to begin. Furthermore, the relation of stat and ait is not constant. Sometimes a stat is a part of an ait as in circles 3 and 4; sometimes a stat will cover two or more aits, as in circle 2; sometimes it will cover more than an ait, as in circle 1.

That a stat and an ait are not coincident fits our argument for the necessity for two concepts, but that the location of a stat depends on the position (the id) with which one starts one's search is disturbing. Indeed, the full extent of this indeterminacy is evident if one happens to take a d value (or corresponding r_p) which happens to cover just two ids in a fairly uniform distribution of ids. The essence of the problem is seen if we imagine a straight line of equidistant points, when it will be evident that they could be grouped either (1,2); (3,4), etc., or (2,3); (4,5), etc., depending on the starting point.

Leaving the reader to digest for a while this quality in one of the concepts at which we have aimed, we must turn to yet another aspect of the grouping problem that has to be clarified before we can hope to converge on a finally meaningful procedure. It involves a return to the resemblance function itself—regardless of whether it enters the definition of stat or ait—and the asking of some almost philosophical questions about the possible meanings of similarity, and about the algebraic or geometrical equivalence which we give to them.

When the logical basis for r_p was originally stated (Cattell, 1949), it was pointed out that customarily we are given to making a distinction between the character of the *thing in itself* (the German philosophers' *Das Ding an sich*) on the one hand, and certain *effects* of the thing, on the other. In literature one encounters it in such comments as in Chesterton's essay on Browning: "The great but now neglected truth, that a man may actually be great, yet not in the least able," and one encounters it again in epistemology and in religion.[4] The psychometrist routinely distinguishes the test and the criterion. Rightly or wrongly he has the habit of thinking of an individual's profile on personality and ability tests as one thing and his criterion performances in everyday life or his social effect on others as another. How does this duality of realm of reference affect the principles for determining the similarity of two people?

A fair number of attempts to type or group people and other ids have been explicitly concerned with a single function and one which would be regarded as a criterion or effect. For example, one might type children in relation to school achievement ("underachievers") or wood saws, for *Consumer Reports*, in regard to their effectiveness for sawing wood. In such a case the transformation from the set of measurements— hopefully factor dimensions—on which one began the original

---

[4] Whether or not this is a defensible division is another question, but it certainly recurs in human thinking, in many contexts, e.g., in the theological "grace" versus "works," and, epistemologically, perhaps in Hume's primary and secondary properties of objects.

type search to the single dimension on which one will now search afresh for modes, is carried out either by a linear specification equation, or some higher order polynomial, known best to predict the specific performance from the traits.

This is illustrated, as a transition from two dimensions to one, in Fig. 5.3, where the linear factor specification equation transformation results in the straight line *wx* and a nonlinear polynomial might be as shown at *yz*. In such cases one can view the transformation of the existing typology on the higher dimensions to that on the single dimension as a projection of the first distribution onto a line, in this case resulting

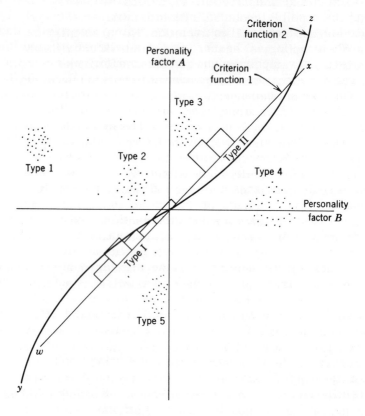

Fig 5.3   Regrouping and reduction of modal types when specific effect (Criterion) functions are used.   Histogram drawn of Criterion Function 1 shows two modes (types) replacing the five modes (types) on the profile elements themselves.   The projections on Criterion Function 2 are too complex to be readily drawn.

in a collapse of five types to two (see histogram on *wx* base). Thus any expression of type function in terms of evaluation by a single purpose will result in a change of type grouping (usually a reduction in number) which will, of course, present a typology peculiar to each function. One can see this at a common sense level if one reflects that to a barber, a brush, comb and pair of scissors have similarities of function, while a screw driver and a bottle opener are something else. But in removing a bottle cap, the screwdriver, pair of scissors and bottle opener form a class to which a comb and a brush no longer belong.

That the nature of the grouping one obtains when one transforms from a multidimensional "thing in itself" to some specific usage or criterion will change considerably is thus readily understood both in the everyday world and in our mathematical scheme of representation. The single criterion is properly viewed as only the extreme case of a general transformation from a k- to a c-dimensional representation, where $k > c$. In practice the c dimensions may be completely predictable as a subspace within the k, or it may present the kind of problem for which we avail ourselves of a best estimate via canonical correlation. With linear relationships there is never any problem, so long as the criterion dimensions are fewer and in a subspace, in passing from one typological grouping to the other.

However, the problem here raised—though we solve it by saying there is *no* difference between the worlds of test and of criterion, and that the thing *is* its performance—emphasizes the importance of what the present writer has maintained in other personality measurement contexts (1957), namely, of *representative sampling*. The criterion behavior is just another way of behaving, but criterion and test behavior can be conceived as sampled from some total population of behaviors. And if we can devise operations to define the population and to reach a stratified sample from it we have a basis for saying that the typology derived from it is *the* typology, from which all typologies in smaller subspaces are mere projections, to fit some specific and limited concept of the purpose of the object.

The transformation we are not considering, in which certain dimensions are lopped off altogether, may in turn be regarded as an extreme example of weighting (with some weights going to zero). Weighting, which is often accidental and unintentional, is properly to be invoked to express some information we have about the relative importance of various dimensions, and must be applied to an ideal initially equally weighted model. The ideal commencement point, regardless of what transformations occur later, is the factor dimensions found from taking an adequate and stratified sample of all purposes, properties and behaviors of the organisms concerned, and using the factors therefrom to provide equally scaled scores for the elements of the profiles to be compared. This is the basis of the meaning of the thing-in-itself. However, this reduction of a world of variables to the most comprehensive set of factors is only a first step to enable us in controlled fashion to apply unequal weights to them according to some rational view of the nature and purposes of the typology. For the psychologist does not usually reside upon Olympus, but in a world of restricted practical objectives. However, the actual calculation of "weighted typologies" is best considered in the next section as we return to the "resemblance" or "nearness" functions themselves.

6. GENERAL FORMULAE IN THE FAMILY OF PROFILE SIMILARITY COEFFICIENTS

The coefficient r_p, as used, for instance, in guidance, to determine an individual's fitness (belonging) to an occupation, or, in clinical work, to diagnose the case in terms of exact resemblance to a standard syndrome mean profile, has two noteworthy mathematico-statistical properties besides those noted in describing its essential usefulness above. First, through use of the quadratic term Σd^2, any deviation from the "ideal" is penalized equally in either direction (which is a generally desired property, for a fitness measure). Secondly, however, it penalizes deviation as the *square* of the deviation magnitude and, of course, without prior research ascertainment, there is no guarantee that the second power is the best for calculating the criterion fitness. The second power has certain practical advantages and it keeps us nearer to Euclidean space, but insofar as the ordinary linear specification equation is widely used in other psychological predictions, and the linear weights are known for various criteria, there is an argument for a second form of r_p in which $\Sigma\,d$ is substituted for $\Sigma\,d^2$ and the expectation value, $2k$, is altered accordingly. One could either preserve the sign of d, in which case one would be essentially comparing two people of the criterion prediction from the specification equation (the "coefficient of criterion closeness") or eliminate it, as in the "coefficient of nearness" proposed below, in which distance remains signless.

Obviously, by adapting to various assumptions, a whole family of r_p coefficients could be derived. While there is much to be said for what the writer has called elsewhere a *coefficient of criterion closeness*, which is consistent with the specification equation, and has positive and negative values according to the direction of deviation, yet here we shall set out only one new variant of r_p . This is the *coefficient of nearness*, which attempts to preserve the above desirable properties of r_p (e.g., 0 = no relation, and so on), while conforming somewhat more closely to Euclidean space. The profile nearness coefficient is simply:[5]

$$r_n = \frac{\sqrt{2k} - \sqrt{\sum_1^k d^2}}{\sqrt{2k} + \sqrt{\sum_1^k d^2}} \tag{3}$$

The greater conformity to Euclidean space (i.e., to a generalized D) is shown in the graphs of Fig. 5.2. As indicated, it nevertheless preserves the capacity to give immediate meaning to similarity coefficients in that it is 0 with no more than average, i.e., chance relationship; +1.0 for exact likeness; and potentially -1.0 for as great an unlikeness as possible. What recommends it less than r_p , however, is that its distribution is more skewed, approaching -1.0 very slowly. (At a 5 sigma difference on every element is still only at about -0.6.) This slowness to approach -1.0 may, however, express a real truth, namely, that in any ordinary population extreme opposites are rare. Nevertheless, until we have more experience of r_n it must be recognized that the averaging of r_n's, and possibly other treatments may have pitfalls. Consequently, until such experience is gained we propose here to stay with r_p.

Published psychological uses of r_p have so far made two main assumptions: (1) that the factor measurements are

---

[5] Strictly, the expected value of $\sqrt{\Sigma d^2}$ is $\sqrt{2k}\,(1 - \dfrac{1}{4k} + \dfrac{1}{32k^2} + \dfrac{1}{128k^3} + \ldots)$ but $\sqrt{2k}$ is a close enough approximation if k is not too small.

orthogonal, and (2) that the elements (factors) are given equal weight. Yet most known real personality and ability source traits are oblique, and if we wish to give such oblique factors exactly equal weight (or known weights, with freedom to give any other weights we may want to the higher strata factors), then strictly we should not be using the ordinary r_p formula— (1) above.

The dependable argument for unequal weights is that with any stratified sampling of the world of total behavior, as in the personality sphere, we are likely to find some factors more "important" than others. That is to say, if we seriously regard prediction over the whole personality sphere as the proper ultimate basis for a typology, then factors *should* be unequally weighted. A precise expression (granted an agreed total population of variables) for that importance can be given by an estimate from the mean variance contribution across the population of variables, i.e., by the root average squared sums of the factor loadings for the given factor (the "latent root" in the orthogonal case) as shown in (4), where b_{jk} is the loading of variable k on factor j.

$$w_{f_j} = \sqrt{\frac{\sum_{k=1}^{k=n} b_{jk}^2}{n}} \qquad (4)$$

Beginning with any agreed weighting system, a generalized r_p for any obliquity and any weight will begin with the essential form behind (2) above, namely,

$$r_{p_{xy}} = \frac{Ek - D_{xy}^2}{Ek + D_{xy}^2} \qquad (5)$$

where D_{xy}^2 is the squared distance apart of two people, x and y (previously written $\sum_1^k d^2$) in a k dimensional Euclidean space and Ek is the expected distance for k dimensions (previously assumed to be $2k$). But D_{xy}^2 can no longer be simply

$$\sum_{j=1}^{j=k} (Z_{jx} - Z_{jy})^2$$

(or, in matrix notation: -

$$Z'_{d_{(xy)}} \; Z_{d_{(xy)}}).$$

For we must now take into account the correlations, $r_{f_j f_1}$ between the source traits (factors) j and l, and others, which we may write as the usual matrix R_f, and we must also include the weights assigned to the factors, which we will write into the k by k diagonal matrix D_w. Then:

$$d^2_{(xy)} = Z'_{d_{(xy)}} \; D^2_w \; R_f D^2_w \; Z_{d_{(xy)}} \tag{6}$$

The expected value of $d^2_{(xy)}$ is no longer $2k$, but is:

$$E_k = \left[\text{trace}\,(D^{1/2} \; L' D^2_w \; R_f D^2_w \; L \; D^{1/2} \,)\right] \tag{7}$$

where D is the diagonal matrix of latent roots of

$$Z_{d_{(xy)}} \; Z'_{d_{(xy)}}$$

and L the matrix of the associated latent roots.

If one wishes to revert to the special case so far employed—the orthogonal, equal weight r_p—it is easily done by inserting $r = 0$ and $w = 1$ in the above. This special case [(2) above], which we have often proposed for more general use, is, it is true, an approximation, justifiable (when actually only minor obliquities exist) because the computing advantage is actually very great. For the user of the oblique formula is compelled to work out afresh for each case the complex expression $Z'_{(xy)} D^2_w \; R_f D^2_w \; Z_{(xy)}$; whereas for the simple approximation it suffices only to enter a nomograph with the individual Σd^2 (Cattell and Eber, 1966). Nevertheless, with a computer program, based on (7), the use of the full formula on numerous individual cases presents no problem.

The formula for the profile nearness coefficient (using d's, without signs, instead of d^2) becomes, correspondingly:

$$r_n = \frac{E_k - [Z'_{d_{(xy)}} \; D^2_w R_f D^2_w \; Z_{d_{(xy)}}]^{1/2}}{E_k + [Z'_{d_{(xy)}} \; D^2_w \; R_f D^2_w \; Z_{d_{(xy)}}]^{1/2}} \tag{8}$$

for oblique and weighted[6] source traits. Here, to a first approximation:

$$E_k = [\,\text{trace}\,(D^{1/2}\,LD_w^2\,R_f D_w^2\,LD^{1/2}\,)]^{1/2} \qquad (9)$$

The distribution and significance limits for r_n, corresponding to those obtained for r_p (Horn, 1961) remain to be worked out, so the ensuing steps here are best considered to employ r_p.

7. THE DEFINITION OF PHENOMENAL AND NUCLEAR CLUSTERS (OR CLIQUES) IN AN INCIDENCE MATRIX

If one is eventually to speak of distinct groups or categories there comes a point where one must substitute a categorical for a continuous function, such as r_p or r_n. Whatever fine decimal values are calculated for the relations of an individual to others, he must eventually be placed either inside or outside a group. Although it is conceivable that a continuous value for "degree of belonging" to a type can be given—indeed, we later propose such a value—yet for most purposes a decision has to be reached whether the individual does or does not belong, and in any case if the definition of the type itself is to be a collection of individuals it must have a topological, nonparametric boundary.

Using r_p, r_n, D, or any other legitimate measure of resemblance of two people it therefore becomes necessary to apply a "cutting point" or "limit," saying that all pairs above this show "adequate or significant resemblance" and all below do not. About the choice of this limit much can be said and much dispute can arise. Wherefore one should never lose sight

---

[6] The weights for source traits, both in r_p and r_n, are typically positive. However, paradoxical though it may at first appear, it is possible for some performance depending on the relations of two people to be better performed where they are more *un*like on some elements of the profile. Sexual attraction is a case in point. In such a case the squared weights in certain elements of D_n^2 must go negative, and the E_k value will be reduced. (In the orthogonal case, with unit weights, it will lose two degrees of freedom for each element reversed in sign.) However, in this use of r_p or r_n we are no longer dealing with the concept of distance among individuals but with estimations of performance of two individuals at a time.

of the original parametric basis, and should constantly consider what the effects would be on the obtained grouping if one were to adopt other levels.

Granted a basis for choosing a cutting level on r_p, the square Q-matrix of coefficients used for the $\bar{Q}$-technique procedures will at this point be transformed to an *incidence matrix*. This has unities as entries when two people resemble each other to the required degree or above (or have a "linkage") and zeros when they do not.[7]

Incidentally, from this point on our model and our program fit both the personality theorist's (or the biologist's and cultural psychologist's) need to find types of organisms, on the one hand, and the sociologist's search for an objective basis for locating cliques and communication networks on the other. In the latter case the unit entries are "ties" (Cattell, 1963), not measures of resemblance, but the formal similarity of subsequent treatment is very high, and both the methodology and computer program are applicable to each. Indeed, there are some very diverse fields of research, having in common only the treatment of some relation—resemblance, interaction, common fate, etc.—between two entities, to which the rest of our model and treatment can usefully apply.

At this point, having completed the promised investigation of the technical issues in measuring resemblance, and reached a systematic use of r_p culminating in the incidence matrix ready for some form of Q-analysis, we return to the difficult

---

[7]Since the practical question will arise at this point whether one should also insert -1.0's, this is perhaps the place to remind the reader that the whole notion of reciprocity of R- and Q-technique practices breaks down in one important respect; namely, that *one can meaningfully reflect tests but not people.* Thus the incidence matrix has +1.0's but no -1.0's, despite r_p itself ranging asymptotally from +1 to -1. It would seem that in some domains we come near to "reversing people," i.e., thinking of individuals with an r_p of -1.0 as nevertheless in some way potentially closely related, as when we talk in one breath of angels and devils, and insist that Lucifer had to be a fallen angel. But what is the opposite of a chair? Opposities to existing objects commonly will not even be logical possibilities or exist in real data. Like D'Artagnan we may assert *"Le diable est mort"* without becoming atheists. In short, in the whole process of mapping similars in real data we are not required to consider opposites in the same framework, nor can we rationally make reflections in Q-matrix entries. Parenthetically, with *correlation of persons,* reflecting even a test upsets the obtained value, as it would not if reversal were a legitimate procedure in the person domain. [See Footnote (3) above.]

question of the elusive homostat. If we are indeed prepared to ask operationally, "What sets of people can be found in which everyone resembles everyone else above an agreed value?", an answer can be given. But, as we have seen earlier, any such operation will normally present a whole series of stats, overlapping in various ways, such that, as a descriptive device, it offers alternatives and redundancies. Only with simple "texture" in the data—notably, a number of well-segregated groups—and a fortunate choice of cutting level on r_p—namely one which gives a sphere of just the right diameter to enclose these nebulae—will analysis by stats straightway yield a useful summary of the types which exist.

How then are we to pass from the plethora of homostats to some more condensed statement? In an earlier treatment (1952) the present writer proposed the term "phenomenal cluster" (or p-cluster) for this first form of homostat and pointed out that an obvious step to a generally more condensed description would be to recognize also a "nuclear cluster" (or n-cluster). An n-cluster is composed of and defined by, the ids in the overlap area of two or more phenomenal clusters, as instanced by (k,n) or (l,o) in Fig. 5.4 (ii) or by (a, b, c, d) in Fig. 5.4 (i). In fact, Figs. 5.4, 5.5 and 5.6 will most quickly give one the initial meaning of p- and n-clusters and also of the segregates which we shall soon discuss. Regardless of ultimate objectives and needs, these n- and p-clusters are at least objective and operational and worthy of recording as a stage in research, to the extent that the same r_p cutting level is accepted.

However, the last phrase must not be forgotten: The number, nature and degrees of overlap found for p- and n-clusters will depend on the r_p cutting point accepted in going from the r_p matrix to the incidence matrix. Different groupings will appear as the limit is dropped, just as the map of sand bars in an estuary will change with the tide. Some typologists have been frankly arbitrary in fixing the limit, taking, for example, +0.5 to +0.8 as "reasonably" high similarity to go into the same group. Since arbitrariness of this degree is unsatisfactory some alternative principles must be sought, and the following are suggested:

1. The taxonomist decides what fraction of his total population he expects to see incorporated in types and fixes on an r_p level which will "rope in" that number. This is arbitrari-

ness only once removed, but, at least, enlightened by pragmatic considerations of what a typology is for.

2. The experimenter uses the mean of the positive r_p's in the matrix as his cutting point. This acceptance of a value taken from the general texture of his domain recognizes that a hundred people shoulder to shoulder constitutes a "subcrowd" in Times Square, but six people within sight of one another indicates a group if in the Sahara. Another version of (2) is to take the mean of a set of random r_p's for k profile elements. Table 5.1 is presented as a first available guide, reached by Monte Carlo methods, for choosing such values.

TABLE 5.1   Values from Distribution of Random r_p 's
Obtained by Monte Carlo Methods (using normal
distribution on each element of profile)

Algebraic Mean			Mean of Positive Values Only		
N/k	2	6	10	N/k	2	6	10
25	0.188	0.135	0.052	25	0.501	0.307	0.223
50	0.174	0.047	0.011	50	0.479	0.263	0.197
75	0.114	0.046	0.017	75	0.450	0.263	0.202
100	0.100	0.031	0.011	100	0.449	0.257	0.199

Incidentally, in considering Table 5.1 the reader may wonder what the effect upon clustering may be of including larger and larger samples from the same population. The question at the moment is not about sampling *variation* but about systematic effects of size. The chances of finding a second person with high resemblance to one first taken are, of course, increased as the sample size increases, but so also are the chances of encountering those with significant negative resemblance. The algebraic mean of r_p would therefore be expected not to alter and Table 5.1 suggests that once k and N get to appreciable sizes this is true. At the same time, a given positive r_p limit will, of course, include more people in the cluster as the total sample size increases. But one would expect the number, form and percentage of the total group included in clusters to stay the same, except for sampling variations. In comparing results from different samples it is thus an obviously necessary first step to express clusters as percentages.

Before asking what further meaning can be extracted from phenomenal and nuclear clusters it may help if the reader familiarizes himself with how they appear in (a) the incidence matrix and (b) in a topological diagram, is shown in Table 5.2,

TABLE 5.2   Incidence Matrix for 15 People

	a	b	c	d	e	f	g	h	i	j	k	l	m	n	o
a	1	1	1	1	1	1	1	1	1						
b	1	1	1	1	1	1	1	1	1						
c	1	1	1	1				1	1						
d	1	1	1	1				1	1						
e	1	1			1	1	1		1						
f	1	1			1	1	1								
g	1	1			1	1	1								
h	1	1	1	1				1							
i	1	1	1	1	1				1						
j										1	1		1		
k										1	1	1		1	1
l											1	1	1	1	1
m												1	1		1
n										1	1	1		1	1
o											1	1	1	1	1

and in Fig. 5.4 (p. 132). As the diagram clearly shows, there are six phenomenal clusters discoverable from the incidence matrix of Table 5.2 but they overlap. Ids a and b are then seen to constitute a nuclear cluster with regard to three phenomenals, but c and d with respect to only two. The resulting printout of nuclear clusters is shown in Table 5.5, (p. 132). Whereas p-clusters require a summary which gives sizes, content and frequencies at the sizes, n-clusters require a series of columns for number of p-clusters overlapping in them, as well as rows for size of cluster. This descriptive phase ends, therefore, with two columns (content and frequency) and s rows (sizes) for p-clusters, and s rows (sizes) and n columns (number of clusters in overlap) for n clusters. (See Tables 5.4 and 5.5.) However, both tables might well be repeated, giving the picture at each of two r_p cutting points.

8. THE BOOLEAN CLUSTER (STAT) SEARCH ALGORITHM CENTRAL TO THE TAXONOME PROGRAM

So far we have described what operational concepts can

be used, and how the results can be summarized, but not just what procedures would be used for locating them. A purely visual search for internally consistent clusters suffices for a small Q-matrix as in the illustration in Table 5.2, but, as a *mechanical* search procedure, for larger matrices, Cattell (1952) proposed the algorithm of the *ramifying linkage method*. Experience has shown that it needs an additional step, best formally expressed as a Boolean multiplication. This whole programmable process for finding homostats will now be briefly described. It first finds p-clusters and then examines them for n-clusters.

The ramifying linkage method proceeds from the original Q_0 incidence matrix[8] by working sequentially through the set of other persons (or other entities) related to the particular person with whom one starts. This means, usually, beginning with column 1 and looking at the successive row values. At each step one deletes those who are not related (linked) to *all* of those already examined. Thus, starting in column 1 in Matrix Q_0 of Table 5.3, the method notes first the set of persons related to person 1, namely persons 5 and 7. It proceeds next, therefore, to column 5 and notes that person 5 is related to person 7, so 1, 5 and 7 in this case form a cluster though in some other case not all those picked up in the first column would themselves prove interrelated.

We can see further how the method works by using it on the hypothetical example of 10 people in matrix Q_0 in Table 5.3. If two persons i and j have adequate resemblance, then the (i, j) and the (j, i) elements of Q_0 are 1, so it would only be necessary to use half the matrix, but it is more convenient for programming to use the whole matrix, recognizing that this will result in our finding the same cluster twice. The procedure involves searching Q_0, column by column and transfering the results to a new matrix, P_1 (for phenomenal cluster) each time we find a set which meets the conditions for a cluster. Thus in this case, P_1 shows that five such clusters are recorded. To search Q_0 we first consider column 1, which gives the set of persons

[8] The expression "Q-matrix" has hitherto been sufficient to designate any (square) interrelation matrix for a set of ids. It now becomes necessary to call the first, experimentally obtained matrix of this class, in incidence form. the Q_0 matrix, since a series of matrices computationally derived from it now need to be designated Q_1, Q_2, etc.

TABLE 5.3 Sequence in the Phenomenal Cluster Search Process

	1	2	3	4	5	6	7	8	9	10
1	1	0	0	0	1	0	1	0	0	0
2	0	1	0	0	0	1	0	0	0	0
3	0	0	1	0	0	0	1	0	0	0
4	0	0	0	1	0	0	0	0	0	0
5	1	0	0	0	1	1	1	0	0	0
6	0	1	0	0	1	1	1	0	0	0
7	1	0	1	0	1	1	1	0	1	0
8	0	0	0	0	0	0	0	1	0	0
9	0	0	0	0	0	0	1	0	1	1
10	0	0	0	0	0	0	0	0	1	1

(1)

Q_0

P_1

	I	II	III	IV	V
1	1	0	0	0	0
2	0	1	0	0	0
3	0	0	1	0	0
4	0	0	0	0	0
5	1	0	0	0	0
6	0	1	0	0	0
7	1	0	1	1	0
8	0	0	0	0	0
9	0	0	0	1	1
10	0	0	0	0	1

P'_1

	1	2	3	4	5	6	7	8	9	10
I	1	0	0	0	0	0	1	0	0	0
II	0	1	0	0	0	1	0	0	0	0
III	0	0	1	0	0	0	1	0	0	0
IV	0	0	0	0	0	0	1	0	1	0
V	0	0	0	0	0	0	0	0	1	1

Q_1

	1	2	3	4	5	6	7	8	9	10
1	1	0	0	0	1	0	1	0	0	0
2	0	1	0	0	0	1	0	0	0	0
3	0	0	1	0	0	0	1	0	0	0
4	0	0	0	x	0	0	0	0	0	0
5	1	0	0	0	1	x	1	0	0	0
6	0	1	0	0	x	1	x	0	0	0
7	1	0	1	0	1	x	1	0	1	0
8	0	0	0	0	0	0	0	x	0	0
9	0	0	0	0	0	0	1	0	1	1
10	0	0	0	0	0	0	0	0	1	1

(2)

=

	1	2	3	4	5	6	7	8	9	10
1	0	0	0	0	0	0	0	0	0	0
2	0	0	0	0	0	0	0	0	0	0
3	0	0	0	0	0	0	0	0	0	0
4	0	0	0	1	0	0	0	0	0	0
5	0	0	0	0	1	1	1	0	0	0
6	0	0	0	0	1	1	1	0	0	0
7	0	0	0	0	1	1	1	0	0	0
8	0	0	0	0	0	0	0	1	0	0
9	0	0	0	0	0	0	0	0	0	0
10	0	0	0	0	0	0	0	0	0	0

(3)

Q_2

P_2

	I	II	III	IV	V	VI
1	1	0	0	0	0	0
2	0	1	0	0	0	0
3	0	0	1	0	0	0
4	0	0	0	0	0	0
5	1	0	0	0	0	1
6	0	1	0	0	0	1
7	1	0	1	1	0	1
8	0	0	0	0	0	0
9	0	0	0	1	1	0
10	0	0	0	0	1	0

P'_2

	1	2	3	4	5	6	7	8	9	10
I	1	0	0	0	1	0	1	0	0	0
II	0	1	0	0	0	1	0	0	0	0
III	0	0	1	0	0	0	1	0	0	0
IV	0	0	0	0	0	0	1	0	1	0
V	0	0	0	0	0	0	0	0	1	1
VI	0	0	0	0	1	1	1	0	0	0

Q_3

	1	2	3	4	5	6	7	8
1	1	0	0	0	1	0	1	0
2	0	1	0	0	0	1	0	0
3	0	0	1	0	0	0	1	0
4	0	0	0	x	0	0	0	0
5	1	0	0	0	1	1	1	0
6	0	1	0	0	1	1	1	0
7	1	0	1	0	1	1	1	0
8	0	0	0	0	0	0	0	x
9	0	0	0	0	0	0	1	0
10	0	0	0	0	0	0	0	0

(4)

128

related to person 1. As we run down this column and encounter a 1 we must next decide if the person in that row belongs in the whole group or not. He will belong if he is linked also with everyone already in the accepted group. That is, if for every 1 entry above him in P_1 (transferred, as accepted, from column 1) there must be a corresponding (i.e., column) entry 1 in his row (or equivalently, column) of Q_0. (The ramifying linkage method as originally described by the present writer (1952) required comparison with all 1 entries below the one being considered, a logically equivalent procedure, though slightly less efficient for computing.)

Thus in Q_0 of Table 5.3, proceeding down column 1, we see that 5 is linked to 1, then going down the column to the next 1 entry we find that 7 also belongs to the group since when we look along the 7 row there are 1's in columns 1 and 5 (i.e., with the two persons already included in the group). Going next to column 2 we find persons 2 and 6 form a group, from column 3 that 3 and 7 form a group. Column 4 contains a single 1 and need not be considered. Working down column 5 we include 1 and 5, but on examining person 6 we find a 0 in the 1 column of row 6, so 6 does not belong in the group. 7 is related to 1 and 5, and so is included. However, the group now found upon being referred for entry in P_1 is found to be identical to group 1 and so we do not include it. Similarly, we work through columns 6 to 10, finding in all the five distinct groups listed in Table 5.3 as the columns of P_1.[9]

As we now recognize, the ramifying linkage method is best regarded as a first extraction step, just as taking out a first factor—sufficient in a Spearman analysis—came to be regarded as only the first step when multiple factor extraction was introduced. Indeed, the formal similarity to factor analysis is considerable, for our procedure is to set down a first

[9]Two points must be noted about the ramifying linkage method. Firstly, some of the clusters found may be subsets of other clusters. This presents no problem, since the referral to P_1 results in recognition of the fact. Secondly, due to the one-way sequential nature of the procedure, not all clusters may be found, at least where certain unusual configurations exist. Thus in Table 5.3(a) the group consisting of persons 5, 6 and 7 is not found at the first processing. This is why the method needs supplementing as now proposed. Of course, we do not include phenomenal "clusters" of only one person, which correspond to a column with only a diagonal element that is nonzero (e.g., columns 4 and 8 of Q_0).

phenomenal cluster matrix, P_1, as shown, from the ramifying linkage "extraction" process, and make therefrom a product matrix, Q_1, which, subtracted from Q_0, leaves a first residual, Q_2. Thus, step 2 in the cluster search algorithm, as shown in Table 5.3 is:

$$Q_1 = P_1 \cdot P'_1 \tag{10}$$

where the prime denotes transposition and the period denotes Boolean matrix multiplication, for example, matrix multiplication with arithmetic addition and multiplication replaced by logical addition ('or') and multiplication ('and').

If P_1 contains all phenomenal clusters, then we must have:

$$Q_0 = Q_1 \tag{11}$$

since a link (other than a diagonal one) in Q_0 indicates that two persons are related and so they must appear together in at least one phenomenal cluster. The operation $P_1 \cdot P'_1$ simply determines which persons appear together in phenomenal clusters. Table 5.3(2) gives Q_1 for the example. Zeros in Q_1 corresponding to ones in Q_0 have been denoted by x's, indicating that in this case not all phenomenal clusters have been found.

Now a new "residual" incidence matrix, Q_2, is formed from the x's of Q_1 plus any element in their columns that was a 1 in Q_0 and for which there is also an x in its row of Q_1. Such an element might form a phenomenal cluster with the x's and so needs to be included. Table 5.3(3) gives the Q_2 for the example. One now, as in the factor analytic analogy, operates upon this residual afresh by the primary method—the ramifying linkage method. Thereupon we find additional phenomenal clusters—in this case one, No. VI—which we include with those already found to form P_2.

Then,

$$Q_2 = P_2 \cdot P'_2 \tag{12}$$

and

$$Q_2 = Q_1 \tag{13}$$

if all phenomenal clusters have been found. We proceed in this way until we find a P_n such that $Q_n = Q_{n-1}$ except possibly for some diagonal elements, which do not count. In the example, Table 5.3, $Q_3 = Q_2$ except for the (4,4) and (8,8) elements, so P_2 contains all the phenomenal clusters in Q_0. This whole process has been programmed for the computer as part of the Taxonome program described below.

TABLE 5.4 Phenomenal Clusters (p-Clusters) Discovered
from Incidence Matrix in Table 5.2*

Raw Size	Identifying numbers (in parentheses)* Actual Ids in the Content (as letters)		Size, if Cluster, as Estimated Percentage of Population	Frequency Distribution of p- Clusters, as to Size
6	(2) a b c d e i		40	16 2/3
5	(1) a b e f g	(3) a b c d h	33	33 1/3
4	(4) k l n o		26.7	16 2/3
3	(5) j k n	(6) l m o	20	33 1/3
2	None			0

*Estimated Percentage of Population in p-clusters = 93.3.

9. THE CONDENSED STATEMENT OF HOMOSTAT FINDINGS AND TEXTURE, AND THE ENSUING SEGREGATE SEARCH PRINCIPLES

Results from applying the above principles, embodied in the Taxonome program, can be exhaustively set out in two kinds of table (potentially three) as in Tables 5.4 and 5.5, or in a drawing, as in Fig. 5.4. (These results are not from the incidence Q-matrix of Table 5.3, which was kept small to illustrate the calculations, but from the Q-matrix data in Table 5.2.)

As previously indicated, the two required kinds of table, one for p- and one for n-cluster structure are:

1. A row by column listing of p-clusters by id-count size, from 2 upward, recording also the actual individuals involved in each, as in Table 5.4 above.
2. A row by column listing of nuclear clusters, arranged by id size, listing actual ids, and recording the number of p-clusters, by columns, overlapping to give the given n-cluster, as in Table 5.5.

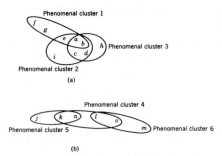

Fig. 5.4   Topological diagram of phenomenal and nuclear clusters present in the incidence matrix in Table 5.2.

An investigator called upon to use or to communicate this information may reasonably object:

(a) That this resolution does not present a particularly simple outcome, of the kind which he can communicate by saying,"There are six types in this region." It may be a correct description of real complexities, but if some reduction and approximation must be made it still leaves him with further decisions to be made. Indeed, the "summary tables" (Tables 5.4 and 5.5 here) may actually contain more particulars than the original data, for example, as the number of things 2 at a time is larger than n. Particularly as far as stats are concerned, if all possible overlapping instances are to be recognized, the number in a k dimensional for n individuals, where k and n approach, for example, 10 and 100, respectively, could be very large indeed. In a circumplex of a "mottled"

TABLE 5.5   Account of Nuclear Clusters*

This Sample	Size As Estimated Population Percentage	Number of Phenomenal Clusters Involved in Overlapping 2	3	4
4	26.7	*(a b c d)*		
3	20	*(a b e)*		
2	6.7	*(k n)*, *(l o)*, *(a b)*		

*Total percentage of estimated population in stats: 60.4.

configuration, for example, the number of n clusters could be quite as large.

(b) The structure found, and the total percentage included in types, must depend upon the particular cut-off level adopted with respect to r_p in arriving at the incidence matrix.

Before deciding how to handle these problems let us complete the general treatment by proceeding to segregates—or "aits" as we have called them for brevity, and symmetry with "stats." Introductorily, to bring out the potential properties, we illustrated in Fig. 5.1 with elongated aits, showing that individuals could belong to the same ait despite even a negative mutual r_p. Though we have to prepare to meet this situation, the general considerations about the origins of types discussed above surely suggest that segregation will occur normally with groups of fairly high homogeneity. (This is already the experience of Sokal and Sneath (1963) in the biological area, at any rate at the species and genus levels.)

But in any case the search for aits is not easy to systematize. A rough approach to them is obviously possible by including in the group of ids located at the largest n-cluster all the satellite p-clusters. One could, for example, read off the instances of the largest order of n-clusters in a summary like Table 5.5 and find its associated p-clusters from Table 5.4. There is a danger that in following this procedure one will run over into some new ait, itself centered on a different, nonoverlapping n-cluster; so a more systematic procedure is here suggested.

This ait search method consists in beginning with stats and grouping them according to contiguity (a form of resemblance) but in a way very different from the design used in grouping individuals to find stats. There we required that each member of a stat should reach a certain minimal resemblance to *every* other. Here, in an ait, we demand only that each member be linked with a minimum of one (or, as later, two) others, above the minimal resemblance value, in the group. However, additionally we now are going: (1) to deal with stats, of an appropriately effective diameter or "grain size" in relation to the number and mean resemblance of ids, *instead* of single ids, and (2) to make the linkage out of *contiguity indices* instead of resemblance (r_p) indices. One stat will be said to be linked, by an adequate contiguity index, to another when some fixed absolute number or percentage of ids (the former is simpler) is minimally shared by the two stats.

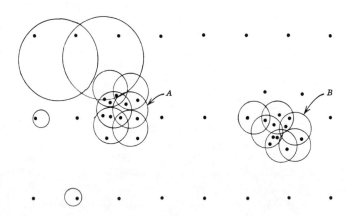

Fig. 5.5   Effect of cutting level of r_p on nature of recorded stats and aits.

The need for the procedure is best seen by glancing at Fig. 5.5.   Let us suppose what is probably most frequent in real data, namely segregates (a couple: A and B) in an otherwise fairly evenly "dilute" field, and that the density of individuals becomes greater toward the center of each segregate. To illustrate the effect of r_p cut-off point let us suppose that values of 0.9, 0.8 and 0.6 correspond to circles of diameter 0.2, 0.5, and 3 cm in Fig. 5.5.   If we make an incidence matrix from 0.9 (since as illustrated at the left 0.2 cm is incapable of spanning two points except at the very centers of the segregates) we may finish with only two or three two id p-clusters, with most people unrepresented.   At 0.8 we still do not span any two adjacent people in the general field but we find a lot of p-clusters in each segregate and they overlap in several n-clusters at the center of each segregate.   The central region is recognizable in a tabular set-out like Table 5.5, by the higher number of p-clusters involved in the n-cluster.   Finally, if we take 0.6, the larger circles yield p-clusters even in the field (only a few are drawn, to avoid confusion).   *Everyone* is in at least one p-cluster, but the region of the segregates (not shown in big circles) is still recognizable at the larger

size[10] of n-clusters and the greater number of p-clusters involved (since these two parameters will generally correlate
as we compare one segregate with another). Thus Fig. 5.5 will
show (admittedly for a somewhat convenient texture of re-
latedness) that if (a) we hit on a reasonably apt r_p cut[11] for
stats to distinguish figures and ground, and, then, (b) start an
incidence matrix for contiguities of stats, we should be able,
by searching the contiguity matrix among stats, arrive at the
main segregations. (For the moment we assume this done by
eye, it can be programmed.)   As Fig. 5.6 brings home, too
large a circle will span distinct segregates and lose the perception of their separation, that is, persons such as a, b, c, d,
e, f, g, h will be included.

Accordingly, the principles expressed in the Taxonome
program now require it to proceed to a new incidence matrix,
but based on a different index from that originally made among
people, and now applying to stats. In this case the incidence
matrix has a plus one entered wherever two phenomenal
clusters (selected above at a certain density from Table 5.3,
for example, a density rejecting two-thirds of the clusters)
overlap by two or more persons. (Experience *may* show that
sampling variations are better reduced by taking a more conservative limit for this "contiguity index," say of overlap by
three or more.)   The matrix so obtained we may call the
phenomenal cluster contiguity matrix and symbolize by Q_{pc} .

The search method for the Q_{pc} matrix is distinctly different from that used to search for stats in the Q incidence

---

[10] It is important to remember that a *large* cluster, in terms of the
number of ids involved, is not a *broad* one, in terms on breadth of psychological domain, but a *dense* one, i.e., a region in which many people are
close together.   For the psychological breadth is kept constant by the
absolute value of r_p kept for the cutting point.

[11] As a glance at Diagram 5.5 will show, the cut at $r_p = 0.8$ would be
appropriate in getting contiguity among the numerous phenomenal clusters
in A and B but not in the field.   Use of the larger circles might more
quickly and stably cover the ground but would not so precisely distinguish
segregate patterns from the field background.   If a higher standard of
"contiguity" were used with the larger circles, say a 50% overlap or more,
the end result should, however, be consistent with that from the smaller.
As with photography or the reproduction of objects over TV, it is a question of choosing a "grain" fine enough for the job, yet not impractically
expensive of time and apparatus.

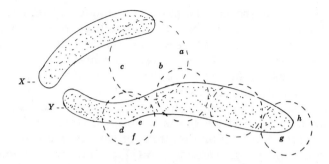

Fig. 5.6   Relation of homostats in mapping a segregate. The narrow homo-stats used in X are in no danger of misperceiving its boundaries, but the large ones (lower r_p) in Y will bring in some ids not belonging and may bridge to X.

matrix. In this "segregate search procedure" any connection encountered as one descends a column (see Table 5.6) is pursued to a tracing of *all* its connections with other variables.[12] Thus a pattern which is a simple chain, or a branching chain or even a circle gets successfully located, not merely the completely internally knit p-cluster pattern. In general it would seem desirable that some restriction be added to eliminate the inclusion as a unitary segregate of two essentially remote types joined by a connection so tenuous that it would be likely to vanish with a slight rise of r_p level or a change of sample. This can be taken care of by the practice—in any case desirable in any important study—of: (a) raising the contiguity index to require a minimum overlap of say, two or

---

[12] Explicitly, in segregate search of Q_{pc}, one proceeds, starting with column 1, systematically through the columns, accruing the groups in a column to the segregate being considered, if the intersection of the segregate and the column is not null, one continues until no new segregates appear. Thus in Table 5.5(b), columns 1, 2 and 3 form a segregate but the intersection of this with 4, 5 and 6 is null. Starting again with 4 one finishes with 4, 5 and 6. Illustrated in Boolean terms, if the columns were as in (a) the Boolean product would be zero, and we should proceed no further. In (b) on the other hand, it is not null, so we proceed to Boolean addition to form the new segregate, in the last column below.

	(a)			(b)			(c)	
0	1	0	0	0	0	0	0	0
1	0	0	1	1	1	1	1	1
1 ·	0 =	0	1 ·	0 =	0	1 +	0 =	1
0	1	0	0	1	0	0	1	1
0	1	0	0	1	0	0	1	1

TABLE 5.6

(a) Phenomenal Cluster Contiguity Matrix*

Phenomenal Cluster Identifying Numbers	1 (6)	2 (5)	3 (5)	4 (4)	5 (3)	6 (3)
1(6)	6	3	4	0	0	0
2(5)	3	5	3	0	0	0
3(5)	4	3	5	0	0	0
4(4)	0	0	0	4	2	2
5(3)	0	0	0	2	3	0
6(3)	0	0	0	2	0	3

*Entries state the count of overlap of persons.

(b) Incidence Matrix among Phenomenal Clusters, * Q_{pc}

Phenomenal Cluster Identifying Numbers	1	2	3	4	5	6
1	1	1	1	0	0	0
2	1	1	1	0	0	0
3	1	1	1	0	0	0
4	0	0	0	1	1	1
5	0	0	0	1	1	0
6	0	0	0	1	0	1

*Converted to Incidence Matrix for 2 overlap and above.

(c) Segregates Discovered by Segregate Search Algorithm Applied to (b)

	S_1	S_2
1	1	0
2	1	0
3	1	0
4	0	1
5	0	1
6	0	1

$S_1 = a\ b\ c\ \ d\ e\ f\ g\ h\ i$
$S_2 = j\ k\ l\ \ m\ n\ o$

137

three ids, or about 25% of a p-cluster content; (b) repeating
the Taxonome program examination of data at, say, each of
three somewhat different levels of r_p cut in the creating of the
contiguity incidence matrices (and at, say, each of two rejection levels of too small and trivial clusters, i.e., below 5% of
sample); and (c) looking for repetition of structure across
samples. What survives such changes of "grain" should constitute a statement of the essential type structure.

10. TRIAL OF TAXONOME ON REAL DATA AND PLASMODES

A preliminary trial of the first part of the taxonome algorithm—before committing it to a computer program—was
originally made soon after r_p was worked out (Cattell, 1950)
on a culture pattern typing problem on the newly found (Cattell, Breul and Hartmann, 1952) 12-factor culture profiles on
each of 69 countries. The ramifying linkage method and the
homostats produced worked out very well, judged by existing
socio-historical views, yielding phenomenal clusters which
condensed to ten major nuclear clusters, of which the five in
Table 5.7 are instances.

TABLE 5.7   Nuclear Types Found among
Nations by Culture Pattern r_p Evaluations

Eastern European	Mohammedan
Czechoslovakia	Afghanistan
Estonia	Iraq
Lithuania	Turkey
Austria	Arabia
	Egypt
Scandinavian	Commonwealth
Denmark	New Zealand
Sweden	Australia
Norway	Netherlands
Switzerland	Belgium
	Canada
Oriental	
India	
China	
Tibet	

The ten types agree so well with the "civilizations" of Toynbee or the culture pattern groupings on historico-anthropological basis that we were encouraged to proceed (albeit all too slowly!) to the development of the further Taxonome features and program here presented.

The urgent need today is for trial of the Taxonome principle and program upon varied examples, not only to check on its effectiveness but also to learn how to modify the parameters to get the best out of different kinds of material. We believe we have the best design of instrument, but we still have to learn how to play it. Especially is it desirable systematically to try it out on a number of what have elsewhere (Cattell, and Jaspars, in press) been defined as "plasmodes." A plasmode is an arrangement of numerical data made to fit a scientific or mathematical model. From the outcome of operations on the plasmode in terms of their revealing the known structure, pre-inserted, the correctness and efficiency of certain strategies of analysis algorithms or programs can be positively evaluated.

Whenever possible the structure submitted in a plasmode should be a concrete, "real" one. That is, it should include with the model the errors and irregularities likely to occur in using the operations on natural data. (Salting in error "regularly" by random numbers does not necessarily reproduce all that the analytical program has to cope with in the distortions of the model in real data.) A concrete plasmode for the present try-out was not easy to find. Measurements on a population sample of mixed insects was tried and abandoned, because the separations are too easy and the measures are all spatial. Eventually we settled on types of ships (in fact, of warships, which have developed such distinct functions) as a suitably definite but not oversimplified "nursery example" for our program. Accordingly, we took measures on 29 ships, from "Jane's Fighting Ships" (1964-65) in the four categories of frigates, cruisers, aircraft carriers and submarines. The measures used were the (1) displacement, (2) length, (3) beam, armament in numbers of (4) light, (5) medium, (6) heavy or (7) very heavy guns, (8) the compliment, (9) maximum speed, (10) submersibility, (11) presence of continuous deck construction, and (12) whether no, some, or many aircraft were carried. These offered an eleven element profile, though it will be recognized that we approximated by using the orthogonal

r_p when these profile elements are in fact somewhat correlated (which may account for some ensuing difficulties).

At the phenomenal cluster level we obtained 9 clusters, as shown in Table 5.8. As our theoretical consideration above of the limitations of stats would lead us to expect, these do not at once correspond to the segregates we know to exist—aircraft carriers, submarines, cruisers, etc. However, except for the aircraft carriers, which yield three overlapping p-clusters, numbers 6, 7 and 8, and for certain mysterious p-clusters of only two or three members, as have turned up in clusters 3,

TABLE 5.8   Phenomenal Clusters Illustrated on *Jane's Fighting Ships* *

		1	2	3	4	5	6	7	8	9
	1						1	1		
Aircraft	2							1		
Carriers	3						1	1		
	4						1	1	1	
	5					1		1		
	6				1					
	7				1	1				
Cruisers	8				1	1				
	9				1					
	10	1								
	11	1								
	12	1							1	
	13	1								
	14	1								
Submarines	15	1								
	16	1								
	17	1		1					1	
	18	1								
	19	1								
	20		1	1						
	21		1							
	22		1	1						
Frigates	23		1							
	24		1							
	25		1							
	26		1							
	27		1	1						
	28		1							
	29		1	1	1					

*Zeros, everywhere else, omitted for clarity.

5 and 9, we are supplied by the program, in clusters 1, 2 and
4, with an excellent separation of submarines, frigates and
cruisers, respectively.

On proceeding to the nuclear cluster print-out(not shown)
we get nothing helpful whatever. One of four vessels and five
of two vessels each appear, and they are obviously fringe
overlaps of the large and clear groups appearing at the p-
cluster level. However, when the program proceeds to its
second phase—that of the segregate search, by chains, of Q_{pc} —
we get a clarification which in certain features is more consistent with the segregates we know. As Table 5.9 shows, the
small, odd nuclear clusters, numbers 3, 5, and 9 are gathered
into the large masses. But these larger masses in some respects represent the expected segregates and in others are an
oversimplification. The placing of the aircraft carriers in
three overlapping p-clusters is now happily resolved by their
all being gathered into a single segregate, number 2. On the
other hand, due to our contiguity index being too generous, the
small bridge of examples common to frigates and submarines
(these vessels are very similar in tonnage, crew and even guns

TABLE 5.9   Result of Search for Segregates by the
Second Part of the Program*

Phenomenal Clusters	Segregates		
	I	II	III
Submarines	1	1	
Frigates	2	1	
Odd Frigates and One Sub-marine	3	1	
Cruisers	4		1
Odd Cruisers	5		1
Aircraft Carriers	6	1	
Aircraft Carriers	7	1	
Aircraft Carriers	8	1	
Odd Submarines	9	1	

*Zeros, everywhere else, omitted for clarity.

in a few instances) has bound submarines and frigates into a single segregate (number 1 in Table 5.9). Segregate number 3, like number 2, cleanly brings together all those of one class, namely cruisers.

A third test of the Taxonome program is in progress with Sixteen Personality Factor Questionnaire profiles on 120 psychotics from the study of Cattell, Tatro and Komlos (1964), but except for indicating the importance of comparing structure for different samples, via the mean attribute profile of the types found, it is in too early a stage to justify conclusions.

Evidently, from these examples, there are occasions (textures) where any one of the three type models—p-clusters, n-clusters and segregates—may make sense in terms of our preconceptions. If one lights on a fortunate size of cutting level for r_p and a domain with naturally discrete groups of about that span, even the p-cluster—despite its Achilles heel in theory—will yield meaningful groupings, as in the clear typing of submarines in frigates in Table 5.8. In other cases, as the national culture patterns, which presumably have some kind of dendritic, phyletic historical growth from a few stems, the n-clusters seem excellently to describe what on other evidence we believe to be the types. And in others, as where Table 5.9 pulls the aircraft carriers into a single type where neither p- nor n-clusters do, the aid seems to offer the best concept and program.

11. THE STRUCTURE OF THE TAXONOME PROGRAM ITSELF

Before proceeding to the final summary it is desirable to make available to readers—since several psychologists have already written in for it—an outline of the program itself such that they may construct it adaptively to their own computers. (Ours is on an IBM 7094.) The construction of the program has been a joint enterprise of the present writer and Dr. Malcolm Coulter of the University of the Witwatersrand, South Africa (while at the author's laboratory) and is republished for convenience here by courtesy of the *British Journal of Mathematical and Statistical Psychology*, in which it first appeared.

Needless, perhaps, to say to those experienced in

computers and programs, we would not claim that the program is in its best final form to meet all requirements indicated by the principles above. In particular, if experience is to be gained in the vital art of "playing" the instrument in skillful relation to the textures in different domains, it will be necessary to make a flexible use of it more easy by building in a variety of tactical subroutines, with ready substitution of values for most initially fixed parameters. However, with these reservations the program is describable in general terms as follows:

This program is a computer realization of the Taxonome Program for the taxonomic classification of a group of subjects, or other entities, into the naturally occurring stats (homostat types) and aits (segregate types) (Cattell and Coulter, 1966).

The program is written in FORTRAN II and requires the following computer configuration: 32K words of core memory, one input tape, one output tape, and two scratch tapes. The 32K memory allows for 100 subjects and 219 variables.

Timing will depend on the computer, the number of subjects, the number of variables and the number of iterations required to find all the clusters of individuals. On an IBM 7094 with off-line printing, a 36-subject, 12-variable problem took under five minutes.

The program allows the user a number of options in the operation of the program. These are:

(a) The number of members that the smallest nuclear cluster of interest must have may be specified.

(b) The cut-off point at which the r_p values are converted to zero or one may be specified, alternatively the program calculates the average of the absolute r_p values and uses this as the cut-off.

(c) The program will accept either scores in the form of a profile for each subject, or an already calculated r_p matrix can serve as the starting point.

(d) The cut-off point may be scaled by a specified constant.

(e) The scores of the r_p matrix may be printed if either or both of these are wished.

(f) The number of members that two clusters must have in common before they will be considered linked when the contiguity matrix is formed may also be specified.

If any of these options is not specified by the user, certain default values will be assumed by the program.

If the input data are scores, these are converted to r_p values using a chi-square value that must be provided by the user as an input parameter.

The r_p matrix of profile similarity coefficients between the subjects is converted to the incidence matrix by using the cut-off, possibly scaling it by a specified constant. Values less than the cut-off are converted to zeros while other values are converted to ones. When the incidence matrix has been calculated it is printed.

The writer wishes to express his great indebtedness to his statistician, Mrs. Anka Wagner, for several improvements incorporated in the latest version of this program.

The phenomenal clusters are now found in the incidence matrix by means of the Ramifying Linkage Method. The clusters are ordered according to the number of members each has and any duplicate clusters, or clusters that are subsets of other clusters, are eliminated. One property of the Ramifying Linkage Method is that it acts serially on the data and this may result, for particular orderings of the subjects, in certain clusters being obscured and missed. This may be tested by forming a reproduced incidence matrix by taking the inner product by rows (using logical or Boolean multiplication). If all clusters have been found then all ones in the incidence matrix will correspond to ones in the reproduced matrix. If not all the ones have been reproduced, then missing clusters exist, and a reduced incidence matrix is formed to which the Ramifying Linkage Method can be applied to find the missing clusters. The process is repeated until all clusters are found. When all the phenomenal groups have been found a list of them is printed in descending order of group size.

Cross-multiplying the clusters (algebraically and by columns this time) we get the overlap matrix whose cells represent the number of members that a pair of clusters have in common. This matrix serves as a basis for finding the nuclear clusters. The overlap matrix is printed, and in addition those subjects who belong to no cluster or only one cluster are listed separately.

The overlap matrix is examined for the largest value. This is the size of the largest nuclear cluster, and its position in the matrix indicates which phenomenal clusters overlap to form the nuclear cluster. There may be several nuclear clusters of this size, and when these have been found a table is printed indicating the membership of each nuclear cluster for this size. The next largest size of nuclear cluster is then found in the same way, and so on until all nuclear clusters with more than a specified number of members have been found.

The overlap matrix is now converted to the contiguity matrix by setting all elements less than a specified size to zero, and the remaining elements to one, and the contiguity matrix gives the graph, or structure, of the relationships between the phenomenal clusters.

Now segregate groupings of the phenomenal clusters are formed, each segregate containing all the phenomenal clusters that make up a single (transitively) linked whole. The segregates are formed by taking a cluster as a starting point and sweeping through the contiguity matrix to find other clusters that are linked to this one. Several sweeps may be required before all clusters belonging to the segregate have been found. A tabulation of the phenomenal clusters which belong to each segregate is printed.

The second-order phenomenal and nuclear clusters are now found in exactly the same way as that described above for the basic phenomenal and nuclear clusters only using the contiguity matrix as a starting point rather than the incidence matrix formed from the r_p matrix. This gives the "clustering of clusters."

When the second order phenomenal and nuclear clusters have been found, the program terminates.

12. DISCUSSION AND SUMMARY

1. The existence of a type—by the most general definition thereof—is recognized by a high relative (modal) frequency of occurrence of individuals at certain positions in a multi-dimensional framework. However, there are two senses in which "unusual frequency" can be interpreted: (a) by reaching a certain absolute frequency (density) as a *stat* (homostat). This is defined by every one of its members being within a defined degree of resemblance (distance) of every other, and (b) by relative frequency and topological properties, as an *ait* (segregate). Therein a natural boundary to the group is set by its being surrounded by a zone of individuals showing less mutual resemblance than exists among contiguous individuals in the ait.

2. A variety of coefficients of similarity exists, but the correlation coefficient, r, is incorrect for this purpose, the values of Mahalanobis's d lack immediately recognizable, universal meaning, and most other available indices have, similarly, more or less serious flaws. The most generally useful indices seem to be the coefficients of *profile similarity*, r_p, and of *nearness*, r_m. They can be adapted to dichotomous, "qualitative" data (e.g., item responses) or to mixtures of continuous and dichotomous dimensions.

3. The distinction between classifying things by "what they are" and "what they do," or by traits and criterion performances has no fundamental basis. It may be useful, however, to classify ids (objects belonging to uniform classes of any kind) at times according to special single purposes or subsets of traits, and when this is done the grouping in the larger dimensionality will become transformed and modified in major ways by the process of projecting it into the smaller dimensionality.

4. Such transformation may be regarded as an extreme case of weighting of dimensions. r_p has hitherto been used for orthogonal factors and equal weighting of the known factors in the given domain. But most source traits, in psychology and elsewhere, are, in any case, oblique, and the freedom to weight them unequally in response to particular required emphases in the properties of objects, is also desirable. For unit (equal) weighting is actually itself arbitrary. However, a "primal," universal weighting system can be worked out which is not

arbitrary. This requires definition of a universe of variables in which the objects function and the weighting of factors by their mean variance contributions to a stratified sample of variables therefrom. This is the nearest we can get to typing by "the thing in itself." Accordingly the formula for r_p has been extended to oblique and weighted factors.

5. So far in this contribution little discussion has been given to the fact that since the coordinates in which the ids are placed are themselves derived from factoring the scores of ids on the variables, there are mutual relations of coordinates and distributions. We encounter, in short, the usual problems of reconciling "test space" and "person space." In particular the departure of the ids from a normal distribution, which the very existence of segregating types implies, *may* result in nonlinear relations among factor scores and changing obliqueness in the coordinate framework. This is a complex issue, which would require also attention to the definition and discussion of in-type and cross-type variables, as made in the text. For the present it will be argued that if segregates are numerous enough the overall multivariate normal distribution will be maintained on cross-type ("between groups") variables and deviations from linearity will be local and restricted. For them the main formulae here will continue to apply.

6. The actual procedures for locating stats and aits can initially be classified into *inter-id-relation* and *cartet or coordinate search methods*. Only the id relation approach is pursued here. It sets up a Q-matrix with similarity indices (r_p or r_m) in the cells and changes this to a Q *incidence matrix* by choosing a suitable cutting point on r_p to give 1's above and 0's below it.

From this one finds p-clusters (phenomenal clusters) by an improved form of the ramifying linkage search method, now incorporated in a "Boolean extraction process" algorithm. A print-out of the distributions giving sizes and content of phenomenal clusters provides our first information on what we have called the "texture" of a domain. Larger clusters mean higher densities (best expressed as *percentages* of the population since with larger samples there are proportionately more people in any one "type"). From this p-cluster table a second programmable process will lead to a listing of the n-clusters (nuclear clusters) recorded in an n-cluster table, arranged by size, content and the number of overlapping p-clusters involved in each n-cluster.

The second main step in the Taxonome program is to proceed from these stats (p- and n-clusters) to aits (segregates). This is best done on a foundation of stats based on a choice of r_p cutting value which leaves the main "field" a blank, that is, not all ids should be in stats and one picks up only the denser clusters (e.g., those above the mode of the size distribution). The new Boolean algorithm—the segregate search—begins now with a Q-matrix of *contiguities* among p-clusters in which an incidence matrix, bounded by the p-clusters of stable, substantial size, is entered by 1's where two p-clusters overlap above, for example, a count of two or three ids. Though no longer arbitrary in beginning and end points—granted a given cut on r_p and the contiguity index—the form of segregates can still vary endlessly. They can be found for example, as chains, circular chains and spherical masses. This is the nature of nature and no mathematical treatment can reduce or simplify these end results if indeed segregates are the object of our search.

7. Although investigators begin by designating "type structure" as the object of their search, one soon recognizes that discovering what might be called the "texture" of a domain is as important a goal as making the (always relative) lists of "types." By "texture" one may designate the absolute frequency of segregates, their densities, their relative frequencies at various sizes, and hierarchical or other relationships of form among them. Reverting to the analogy of clouds (now back in a 3-dimensional sky) texture is equivalent to what the meteorologist finds it convenient to designate by such terms as cumulus, alto-stratus, cirrus, etc. In connection with developing various parameters for texture, an index of the degree of compactness-vs-ranginess of a segregate can be obtained by dividing the total number, t, of significant ties between people in the segregate by the total number of possible ties, n_{C_2}, where n is the number in the segregate.

8. A description of the Taxonome[13] program, at the "flow"

---

[13] Taxonome, on our IBM 7094, is programmed up to Q-matrices of 120 x 120. One might, in clinical or social research on types, even with groups deliberately sampling apparent heterogeneous subgroups to test certain hypotheses, prefer rather to work with 500 to 1000 cases. Reduction to 120 may, however, be a blessing in disguise—at least where not more than about half a dozen main types are to be expected. For the comparison of structure across them gives some evaluation of what is due to

level, extending through the r_p computations, the phenomenal and nuclear cluster listing and so to final segregate listing is given in Section 11, and it is pointed out that much experiment is necessary, with flexible derivatives of the program "plugging in" varying parameters, to discover the art of playing the instrument in relation to all kinds of typing domains and problems. For example, in the practical pursuit of types and texture the investigator will in general need: (a) To experiment with two or three different cutting points for r_p, and for the contiguity measure (which decides the "grain size" of the picture), generating resolutions from the somewhat different incidence matrices. The best resolution requires comparison of all these and the best set for classifying most ids in a given domain can only be found in this way. Especially, he will thus discover what main features are most stable across the different resolutions. This views type search as an iterative procedure. (b) To do separate analyses also over different samples. On the theoretical side much remains to be worked out regarding the nature of sampling effects, and the resulting practical adjustment of programs to handle an adequate size of Q-matrix.

9. Application of the program to plasmodes, that is made-up examples where the solution is already in some sense known, shows, in cases as diverse as ships and culture patterns, that with fortunate choice of parameters and simple texture in the material, the first set of p-cluster stats may be quite meaningful. In another instance the nuclear clusters are more meaningful. In another the latter may be trivial and meaningless while the segregates—as one would in general expect—provide the most intelligible typology.

sampling. The fitting together and checking afterwards can be done either (a) by taking sufficient "market individuals" as in factor analysis we take "market tests," from analysis to analysis, or (b) by taking the centroid profile of the group in each given ait or stat—that by which in the end one quantitatively defines the type—and working out r_p congruences of what are supposedly the same types in the two samples.

CHAPTER 6

Benjamin Kleinmuntz

Carnegie-Mellon University

THE PROCESSING OF
CLINICAL INFORMATION
BY MAN AND MACHINE*

Clinical intuition, it is often said, is an art and as such it
cannot be subjected to the rigors of scientific study. Clinicians
tenaciously cling to the opinion that patients communicate
with, or signal to, them in numerous nonverbal modes, and
they tend to believe that they must see, and sometimes even
"smell out," their patients' diseases in order to arrive at an
accurate diagnosis. Some clinicians, especially in the psychiatric areas, report that they "resonate" to patients with their
unconscious and claim to gain some special understanding of
persons' motivations and dynamics in this way. Other clinicians believe that they possess special powers of intuition
which permit them to find hidden meanings beneath even the
most neutral gestures. It is probably true that a certain
amount of nonverbal, or even emotional, communication contributes some information to the clinical diagnostic process,
but these communications do not remove clinical intuition from
the arena of scientific scrutiny. If anything, they contribute to
my conviction that these phenomena deserve further study. It
is the aim of this paper to argue that clinical intuition generally and clinical diagnosis in particular are amenable to
methods of scientific study, and to present evidence that for
certain classes of clinical prediction problems a set of rules
or formal procedures can perform equally as well as the
human diagnostician. Further, it is the intent of this paper to
present a glimpse of the complexity of some forms of clinical
diagnostic decision-making.

*The research reported in this chapter and the time devoted to its writing
was in part supported by a grant from the Maurice Falk Medical Fund, and
the author gratefully acknowledges this support.*

149

CLINICAL VERSUS STATISTICAL PREDICTION

Most of you undoubtedly recognize that this paper is related to the "clinical versus statistical prediction" controversy. Before proceeding with the main topic of this paper, it may be helpful to review briefly the issues and the emotional tone of that controversy.

The problem posed by Professor Paul E. Meehl (1954) in his monograph on clinical versus statistical prediction can be stated simply as follows: *In any given prediction situation, which procedure is more accurate—that of the clinician or that of the actuary?* By clinical procedure, Meehl referred to the clinician who proceeds by arriving at a diagnosis or prediction by formulating a set of hypotheses about the possible significance of impressions and data collected about a patient. Essentially, the emphasis here is on the fact that the clinician combined his data in an intuitive, judicious and possibly haphazard way. The actuary, in contrast to the clinician, when given the identical data, proceeds by combining them in a mechanical way according to a set of prespecified decision rules; or, he submits the data to a statistician who processes them by means of prediction equations or computer programmed rules in order to arrive at a prediction. Then, when a diagnosis has to be made, for example, whether a patient is psychotic or neurotic, the problem becomes one of choosing between a method of classification which relies on the clinician's thinking about the problem in a judicious rational and informed way and a method which consists of turning the test and file data over to a statistician or computer.

Although Meehl addressed himself mainly to prediction problems within clinical psychology, the implications of his theoretical analysis are broad. The fundamental methodological issue boils down to whether it is better—that is, more accurate and more informative in a scientific way—to intuit or not about clinical data. This consideration, of course, extends to prediction in all diagnostic problem-solving situations since no logical distinctions could be drawn among a diagnosis made by a physician of his patient, a prediction by a psychologist of his client's grade point average, or trouble-shooting for defects in a television set or automobile engine.

For reasons that are only partly clear to me, however,

some ways of proceeding with the enterprise of understanding certain aspects of human behavior engender resistance and highly emotional responses. This methodological problem seems to be such an issue, and the preferences most clinicians feel toward one or the other modes of combining data are reflected in much of the writing on the topic. To capture some of the emotional flavor of the clinical versus statistical prediction controversy I am listing here some of the honorific and pejorative adjectives applied by proponents of one side or the other (Meehl, 1954, p. 4).

By its proponents, the statistical method has been described as operational, verifiable, objective, testable, precise, empirical, mathematical and sound. Those who are opposed to it consider it mechanical, artificial, pedantic, trivial, fractionated, forced, static, and sterile. Adherents of the clinical method refer to their approach as dynamic, global, meaningful, configural, patterned, sophisticated and sensitive; and its critics call the clinical method mystical, metaphysical, muddleheaded, private, primitive, prescientific and sloppy. But stripped of its honorific and pejorative labels, the problem of intuitive versus statistical or mechanical processing of diagnostic data is an important one. A clinician's orientation on the matter influences the way he collects information and the way he sorts that information.

My own biases on the matter tend to favor a view which holds that there are certain classes of prediction problems where the clinician's personal touch—no matter how rational or judicious—adds error variance to the prediction. There is much evidence in the literature to support this view (Halbower, 1955; Marks, 1961; Meehl, 1956; Sarbin, 1943); and for these prediction problems it might be best to submit the predictors to a statistician or a computer for processing. Such a view assumes, of course, that the clinician frequently functions in the manner of a regression equation or a computer. And if such an assumption is warranted, then the clinician should be encouraged to explicate his method of procedure or heuristics, so that a computer could be programmed to carry out similar processes.

The two studies that are reported here reflect attempts to have the clinician spell out his rules of thumb or heuristics, and to apply these rules to clinical problems similar to those that confront him. In the first of these studies—the one dealing with MMPI interpretation—considerable success was achieved in demonstrating that clinicians can publicize their modes of operation and that it is reasonable to turn that clinical problem over to a machine. The second study, focusing on the somewhat more complex problem of diagnosing neurological diseases, has been less successful than the MMPI work, but has yielded much information about neurological diagnosis.

MMPI PROFILE INTERPRETATION

My first example considers the situation where a personality test interpreter perceives and responds to cues provided by the profile sheets of emotionally maladjusted and adjusted college students. The test used for this purpose was the Minnesota Multiphasic Personality Inventory (MMPI) constructed by Hathaway and McKinley (1951) more than twenty years ago. Since the construction of the MMPI the emphasis has gradually shifted from test interpretation based on single-scale analysis to interpretation using the configural properties of the test profile. The most significant contribution toward a configural approach of the MMPI has been made by Meehl and Dahlstrom (1960), who devised a set of sequential decision rules which successfully classified between 61% and 93% of the MMPI profiles of psychotic and neurotic psychiatric patients in eight cross-validation samples.

METHOD

The present study was designed with the specific purpose in mind of demonstrating that clinicians can be encouraged to describe their own profile-analytic decision processes; and that these processes can be made sufficiently explicit so that a computer can carry them out with some success. Accordingly the design of the study was as follows:

After collecting 126 MMPI profiles of maladjusted and adjusted college students, these profiles were prepared for Q-sorting by 10 experienced MMPI users. The criteria of maladjustment and adjustment consisted of selecting college students from a sample of persons who were counseled for varying reasons at the Carnegie Tech Bureau of Measurement and Guidance. The selection criteria are described elsewhere (Kleinmuntz, 1963a; 1963b; 1963c) and will not be detailed here. The Q-sort, a technique developed by Stephenson (1953), calls for the preparation of a set of phrases covering, for example, certain personality traits; and these statements are placed on cards and sorted along a forced normal distribution. In this study, instead of using cards on which were printed phrases or statements, the MMPI profile sheets served as Q-sort items.

The Q-sort technique was selected in this study because the data obtained this way lend themselves to the kinds of analyses which were deemed most essential for the accomplishment of our goals. For example, in order to force the clinician to "think aloud" and to elicit from him information about the way he believes he utilizes profile data, the Q-sort method's multistep rating scale was ideal. It allowed the interpreter to shift profiles back and forth, as he changed his mind about the profile's classification, and it lent itself to a number of statistical computations necessary for determining each sorter's reliability and validity coefficients.

Specifically, the Q-sort procedure used was as follows: Each of the 126 MMPI profiles of the criterion sample was prepared for Q-sorting by cutting away the profile from the larger sheet containing identifying information. Each profile was then identified by a code number, which became the sorter's only means of identifying a particular profile. On these profile sheets the T-scores for each of the following 16 scales were presented: the four validity scales ?, L, F, and K; and the clinical scales, Hs, D, Hy, Pd, Mf, Pa, Pt, Sc, Ma, Si, Es, and Mt (Kleinmuntz, 1961).

The profiles were then sorted by 10 experienced MMPI interpreters across the United States, and these sorters were instructed to place the 126 individual profiles along a 14-step forced normal distribution. The Q-sorters were instructed to place at the left end of the continuum the "least" adjusted profiles, and at the right end of the continuum the "most" adjusted profiles. They were further instructed to start with two piles and then to fan out from the middle until they completed 14 piles. Such a distribution, after sorting, is illustrated in Table 6.1. In analyzing the hit and miss percents of the experts' Q-sorts, a cut-off line between maladjusted and adjusted was arbitrarily drawn at the middle of the distribution. Accordingly, piles 1-7 ($N = 63$) were considered maladjusted and piles 8-14 ($N = 63$) were considered adjusted in the analysis of the Q-sorts.

TABLE 6.1   Fourteen-Step Forced Normal Distribution (Q-sort) of 126 MMPI Profiles

	Least Adjusted										Most Adjusted			
Pile:	1	2	3	4	5	6	7	8	9	10	11	12	13	14
No. of Profiles:	2	3	4	9	12	15	18	18	15	12	9	4	3	2
						(N = 126)									

On the basis of having achieved the highest valid positive (80%) and valid negative (67%) hit rates, and the highest sort-resort reliability coefficient (.96), one MMPI expert was selected for intensive study, and he was instructed to "think aloud" into a tape recorder while he was Q-sorting.

Computer Programming of Tape-Recorded Protocols

Approximately 60 hours of tape-recorded protocol was obtained from the expert Q-sorter, and the recorded material was carefully edited and compiled in order to construct a set of sequential decision rules. During tape recording, the MMPI interpreter was permitted to work at his own pace and a minimum of coaching was necessary. It was anticipated at the outset of this phase of the study that considerable verbal interchange between the researcher and the interpreter might have to be tape recorded, but the ease with which explicit verbalizations were obtained obviated the need for such verbal exchange. The only coaching that was necessary was an occasional reminder to the Q-sorter that he call out the code number of the profile he was considering and that he clarify a particular classification decision (e.g., sometimes the interpreter would neglect to mention the reason(s) he called a profile "adjusted" or "maladjusted"). The information about the code number of a profile was important because the Q-sorter often changed his mind about his adjustment-maladjustment decision of a particular profile after getting midway through his scoring task.

After the interpreter had completed all the Q-sorting, the experimenter played back the tape recordings and notes were taken of the particular scales and scale interactions that were utilized by him in arriving at his decisions. Also, tallies were made of the number of times scales and their interactions were used by the interpreter.

The MMPI profile information thus obtained from the Q-sorter was then compiled into a set of sequential decision rules and a flow chart was made of these rules. The portions of the taped protocol that were used and their corresponding MMPI decision rules are reproduced in Table 6.2

The flow chart of the decision rules is presented in Fig. 6.1. Inspection of this flow chart and of Table 6.2 suggests that the MMPI interpreter considered approximately 16 different combinations of scales and used rather gross cut-off scores in arriving at his decisions (e.g., primarily the T-scores 40, 60, and 70 were used). It was frequently impossible to ascertain the cut-off scores used by the interpreter unless a check was made back to the reference MMPI profile. The highest level of arithmetic used by the expert and formalized in our decision rules was $(Pa + Sc - 2 \cdot Pt)$.

The flow-charted information was then programmed into 20-GATE, which is one of the languages in use at Carnegie Tech and is an algebraic coding system which facilitates the writing of computer programs for the CDC-20 model digital computer. The input data of the program consisted of a profile identification number, sex identification, criterion classification (adjusted or maladjusted), and 16 MMPI raw scores (K-corrected) which were converted to T-scores by the program. The output of the program, part of which appears in Table 6.3, consisted of the aforementioned input variables and approximately 21 computations of various indices (e.g., Anxiety Index, Internalization Ratio, and Hathaway Code) and scale combinations (e.g., Es/Mt, Pa/K, $Hs + Hy - 2 \cdot D$). The program also specified the number of MMPI rules which were applied to a specific profile and the decisions reached by these rules. Also printed out were the hit rates of each of the rules and a 2×2 table of valid negative and positive and false negative and positive hit percents achieved by the computer programmed decision rules. The latter format is reproduced in Table 6.4.

TABLE 6.2 MMPI Decision Rules and Tape-Recorded
Protocol*

Rule	Protocol
1. If four or more clinical scales ≥ T score 70, call maladjusted.	1. Now I'm going to divide these into two piles . . . on the left (least adjusted) I'm throwing all mults with at least four scales primed.
2. If scales Hs, D, Hy, Pd, Mf, Pa, Pt, Sc and Si are ≤ 60 and if Ma ≤ 80 and Mt ≤ 10ᵣ, then call adjusted.	2. I'll throw all mults to the right (most adjusted) if there's no clinical scale above a T score of 60. I'll let Ma go up as high as 80 . . . maybe a raw score of 10 on Mt would be playing it safe . . . so I'm looking at three things now and sorting according to these conditions.
3. If the first two scales in the Hathaway Code include Pd, Pa, or Sc, and at least one of these is ≥ 70, then call maladjusted (if Mt) is among the first two scales, then examine the first three scales in the Hathaway Code).	3. If either Pd, Pa, or Sc is primed, I'm putting it on the left side (least adjusted) . . . it would also be nice to have all of these scales slightly more elevated than the others.
4. If Pa or Sc ≥ 70 and Pa, Pt, or Sc ≥ Hs, D, or Hy, call maladjusted.	4. If the elevations are lopsided to the right with the left side of the profile fairly low. I'm throwing the mults to the left (least adjusted).
5. Call maladjusted if Pa ≥ 70 unless Mt ≤ 6ᵣ and K ≥ 65.	5. Here's a paranoid character. I wish his K score were not quite so high and he could use more Mt . . . when that Mt score is less than 10. I figure something must be stabilizing him. I like an inverted ∨ with F high on the validity scales.
6. If Mt ≤ 6, call adjusted.	6. Boy, I don't know that Mt is too low to call her maladjusted. I'll settle for calling them adjusted if Mt is at a raw score of 6 or lower.
7. Call maladjusted if (Pa + Sc - 2 · Pt) ≥ 20 and Pa or Sc ≥ 65.	7. Here's a nice valley between Scales 6 and 8 and both 6 and 8 are high. I'll call this one maladjusted.

156

8. These 27 profiles are giving me a pain . . . if 2 or 7 is too elevated like, say, higher than a T score of 80 and if the Es scale is approaching a raw score of 50 . . . I'll call it adjusted.

9. A primed Pd and an Mt raw score of 15 or more is going over to the left pile (least adjusted). I guess on a male profile an Mt of 15 or more will do . . . and an Mt of 17 or more on a female profile.

10. With Mt high and Es low. I'll call maladjusted at this stage of the game.

11. Everything's up on this girl's MMPI. I'm especially bothered by the high Pa . . . here's a high Sc . . . everything else is up too . . . over to the left (least adjusted).

12. Here are a couple of nice, normal looking mults. All scales hugging a T score of 50, and Es is nice and high . . . over to the right (most adjusted).

13. An elevated Mf is pretty common for boys around colleges, but when it's primed and when Sc is up and is higher than Pt, I'll throw it to the left (least adjusted).

14. That's a fairly high Si and Pa is up. I'll call it maladjusted . . . here's one with a high Si and Sc is also up. I'll call this maladjusted.

15. Here's a pretty good-looking MMPI, but that low Es makes me think something might be wrong . . . to the left (least adjusted).

16. These are all pretty bad looking mults. I'll call adjusted if the Mt is lower than 10.

8. If D or Pt are the primary elevations and $Es \geq 45_R$, call adjusted.

9. If $Pd \geq 70$ and (a) male Mt $\geq 15_R$ or (b) female Ml > 17_R call maladjusted.

10. If $Ml \geq 23_R$ and $Es \leq 45_R$, call maladjusted.

11. If five or more clinical scales ≥ 65 and if either Pa or $Sc \geq 65$, call maladjusted.

12. Call adjusted if at least five clinical scales are between 40 and 60 and $Es \geq 45_R$.

13. Call maladjusted if the profile is male and $Mf \geq 70$ and $Sc \geq Pt$ and $Sc \geq 60$.

14. If $Si \geq 60$ and $Pa \geq 60$ or $Sc \geq 70$, call maladjusted.

15. Call maladjusted if $Es \leq 35_R$.

16. Call adjusted if $Ml \leq 10_R$.

*The subscript R refers to raw scores.

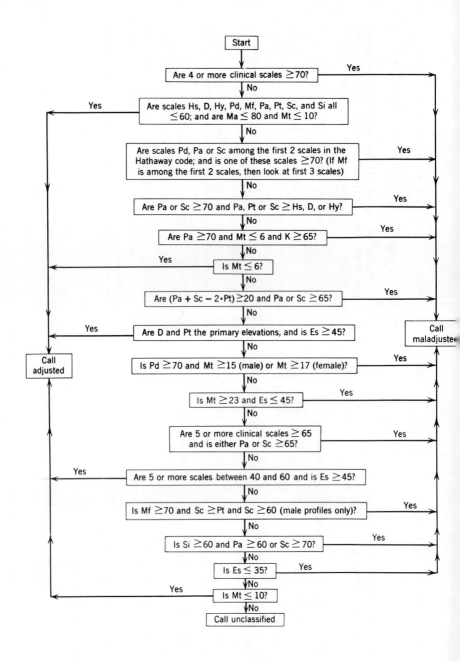

Fig. 6.1   Flow chart of MMPI decision rules.

158

TABLE 6.3 A Print-Out of Three Cases on Which the Computer
Yielded Clinical Judgments

New Case

Identification No. 209   Male   Criterion is Adjusted

Ques.	L	F	K	Hs	D	Hy	Pd	Mf	Pa	Pt	Sc	Ma	Si	Es	Mt
41	47	51	77	57	53	64	69	61	62	60	63	58	40	72	27

Raw Score   58   1

Beta = 13   Band 4   Delta = 10   AI = 50   IR = 0.89

$Pa + Sc - 2 \cdot Pt = 5$ $Hs + Hy - 2 \cdot D = 15$ $Mt - Es = -45$

$2 \cdot F - L - K = -22$

43, 8, 6, 5, 7-9, 12/0   Hathaway Code

Rules   Call this person maladjusted

Rules 18, 26, 22, Call this person normal

This person is called normal on the basis of precedence rule   0

New Case

Identification No. 210   Male   Criterion is Maladjusted

Ques.	L	F	K	Hs	D	Hy	Pd	Mf	Pa	Pt	Sc	Ma	Si	Es	Mt
44	43	53	46	39	60	60	74	59	64	52	44	68	42	54	56

Raw Score   44   19

Beta = -3   Band 3   Delta = 39   AI = 66   IR = 0.75

$Pa + Sc - 2 \cdot Pt = 4$ $Hs + Hy + 2 \cdot D = -21$ $Mt - Es = 2$

$2 \cdot F - L - K = 17$

4'963, 2-, 57/80:1   Hathaway Code

Rule   6,   Call this person maladjusted

Rules   Call this person normal

This person is called maladjusted on the basis of precedence rule   0

New Case

Identification No. 211   Male   Criterion is Maladjusted

Ques.	L	F	K	Hs	D	Hy	Pd	Mf	Pa	Pt	Sc	Ma	Si	Es	Mt
41	43	55	64	52	65	62	55	76	47	62	69	45	46	59	49

Raw Score   48   12

Beta = 14   Band 4   Delta = -12   AI = 73   I R = 1.10

$Pa + Sc - 2 \cdot Pt = -8$ $Hs + Hy - 2 \cdot D = -16$ $Mt - Es = -10$

$2 \cdot F - L - K = 3$

5'827, 3-41/6, 0, 9   Hathaway Code

Rules 11, 14,   Call this person maladjusted

Rule 22,   Call this person normal

This person is called maladjusted on the basis of precedence rule   2

TABLE 6.4　A Computer Print-Out of the Hit Rates
of Each Rule and of the Entire MMPI Program

Rule No.　1 has a hit rate of 0.83; it applied to 18 profiles

Rule No.　2 has a hit rate of 0.86; it applied to　7 profiles

Rule No.　3 has a hit rate of 1.00; it applied to　7 profiles

Rule No.　4 has a hit rate of 0.88; it applied to 17 profiles

Rule No.　5 has a hit rate of 0.78; it applied to　9 profiles

Rule No.　6 has a hit rate of 0.73; it applied to 15 profiles

Rule No.　7 has a hit rate of 0.77; it applied to 13 profiles

Rule No.　8 has a hit rate of 0.75; it applied to　4 profiles

Rule No.　9 has a hit rate of 0.89; it applied to 18 profiles

Rule No. 10 has a hit rate of 0.50; it applied to　6 profiles

Rule No. 11 has a hit rate of 1.00; it applied to　7 profiles

Rule No. 12 has a hit rate of 0.79; it applied to 14 profiles

Rule No. 13 has a hit rate of 0.71; it applied to　7 profiles

Rule No. 14 has a hit rate of 0.33; it applied to 21 profiles

Rule No. 15 has a hit rate of 1.00; it applied to　8 profiles

Rule No. 16 has a hit rate of 0.54; it applied to 13 profiles

	Valid	False
Positive	0.63	0.14
Negative	0.86	0.27

The overall hit percents achieved by the computer pro-grammed rules, as indicated in Table 6.4, were 63 and 86 in the valid positive and valid negative categories, respectively. Thus encouraged by the fact that an MMPI interpreter's rules of thumb and heuristics could be "frozen" and translated into a set of programmed instructions, the next step of the study was undertaken.

Revision of the MMPI Decision Rules

Up to this point the MMPI decision rules were devised

primarily by utilizing information that the expert furnished in his tape recordings. In an effort to improve upon the expert's Q-sort performance and to sharpen the existing decision rules, the method used consisted mainly of statistical searching and shuttling back and forth between intuitive hunches about combinations of various scales and their possible effect on the criterion hit percents. A number of developed and available MMPI indices were tried and some of these helped to improve the rules. Among those which were adopted were Welsh's Internalization Ratio and Anxiety Index (1952), the 4-prime rule of Meehl and Dahlstrom (1960), and the Hathaway Code (1947). Most important, in the derivation of the new rules, the computer's capabilities for storing and retrieving large quantities of information and its facility for high-speed arithmetical operations were exploited to the utmost. For example, one of the techniques that was used was to let the computer apply all the rules to a particular MMPI profile and to withhold its maladjusted or adjusted decision until a vote could be taken of the number of rules that favored one of the two classifications. In this way, if six rules called a profile adjusted and two rules classified it as maladjusted, then the former diagnosis would be made. Also, on the basis of an empirical determination of the relative strength or weakness of a particular decision rule, the computer program was "taught" to attend to specific patterns of rules rather than just to the number of votes that each profile received. The pattern analytic approach to the rules themselves was made possible by writing the computer program in such a way so that it printed the hit rates and the number of profiles to which each decision rule applied. (See Table 6.4.)

Finally, the completed set of MMPI decision rules included the original expert interpreter's information, a number of intraprofile slope characteristics that the expert failed to observe, and optimal ordering of the various components that comprised the whole. The hit percents for the total sample of 126 profiles are reported in Table 6.5. As can be seen from the results in this table, the programmed decision rules were a considerable improvement upon the original MMPI rules and upon the expert's Q-sort.

The MMPI decision rules, which consist of 35 sequential steps and instructions that govern the application of specific rules, are presented in Table 6.6 and Fig. 6.2. Although it is

TABLE 6.5   Hit and Miss Percents of Revised MMPI
Decision Rules with Total Sample (*N* = 126)

	Valid	False	Unclassified	Total Unclassified
Positive	91	12	4	
				2
Negative	84	9	0	

not advisable for practical reasons of time to attempt to apply these rules without the aid of a computer, it can probably be done. To process each MMPI profile by hand could take up to 30 minutes. The total estimated time in which the computer can do a similar job lies within the range of 1/10 of a second to $2\frac{1}{2}$ seconds; and these computer times depend on the ingenuity used in writing the program and on the speed of the particular model of electronic digital computer to be used.

Cross-Validation Samples

The proof of the efficacy of any psychological measuring instrument, mathematical model or set of rules lies in its ability to hold up when applied to new samples. Four new groups of college students served as cross-validation samples. The MMPI profiles and the accompanying diagnostic judgments as to their adjustment-maladjustment status were drawn from Brigham Young University (*N* = 100), University of Nebraska (*N* = 116), University of Iowa (*N* = 155), and the University of Missouri (*N* = 198). MMPI test administration to these students had taken place at the time that they sought counseling. In almost all instances the maladjustment-adjustment judgment was arrived at by accepting the consulted counselor's decision.

A report of the valid and false positive and negative findings is presented in Table 6.7. The proportion of maladjusted students who were correctly classified as such (e.g., the valid positives) ranged from 68% to 84%; and the percent of adjusted students correctly classified (valid negatives) ranged from 53 to 94. The percent of MMPI profiles left unclassified by the rules is almost negligible in three samples, but it did reach 7% in the Iowa sample. The size of the cross-validation "shrinkage" is not large and attests rather well to the validity

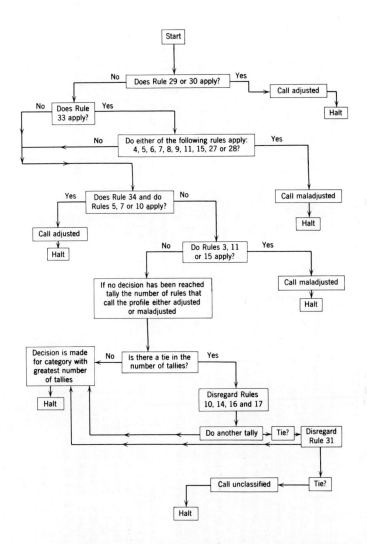

Fig. 6.2   Flow chart of the operation of some of the decision rules presented in Table 6.6.

163

TABLE 6.6 College Maladjustment Rules for MMPI Interpretation*

The MMPI should be scored on 16 scales, and these include: ?, L, F, K, Hs, D, Hy, Pd, Mf, Pa, Pt, Sc, Ma, Si, Es, and Mt (Kleinmuntz, 1962, p. 396). The latter two scales usually do not appear on the conventional MMPI profile sheet and should be notated and are reported here as *raw scores*. K correction is assumed for scales Hs, Pd, Pt, Sc, and Ma. All scores except those for Scales Es and Mt are reported here as T scores.

Application of these rules without the aid of an electronic digital computer may be exceedingly cumbersome due to the pattern analytic approach to the decision rules themselves.**

The following calculations will be needed:

1. Hathaway Code
2. Band location $(Pt + Sc) - (D + Hs) =$ beta
   Band 1: beta = - 31 and less
   Band 2: beta = -30 thru - 11
   Band 3: beta = -10 thru 6
   Band 4: beta = 7 thru 25
   Band 5: beta = 26 and above
3. Delta = $(Pd + Pa) - (Hs + Hy)$

4. Anxiety Index (AI) $= \dfrac{Hs+D+Hy}{3} + (D + Pt) - (Hs + Hy)$
5. Internalization Ratio (IR) $= \dfrac{Hs + D + Pt}{Hy + Pd + Ma}$

Note: Proceed to the next rule regardless of the maladjustment versus adjustment decision. Since a tally must be kept of the number of rules that apply to an MMPI profile, the rule number must be notated.

Call maladjusted if:

1. Four or more clinical scales ≥ 70 (Mt and Es excluded).
2. The first two scales of the Hathaway Code are among the Scales Pd or Pa or Sc and one of these ≥ 70. If Mf is one of the first two scales in the Hathaway Code, then examine the first three scales.
3. Pa or $Sc \geq 70$ and Pa or Pt or $Sc \geq Hs$ or D or Hy.
4. $Pa \geq 70$, unless $Mt \leq 6$ and $K \geq 65$.
5. $(Pa + Sc - 2 \cdot Pt) \geq 20$, if Pa or $Sc \geq 65$ and if Pa and/or $Sc \geq Pt$.
6. $Pd \geq 70$ and (a) $Mt \geq 15$ (males); (b) $Mt \geq 17$ (females).

7. $Pd \geq 70$ and (a) Band 4 or 5 and $\Delta \geq 0$ or (b) Band 1 or 2 and $\Delta \leq 0$.
8. $Mt \geq 23$ and $Es \leq 50$.
9. $Mt \geq 23$ and $Es \leq 45$.
10. Five or more scales ≥ 65 and Pa or $Sc \geq 65$.
11. Male profile with $Mf \geq 70$ and $Sc \geq 60$ with $Sc \geq Pt$.
12. $Sc \geq 70$ and either Si or $Pa \geq 60$.
13. $Es \leq 35$.
14. $IR \geq .90 \ \Delta \leq -10$.
15. Sc is primary elevation (first in Hathaway Code) and is ≥ 65 and $F \geq L$ and (not plus) K.
16. Band 2 profile.
17. Band 3 and $IR \geq 1.00$.
18. $K \geq 50$ and any scale except Es or $Ma \geq 70$.
19. Male profile and $Mf \geq 65$ and $Pd \geq 63$.
20. $Sc \geq 60$ and $Si \geq 50$ and $AI \geq 60$, unless Ma scale ≤ 65.
21. $Sc \geq 60$ and $Si \geq 50$ and $Ma \leq 70$ and $AI \geq 50$.
22. $Pd \geq 63$, and $Hs \leq 48$ and $AI \geq 65$.
23. Male profile and $Pd \leq 54$, $Hs \geq 58$, and $Si \geq 44$.
24. $Hs \geq 58$, $Hy \leq 61$.
25. $Hy \leq 61$ and $Pd \geq 63$; also hold for female profile if

Pd is not the primary elevation.
26. Pa and $Sc > 60$ if male, or > 65 is female.
27. $(Hs + Hy - 2 \cdot D) \geq 10$, $Pa < 50$, $Pt \geq 50$, and $Mt \geq 10_R$.
28. $(Mt - Es) \geq 4_R$.

Call adjusted if:
29. $Mt \leq 6_R$.
30. All scales ≤ 60 except $Ma \leq 80$ and $Mt \leq 10_R$.
31. D or Pt are primary elevations and $D \geq Hs$ and $\geq Hy$; and $Pt \geq Pa$ and $\geq Sc$; and $Es \geq 45$.
32. $Mt < 10_R$.
33. Five scales between 40 and 60, and $Es \geq 45$.
34. $(Hs + Hy - 2 \cdot D) \geq 20$; and $Pt < Pa \leq 70$ or $Mt \leq 10_R$.
35. $(Mt + Es) \leq 0_R$ if female, $\leq -20_R$ if male, unless Rule 5 calls profile maladjusted.

**Up until this point only tentative decisions have been made. The flow chart of Fig. 6.2 specifies the conditions for the final clinical decisions. The decisions are one of three: (a) call adjusted, (b) call maladjusted, and (c) call unclassified.

*The band locations, the beta and delta computations, the Anxiety Index and the Internalization Ratio mentioned as basic calculations were adopted from the Meehl-Dahlstrom (1960) rules. It may be helpful to the reader who is not familiar with MMPI literature to consult Dahlstrom and Welsh's *An MMPI Handbook* (1960) for complete explanations of some of the indexes used in these rules.

generalization of the MMPI decision rules to other college populations. Nevertheless there is shrinkage for which an account must be given in order to help increase the applicability of the rules to new situations.

TABLE 6.7   Hit and Miss Percents of Revised MMPI
Decision Rules with Four Cross-Validation Samples ($N = 569$)

Sample		Valid	False	Unclassified	Total Unclassified
Brigham Young University ($N = 100$) Adjusted ($N = 50$) Maladjusted ($N = 50$)	Positive Negative	80 64	36 18	2 0	1
University of Nebraska ($N = 116$) Adjusted ($N = 80$) Maladjusted ($N = 36$)	Positive Negative	72 94	6 25	3 0	1
University of Iowa ($N = 155$) Adjusted ($N = 98$) Maladjusted ($N = 57$)	Positive Negative	84 53	38 12	4 9	7
University of Missouri ($N = 198$) Adjusted ($N = 141$) Maladjusted ($N = 57$)	Positive Negative	68 70	28 26	2 5	3

There are at least two possible explanations for the size of the cross-validation shrinkage: (1) There are certain obvious differences between the criterion group and the new samples; and (2) the diagnostic judgments rendered by the counselors on the criterion and cross-validation adjusted and maladjusted students may be inaccurate.

Man versus Machine

Recently, this MMPI study was extended in a manner that permitted a comparison of the relative superiority of the computer programmed rules and eight test interpreters (Kleinmuntz, 1967). The purpose of this study was to determine whether a set of formal rules can equal or surpass clinicians' judgments for the particular prediction problem under consideration.

Again, using five samples of MMPI profiles, similarly prepared for Q-sorting, the subjects for this study were a group of eight MMPI interpreters, with varying lengths of clinical experience, but with substantial reputations for their interpretive skills with the MMPI. They were solicited by mail to perform the required task, and were not paid for their services. Also, they were assured of the confidentiality of their identities and the outcomes of their participation. The total number of persons contacted was four more than responded.

The samples were drawn from Brigham Young University ($N = 100$), the University of Nebraska ($N = 116$), the University of Iowa ($N = 155$), the University of Missouri ($N = 198$), Bucknell University ($N = 151$), and Carnegie Institute of Technology ($N = 126$). The students from the last of these schools served as the criterion subjects on whom the computer programmed rules were originally developed, and therefore their MMPIs were not used in comparison between computer and clinician. With the exception of the Carnegie Tech sample, MMPIs were administered when the students sought counseling and the criterion of maladjustment or adjustment was based on the consulted counselors' judgments.

Each of the eight MMPI interpreters was instructed to Q-sort the profiles of the five samples (i.e., all groups except Carnegie Tech) along a prescribed continuum from "most" to "least" adjusted, and to record his sortings on specially prepared coding sheets. The number of piles (i.e., discrete steps along the continuum) to be sorted varied from a 10-step continuum for the smallest sample ($N = 100$) to a 16-step continuum for the largest sample ($N = 198$). Additionally, Q-sorters were asked to draw a line at some point along the Q-sort distribution. They were told that this line demarcated that portion of their Q-sort in which they had the greatest confidence about their maladjusted vs. adjusted decisions. In our analyses of the data, each Q-sorter's line was used as the point at which his judgments were dichotomized into either the maladjusted or adjusted category.

No information was given the sorters about the criteria used to determine maladjustment or adjustment; nor were they given any description of the particular samples beyond the statement, "emotionally maladjusted and adjusted college students."

The results of the comparisons are summarized in Table 6.8. The differences in hit percents between the computer and the best clinician from among the eight (i.e., the clinician who achieved the highest overall success rate) are not statistically significant. Likewise, the hit percents between the computer programmed rules and the average of the eight clinicians are not statistically significant. However, the direction of the differences between the computer and the average clinician are consistently (5 out of 5) in favor of the computer programmed rules. These differences are statistically significant at the 0.03 level according to the nonparametric "sign test" (Wilcoxon, 1949) for small samples.

TABLE 6.8   Percents Hits and Misses of Computer Programmed Rules and Clinicians with Five MMPI Samples

	Computer		Best Clinician		Average Clinician	
Sample	Hits	Misses	Hits	Misses	Hits	Misses
Brigham Young (N = 100)	72	28	68	32	63	37
Nebraska (N = 116)	86	14	78	22	74	26
Iowa (N = 155)	65	35	65	35	61	39
Missouri (N = 198)	71	29	75	25	70	30
Bucknell (N = 151)	62	38	65	35	60	40

Taken as a whole, the results of this study indicate that for the prediction problem under consideration the computer does about as well as the best MMPI interpreter, and surpasses the average clinician. Moreover, our results suggest that the overall hit percents achieved by both the computer programmed rules and the best of eight clinicians in all but one of the five samples (i.e., Nebraska) are not especially high.

DISCUSSION

The findings of the MMPI studies have a threefold

significance for future use of computers: (1) Since computers
are more accessible than clinicians for the tedious data processing task that is entailed in MMPI profile interpretation, it
may be well to assign this task to machines rather than trained
clinicians. (2) The computer has an advantage over the clinician for this type of screening assignment in that it can accept
and utilize such programmed instructions as "here comes an
Iowa" sample (or Minnesota, Yale, Brigham Young), and can be
easily programmed to make proper normative adjustments in
order to achieve maximal hit rates. The clinician, on the other
hand, is severely limited by his experience with one or at most
two types of samples. (3) Finally, the special powers of the
computer for the type of decision task presented in this study
is its relatively greater consistency. Whereas the human may
apply certain hypotheses or rules occasionally, the machine
will apply such rules always and consistently, and therefore
does not add "error variance" to its judgments. All of these
considerations lead to the speculation that the computer
potentially is superior to the human for this and similar types
of prediction problems.

    At the outset of this paper it was suggested that the profile
analytic decision process could be studied, and that computer
programming of an interpreter's heuritics would lead to an understanding of that process. We now can ask the question:
What was learned about the test interpretation process from
our thinking aloud approach? For a partial answer to this
question, it can be said that not very much was learned about
profile analysis except that the problem at hand—that is, the
simple problem of predicting maladjustment and adjustment
from MMPI profiles—is not an enormously complex one. Certainly, judging from the fact that the entire process can be
summarized by a set of 16 formal rules for combining the
MMPI scales (see Table 6.2), it is apparent that there is no
justification for shrouding the profile analytic procedure in a
veil of mystery. But that is not much of a lesson, and in order
to learn in more detail about the complexities of clinical
decision making, we turned to investigating a much more
complex diagnostic problem-solving venture.

DIAGNOSIS IN CLINICAL NEUROLOGY

The profile analytic problem, as Newell correctly pointed

out several years ago (1963), is relatively simple because the MMPI search is a fixed and predetermined one, where the test interpreter operates within a closed environment. Furthermore, the objective of his search is simply a classification. No predictions of specific behavior or sequential decision-making that require subsequent readjustments of the decision scheme are required. Moreover, the use of an expert, who knows all the MMPI scale interactions, and who is totally familiar with MMPI profiles, explains little about the complexities of discovering scale interactions.

In the next set of studies to be reported here, a more complex task environment than profile interpretation was selected with the idea that such complexity would serve to reveal a richness of cognitive behavior more interesting than MMPI profile analysis. As an example *par excellence* of diagnostic problem-solving we chose to focus on the cognitive activities of diagnosticians within the clinical specialty of neurology. This particular specialty was selected because of the highly structured nature of clinical data within it and because of the importance placed by neurologists on arriving at a correct diagnosis.

Before proceeding to a consideration of these studies, some preliminary definitions are in order. Up to this point the terms diagnosis, clinical intuition and cognitive clinical activities have been used interchangeably. We are concerned in this portion of the paper only with formal diagnosis, which we shall consider to be a special instance of problem-solving which confronts the clinician with an array of data through which he searches and sifts, rejecting some of its aspects and calling for more information to supplement existing data. The problem to be solved by the diagnostician is in the form of a patient about whom certain biographical data, symptoms, signs, laboratory test results and other observable or elicited cues are available. The solution to the problem consists of an etiologic formulation, a classification of the patient into a taxonomic category, and the prescription of some treatment recommendations. It is recognized that the diagnostic problem-solving that intervenes between the beginning and end may be for each diagnostician a highly idiosyncratic process, and we will be interested in these differences, as well as in the similarities among certain kinds of diagnosticians.

Specifically, the questions we would like to answer are: 1) How does the diagnostician represent information in his memory; 2) how does he process that information during diagnostic problem-solving; and 3) does level of experience influence his information-processing? Answers to these questions might serve as an aid in the education of aspiring diagnosticians, should enable us to modify existing diagnostic search strategies, and could provide the elements of a computer program designed to simulate the human neurology diagnostician. Such a computer program would constitute the beginnings of a theory of neurological diagnostic problem-solving. In principle the theory is testable in the sense that it may or may not process neurological information (i.e., symptoms and signs) in a manner indistinguishable from that of the human diagnostician. Moreover, it will be a good theory only to the extent that it could predict a particular diagnostician's problem-solving behavior for a set of new diagnostic situations.

METHOD

In order to discover the neurologist's search strategies we devised a scheme which allows him to "think aloud" during his diagnostic problem-solving sessions. This scheme was our analogue to the Q-sort which was used successfully in the MMPI study. In the neurology problem we found a variant of the childhood game of Twenty Questions to be a useful technique that lends itself readily to the systematic study of a number of variables.

The game is played by having one player, called the experimenter, think of a disease, while the other player, or subject, tries to diagnose the disease the experimenter has in mind. The experimenter can play any of a number of roles: he can pretend, for example, that he is a patient suffering from symptoms x, y, and z; or he could assume the role of the neurologist who is thinking of a particular disorder which is characterized by symptoms x, y, and z. The diagnostician's job in either case is to inquire about the presence of certain symptoms, signs, or biographical data and he may, if he chooses, ask for certain laboratory test results. It is necessary that the experimenter be an experienced neurologist in order to answer the subject's questions, because he must be able to recognize the appropriateness of many symptoms, signs and laboratory tests that might possibly be relevant for a particular disease. The emphasis in these games is always on the manner in which the subject solves the diagnostic problems presented to him.

These games of Twenty Questions are tape recorded, and the end product, after appropriate editing resembles a tree structure (see Fig. 6.3). The way the game was described above a binary tree is obtained in which each point, or node, in the tree has exactly one connection to a point closer to the root of the tree. The starting point, or the root of the tree, is the subject's first question. All subsequent questions are the tests that are performed at the various nodes of the tree. Unless a diagnosis has been reached, each node is connected to exactly two lower nodes and through them to any number of still lower nodes. A path is a collection of lines from the root of the tree to a terminal node and is the schematic representation of the search strategy used by the neurologist to arrive at a diagnosis. In other words, the tree structure, or, as it is sometimes called, the discrimination net, represents the diagnostician's solution path from a certain set of givens to the diagnosis.

For illustrative purposes consider the game in Fig. 6.3 in which the subject was given the information that he is to diagnose the case of a 55-year-old patient who suffered from a sudden left central scotoma and a right hemiparesis. From the point at which the diagnostician asked the first question (i.e., "Is this the first episode?") until a diagnosis was reached, there were exactly nine test nodes and eight binary branchings.

From inspection of this binary tree structure we can readily see the types and the number of questions that were asked by the diagnostician as he worked his way toward a diagnostic solution. We recognize that the artificial situation of the psychology laboratory placed certain constraints on the functioning of these diagnosticians, but these conditions were roughly parallel for all participating subjects. For the series of studies reported here, particular attention was paid to the number and types of subgoals used by neurologists of varying levels of experience in arriving at a solution to diagnostic problems.

The diagnostic games consisted of eight sets of givens—

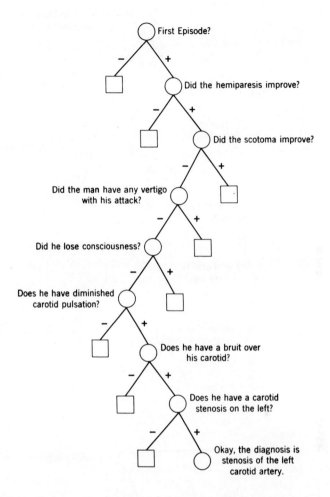

First Episode?

Did the hemiparesis improve?

Did the scotoma improve?

Did the man have any vertigo
with his attack?

Did he lose consciousness?

Does he have diminished
carotid pulsation?

Does he have a bruit over
his carotid?

Does he have a carotid
stenosis on the left?

Okay, the diagnosis is
stenosis of the left
carotid artery.

Fig. 6.3 A tree structure of a neurologist's diagnostic game in which the information given was: Sudden left central scotoma and right hemiparesis in a 55-year-old.

that is, information given to the subjects or diagnosticians by the experimenter to represent each of the following eight neurological disease categories: Inflammation, degeneration, malformation, vascular disorders, neoplasm, metabolic disorders, toxic disturbances, and disorders due to head trauma.

The diagnosticians were 12 neurologists, ranging in experience all the way from juniors in medical school to persons

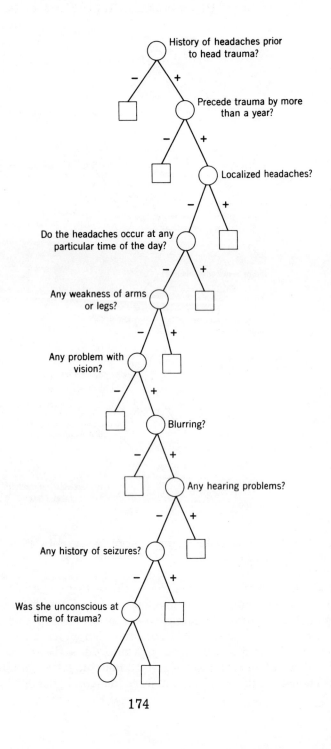

History of headaches prior to head trauma?

Precede trauma by more than a year?

Localized headaches?

Do the headaches occur at any particular time of the day?

Any weakness of arms or legs?

Any problem with vision?

Blurring?

Any hearing problems?

Any history of seizures?

Was she unconscious at time of trauma?

174

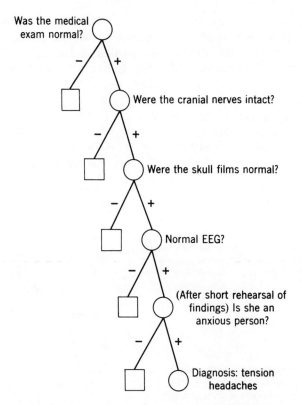

Fig. 6.4   Information given to a *first year* neurology resident was: History of head trauma and severe headaches in a 40-year-old female.

with three or more years post-residence hospital-ward practice.   Since each of 12 subjects played 8 diagnostic games twice—that is, since a total of 192 games were played, and about an equal number of tape-recorded hours were collected— only the highlights of these findings can be summarized here.

RESULTS

Level of Experience and Number of Subgoal Questions

The most obvious finding obtained relating the effects of experience to diagnosis was that hospital ward experience made a significant difference in both accuracy of diagnosis and in the number of questions asked. In other words, subjects who had not had experience with neurologically ill patients missed more than half the diagnostic games. In terms of their tree structures, this means that they either arrived at a mistaken diagnosis, or that they conceded "being at the end of the rope" somewhere along their solution paths.

An interesting finding was obtained when these subjects returned for a second diagnostic session using the identical games. One would expect that since they were all instructed

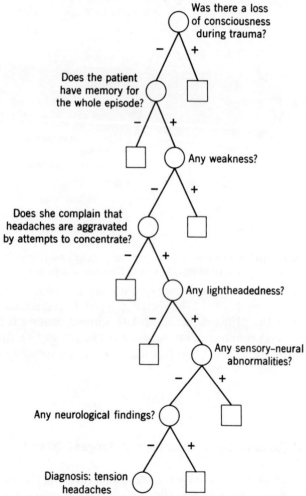

Fig. 6.5 The same information as that given in Fig. 6.4 was presented to a *second year* neurology resident.

that they would return for another session, that they might study, look up, or rehearse the diseases missed by them. But the fact of the matter was that they misdiagnosed the same diseases in almost identical fashion.

When the factor of experience on the ward was held constant, but the amount of that experience was varied—that is to say, when all our subjects had had hospital experience, but the length of that experience became the independent variable, then it was observed that the number of questions asked decreased with greater ward experience. This is illustrated in the three binary tree structures shown in Figs. 6.4, 6.5, and 6.6, which represent three levels of neurology experience— viz., first-year, second-year, and post-residency training.

The information given for the problem presented in these figures consisted of: "History of head trauma and severe headache for five months in a 40-year-old female." The various tree structures generated by our neurology diagnosticians differ from one another in length, that is, in the number of

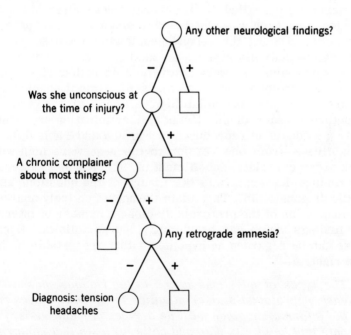

Fig. 6.6 The same information as that given in Figs. 6.4 and 6.5 was presented to a *post-resident* neurologist.

steps required for solution. The subjects of Figs. 6.4, 6.5, and 6.6 required 17, 8 and 5 questions to arrive at a diagnosis. Accounting for the first diagnostician's lengthy questioning was his tendency to rehearse and to summarize all of his findings at every other node in the tree. Whether or not this tendency disappears with experience, or whether it was a stylistic pattern of the individual, is subject for further study. Incidentally, when he returned several weeks later, and was challenged by the identical set of games, he continued to ask similar questions and make similar errors.

Levels of Experience and Types of Subgoal Questions

What the diagnostician says while he is solving a problem reflects in many ways what he has in memory and the way he uses information stored in memory. In order to gain some glimpse of the diagnostician's reasoning process, the game of Twenty Questions was modified somewhat. Each of the diagnosticians was called back several weeks after his initial session, and each was instructed to diagnose the same set of problems. During the second session the diagnostician was expected to state his reasons for asking each of his questions. By this procedure we were able to obtain a rather rich "thinking aloud" protocol, while at the same time it enabled us to secure a test-retest reliability estimate of the size and structure of each diagnostician's discrimination net. One of these protocols is reproduced in Fig. 6.7 and Table 6.9. The reliabilities from one session to the next were high with a rank order correlation coefficient of .92. The more interesting finding, however, was the nature of the questions asked by the diagnostician. These data are not yet entirely analyzed, but inspection of the protocols disclose a number of interesting findings which can be summarized as follows. Each of these can be regarded as hypotheses that are testable in their own right:

1. *The types of questions asked at the various nodes within each neurologist's discrimination tree, as he moves from the information given until he arrives at a diagnosis, indicate that he elicits data and calls for tests that conform to a pattern that moves from general to specific questioning.* Thus, typical questions at the outset of any given diagnostic

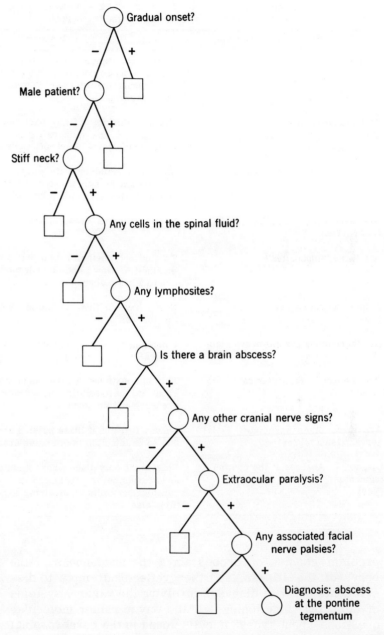

Fig. 6.7 The information given was: fever, obtundation, and diplopia (See Table 6.9).

TABLE 6.9   Questions and Their Stated Reasons in the Diagnosis of a Disease
Characterized by Fever, Obtundation, and Diplopia

Question and Answer at Test Node	Stated Reason for Question
Was the onset gradual? (No)	Generally, tumors or degenerate diseases occur gradually. Infections and vascular disorders are very sudden and abrupt
Is the patient a male? (No)	I'm not thinking of any particular disease. I just want to get some picture of some kind of person
Does the patient have a stiff neck? (Yes)	Stiff neck would indicate either inflammation or hemorrhage, both of which would give you obtundation
Are there any cells in the spinal fluid? (Yes)	Inflammation vs. hemorrhage
Are these lymphosites? (Yes)	To find out whether it is a primary meningitis. Now I know it is secondary to a brain abscess
Is there a brain abscess? (Yes)	Now I have to find out the locus of the abscess
Are there other cranial nerve signs? (Yes)	I must now narrow this down anatomically
Does he have extraocular paralysis? (Yes)	This is a sixth nerve sign, but I must eliminate the possibility of increased pressure on this nerve
Are there other associated facial nerve palsies? (Yes)	I must find out if these palsies are due to an infection in the same area
Diagnosis: Abscess at the pontine tegmentum? (Yes)	This is the only place where a sixth and seventh nerve paralysis can occur together without involving anything else

problem consist of probes about the suddenness of the
onset of the illness, and then reflects attempts to discriminate between diseases involving the various systems
of biological functioning, all the way to rather molecular
questions about types of cells found in the cerebrospinal
fluid.   The phenomenon especially noted among the

protocols of inexperienced neurologists was that this general-to-specific search strategy was disrupted about halfway along their diagnostic games, usually as a result of discovering that they were pursuing the wrong hypotheses. Such disruption does not occur among more experienced diagnosticians.

Such lack of disruption during the experienced diagnosticians' search can be explained on the basis of their using a disease categorization scheme. Paul Wortman (1965) conducted a study in this regard where he instructed three experienced neurologists to sort 115 common neurological diseases into major disease categories. The neurologists displayed a high degree of consistency in the way they assigned diseases to categories. A discrimination net to depict such a scheme is presented in Fig. 6.8. This suggests further that within such categorization schemes, there may be subroutines that serve to specify even further the disease categories into disease entities.

2. *The neurologist has learned to search his problem environment for those symptoms and signs that yield the greatest amount of information.* This is more true about the experienced diagnostician than the beginner. The more experienced neurologist's overall search strategy is guided by a maximization principle in which he radically reduces his

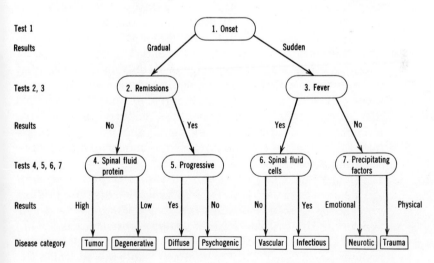

Fig. 6.8   Discrimination net sorted to disease categories.

problem environment with each question until he has zeroed-in on a differential diagnostic judgment. In order to illustrate this point we will digress for a moment from the field of neurology and consider the game of Twenty Questions as it might be played in geography. If an experimenter asserts that he is thinking of a city in the U. S. A., a poor diagnostician might ask several specific, but low information-yield, questions such as "Is it City X?", "Is it City Y?", "Is it north?", and so forth, before arriving at an incorrect or correct solution. The experienced diagnostician, who would be the counterpart of our competent neurologist, might ask whether the city was east or west of the Mississippi River, and thus with one question cut his problem environment in half. The next high-yield question about U. S. A. geography might be whether the city is north or south of the Mason-Dixon line. Again his problem space is cut in half, and he might continue in this manner until a diagnosis is reached. In our neurology tree structures we have observed that this type of optimization leads to solution paths that tend to be shorter than those of the inexperienced neurologists.

3. *The neurologist's search strategies involve the use of both short-term and long-term memory storage.*   After the diagnosticians proceeded about one-half way down a particular diagnostic tree, they were asked to recall or recite all information that they have accumulated prior to that point. They were not able to remember those data that did not substantiate a particular differential diagnostic hypothesis. In other words, they can recall only information that is relevant to a particular diagnosis and seem to selectively forget irrelevant data.   Therefore, it may be assumed that their short-term memories undergo moment-to-moment modifications and revisions, and we may postulate that their long-term memories are much less subject to such modifications.

4. *The neurologist has in memory a visual representation of the central nervous system and much of his information processing involves a shuttling back and forth between symptoms, test findings and neuroanatomical locus.* This observation is well-illustrated in the tree structure and protocol reproduced in Fig. 6.8 and Table 6.9, in which the neurologist was asked to specify his reasons for asking

particular probing questions. For example, in Table 6.9, the neurologist asks, "Are there other cranial nerve signs?" and upon receiving an affirmative reply continues this line of questioning until it is discovered that the anatomical locus of the abscess must be at a particular area of the pons because "This is the only place where a sixth and seventh nerve paralysis can occur together without involving anything else."

DISCUSSION

In terms of the questions raised earlier regarding the way the neurologist represents information in memory, the manner he processes that information, and the influence of experience on such processing, we can now offer a number of tentative conclusions. It was noted that level of experience makes a considerable difference in the number and types of questions, and in the extent of accuracy of neurological diagnosis. Not surprisingly with greater amounts of experience comes a higher level of competency.

Further it was demonstrated that the specific types of questions asked by a neurologist reflect an active hypothesis-testing procedure whereby specific patterns of diagnostic search are discernible. Again, with greater experience there is associated a higher degree of expertness in diagnostic problem-solving.

Future studies in neurology diagnosis should be designed to explore further the differences between experienced and inexperienced diagnosticians, and between competent and poor diagnosticians, with the factor of experience held constant. More specifically, among the important questions that remain to be explored are the effects of noise on differential diagnosis and the problem of whether or not information obtained in a psychology laboratory generalizes to the neurologist's behavior on the ward.

Noise can be added to our game of Twenty Questions by introducing, in the information given to the diagnostician, certain symptoms and signs that do not make diagnostic sense. This is comparable to the real-life situation where a patient presents himself to the physician with a set of complaints, and with the attitude "While I am here," he also volunteers information that is not relevant to the major complaints. Noise can also consist of information that is withheld or improperly described. In the light of our findings reported so far we would predict that noise will have less effect on experienced neurologists than on those who are inexperienced.

Another form of noise that is worthy of further study is the type that is specific to a particular neurologist. That is to say, if certain neurologists indicate that various signs and symptoms have a low probability of occurrence in association with particular diseases, then the introduction of the low-likelihood (subjective probability information obtained from the physician under controlled laboratory conditions) symptoms constitute noise in his diagnostic system. Paul Wortman is currently collecting data on the relationship between a neurologist's assignment of probabilities to symptom-disease occurrences and the way he actually elicits symptom information in his diagnostic searching.

SUMMARY AND CONCLUSIONS

The major thrust of this paper was aimed at demonstrating that clinical intuition is amenable to rigorous scientific study. Accordingly, we examined the behavior of clinicians in two types of decision-making tasks. In the first of these studies, MMPI profile interpreters served as subjects; and in the second set of studies, the subjects were clinical neurologists.

Our first example considered the situation where a test interpreter perceives and responds to cues provided by the profiles (e.g., scale elevations) of emotionally maladjusted and adjusted college students. The test interpreter selected to serve as a subject in this study was one who had achieved the highest success rate from among several MMPI experts. Our subject was then instructed to "think aloud" into a tape recorder while he was performing Q-sorts of a sample of 126 MMPI profiles.

On the basis of the test interpreter's protocol, a set of sequential decision rules was developed, and these rules were written into programmed instructions for computer processing. It was then demonstrated that the computer rules achieved a success rate that closely approximated that of the expert.

Thus encouraged by our initial success, we set out to improve upon the expert's hit rate, and after using the computer's brute force arithmetic powers, we obtained MMPI decision rules which were superior to the test interpreter. However, upon cross-validation of these rules, it became evident that the computer performs about as well as an expert interpreter, but nonetheless could profit from further efforts aimed at improvement.

The second study of clinical intuition in the laboratory consisted of research designed to investigate diagnostic problem solving by clinical neurologists. From verbal reports of physicians diagnosing neurological diseases we obtained binary tree structures that represented the physicians' diagnostic search strategies. These trees were secured by allowing subjects to "think aloud" while diagnosing a patient (the experimenter) in a simulated clinical setting. It was then possible to examine the length of the tree structure—that is, it was possible to count the number of test nodes—and the types of questions asked at each node, which were obtained from various diagnosticians. In the set of studies reported here, the level of experience was the major independent variable, and the number and types of diagnostic tests performed were the dependent variables. Further, the tree structures enabled us to gain valuable information about the way in which neurologists represent information in memory and the strategies they use in arriving at diagnostic decisions.

From the point of view of programming the cognitive activities of neurologists, we achieved less success in the latter studies when these are compared to the MMPI work. No computer program has as yet evolved from the neurology studies. The major reasons for this are twofold: (1) Diagnosis in neurology does not involve an all-or-none, maladjusted-or-adjusted decision; rather it is a complex concept attainment task where the diagnostician must sift and sort through an array of data, accepting some aspects of it, and rejecting others. And (2) our goals were different in the two studies: In the MMPI work, we were willing to settle for a computer program that accomplishes the task of profile analysis; whereas in the neurology studies our concern was mainly to obtain a model of the neurologist's diagnostic problem solving. Such a model would be a high-fidelity replica of the neurologist's cognitive processes while diagnosing patients' diseases, and in principle, a computer program based on it should be able to diagnose the same neurological diseases as the human clinician.

We now can ask the question: What was learned about clinical intuition from the two approaches taken in this paper? For a partial answer to this question we can state that, most basic perhaps, we learned that clinicians can be encouraged to verbalize, in fairly unambiguous terms, the way they utilize information in arriving at decisions. In the MMPI profile task, we focused on the best interpreter available to us, and if we can assume that there are qualitative similarities among "good" interpreters, then we have a partial explanation of MMPI profile analysis.

We learned also that there are certain classes of prediction problems that do not tax to the utmost the ingenuity of the clinician. For example, by using only 16 rules for combining the MMPI scales, the computer program achieved a respectable success rate. Such a finding suggests that some of the clinician's subjective weighting of predictor variables and his inconsistencies in the way he performs from one time to the next add error variance to the judgment process.

When we move away from the straight prediction situation, however, some of the simplicity of the MMPI task is lost. The neurology task, as noted earlier, required an active shuttling back and forth between elicited data and the patient. Moreover, this task demanded the formulation of transitory and tentative hypotheses that are confirmed or disconfirmed by additional questions and findings. When these factors are considered together, we obtain a diagnostic situation where cognitive behavior is displayed in all its richness. However, it is important to emphasize here that this complexity does not remove it from within the realm of rigorous methods of study.

Finally, this paper aims at the clinical versus statistical prediction controversy, but in another way than just providing another tool for the "statistical" or "clinical" sides of the argument. By attending specifically to how the clinician processes data, we are asserting, not that statistics are as good as clinicians, but that the clinician himself is simply another variant of "statistical" predictor. This assertion is not made at an armchair or philosophical level, but in terms of detailed descriptions of how clinicians perform.

CHAPTER 7

Joshua Lederberg
and Edward A. Feigenbaum

Stanford University

MECHANIZATION
OF INDUCTIVE INFERENCE IN
ORGANIC CHEMISTRY*

INTRODUCTION

A paradigm of the scientific method is the successive alternation of reference to hypothesis and datum. We start with a hypothesis, which moves us to select some aspect of the real world for empirical enquiry. Sensory impressions are translated by convention into data. More refined hypotheses are then *induced* by a poorly understood process which contains at least two elements: (1) the data somehow suggest a hypothesis, and (2) deductive algorithms are applied to the hypothesis to make logically necessary predictions; these are then matched with the data in a search for contradictions. A hypothesis is regarded as inductively proven (i.e., we have achieved a scientific discovery) when its predictions are satisfied, and when we have the illusion of inductive exhaustion that no other hypothesis will lead to equally concordant predictions. It is rare for inductive exhaustion to be rigorously justified. Usually, the process is reiterated many times: each refinement of hypothesis suggests the examination of new data; each new datum leads to a discrimination among existing hypotheses, or suggests another refinement.

Our main contribution is, perhaps, the suggestion that organic chemistry is an apt field for the mechanization of the process of scientific induction. It can be circumscribed so that the first studies are simplified without undue loss of

*The research reported here was supported in part by the Advanced Research Projects Agency of the Office of the Secretary of Defense (SD-183), and in part by the National Aeronautics and Space Administration (NsG 81-60).

187

utility or generality.   Real data of any desired level of complexity can be adduced. Few natural sciences are so rich in
inductive analysis from information that can be presented in a
simple, uniform format. By contrast, genetics or embryology
are sciences that might invoke models of most of external
reality. Above all, the hypotheses of organic chemistry can be
abstractly represented, that is, as structure diagrams. These
lead, in turn, to an algebra for inductive exhaustion rarely
available in any other scientific field at the present time.

As will be seen, our program (named DENDRAL) is
firmly rooted in this algebra which can generate an exhaustive
and irredundant list of hypotheses from initial contextual data
(1,2,3,4). The problem of induction is then reduced to efficient
selection from this prospective list. This is only feasible if
the experimental data are recurrently consulted to guide the
hypothesis-generator. Unproductive branches of the generation tree are anticipated and avoided as soon as possible;
conversely, the data are used for heuristic reordering of the
priorities with which the hypotheses are brought up for examination. The program thus simulates a systematic idealiza-
tion more than it does the haphazard evocation of new concepts
in human intelligence.

HEURISTIC DENDRAL: A SUMMARY FROM THE
STANDPOINT OF ARTIFICIAL INTELLIGENCE RESEARCH

The intent of this section is to present in a succinct and
compact fashion information relevant to a general understanding of what our program does and how it does it.

Motivation and Task Environment

We have been interested in exploring processes of empirical inquiry, particularly discovery processes involved in
searching a hypothesis space for hypotheses meaningful and
relevant to the explanations of real-world data. Some practical
considerations concerning the automation of routine scientific
endeavor in particular environments, using heuristic programming techniques, also supplied some of the motivation.
We were interested also in exploring man-machine interaction
in the context of scientific problem solving, not only as an

augmentation to human problem solving processes ("smart scratch paper") but also as a means for "educating" a suitably receptive program, by making it easy for a human skilled in the task area to impart to the program his heuristic search rules and other information relevant to good performance in the task.

The task area chosen was the analysis of mass spectra of organic molecules. The hypotheses relevant to explaining mass spectral data in organic chemical analysis are essentially graphs--molecular graphs consisting of atoms and bonds, such as are seen in textbooks on organic chemistry.

The main tasks presented to the program at present are:

1. Given a chemical (compositional) formula, output a list of the chemically most plausible isomers (structural variants) of the composition, ordered from most plausible through least plausible if that is requested.

2. Given a mass spectrum and a composition, output a list of the most plausible isomers of the composition in the light of the spectral data given. Restated, generate a hypothesis or list of hypotheses to best explain some given spectral data.

Processes, Algorithmic and Heuristic

The program that solves these problems is called Heuristic Dendral. It is a LISP program of some 30-40 thousand words, developed on the SDC Q-32 time-sharing system and presently operating on the PDP-6 at the Stanford Artificial Intelligence Project. Though the program consists of many functions, the most important activities can be summarized as follows:

1. At the most basic level, there is an algorithm, called the Dendral Algorithm, rarely exercised without constraints. Given a chemical composition, it will generate all of the topologically possible noncyclical connected graphs that can be made from the atoms of the composition, given the valences of these atoms. Associated with the Dendral Algorithm is a notation for these graph structures, called Dendral notation. Canonical forms of the graph structures in Dendral notation exist and are used. The Dendral Algorithm is a systematic

and exhaustive "topologist" and knows nothing about chemistry, except the valences of atoms. But, using a chess analogy, it is the "legal move generator," the ultimate guarantor of the completeness of the hypothesis space.

2. Heuristic processes control and limit the generation process (i.e., prune the implicit generation tree). Taken together, these heuristics constitute the program's "chemical model." This model includes: a list of denied embedded subgraphs, the existence of any one of which in a strucutre rules out that structure as a plausible hypothesis; a list of well-known, stable, and generally highly significant radicals which are treated in an aggregate fashion as "superatoms," or essentially higher level concepts; an evaluation function not dependent on spectral data that evalutes the potential fruitfulness of attempting to generate structures from a collection of as yet unassigned atoms (i.e., evaluates the worth of pursuing a particular subproblem); a data matching process that we sometimes call "the zero-order theory of the mass spectrometer" that makes decisions about the relevance of the subproblems based on the actual mass numbers present in the given spectrum; a "rote memory," called the Dictionary, which is the memory of previously solved subproblems, corresponding to the theorem memory in theorem-proving programs; and a few other heuristic processes of lesser importance.

3. Learning processes in Heuristic Dendral are relatively simple, and a high order of learning by the program itself remains more of a goal than an accomplished fact. The main "internal" learning process is the Dictionary building activity. Learning on the subproblem evaluation function a la Samuel's Checker Program is possible, but not implemented. "Extrinsic" learning, in the sense of a human expert communicating to the program the elements of the chemical model, has been extensively and successfully used. Perhaps this is high level programming, but in the same sense that pedagogy in general is high level programming activity.

ORGANIC CHEMISTRY   THE PROBLEM-CONTEXT
OF DENDRAL

The fundamental problem of organic chemistry is the topological structure of a molecule. This was first brought into focus by the Swedish chemist, Jons Jakob Berzelius (1779-1848) when he established the occurence of chemical isomers. These are different organic molecules having the same chemical composition or ensemble of atoms; hence they have different structures (i.e., connectivities of the atoms with respect to atom-to-atom bonds). For one of the simplest examples, take C_2H_6O, which has the two isomers, dimethyl ether and ethanol (Fig. 7.1). To determine that the composition of a compound once obtained as a pure sample, say C_2H_6O, is essentially a mechanical process of quantitative analysis. To assign it to one of the possible isomers is a much more demanding intellectual exercise.

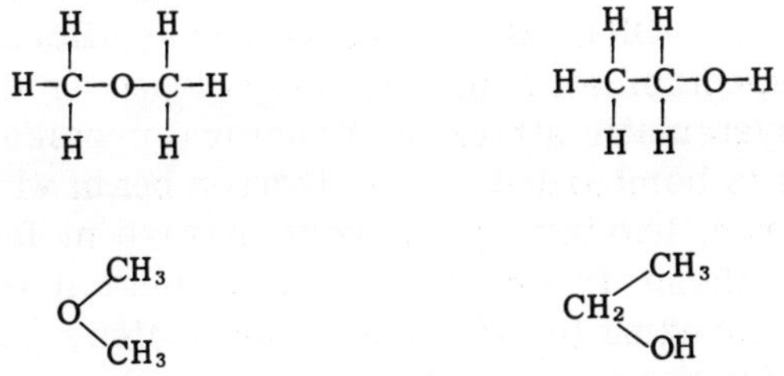

(a)   (b)

Fig. 7.1   Two isomers of C_2H_6O: (a) Dimethyl ether (O..CH3 CH3), (b) Ethanol or ethyl alcohol (CH2..CH3 OH).

   Each of these may also be represented by isomorphic graphs, for example, for ethanol: (CH3.CH2.OH) or (OH.CH2.CH3) or (CH2..OH CH3). The previous notation is in canonical DENDRAL form, being initialized by the center of the graph, followed by a dot for each radical, and then a list of radicals in order of an algorithmically defined value. For internal representation or more compact coding, the H's can be dropped, leaving us with O..CC and C..CO respectively. Where symmetries prevail, we can go one step further, using the '/' as a ditto mark, as in (O./C) for (O..CC). This economy is, of course, trivial here, but not so in more complex formulas.

At this level of analysis, structure means connectivity, not geometry. In fact, with the help of X-ray diffraction analysis, a great deal can be learned about the actual disposition in space of the atoms in a molecule in the crystalline state. However, the molecules, especially in the liquid or gaseous states, may be undergoing a variety of dynamic transitions—linear, rotational, and rocking modes about every chemical bond. Chemical geometry is beyond the scope of the present discussion, but what we know of it could be superimposed upon the topological frameowrk developed below.

The preceding paragraph can be summarized: a chemical structure is represented by an undirected graph whose nodes are atoms, whose edges are chemical bonds. While the analogy was recognized 100 years ago, this outlook has still to penetrate the teaching of organic chemistry.

In practical problem solving the chemist uses every possible datum. For example, smell can help him decide between dimethyl ether and ethanol, if he did not already recognize that the ether would be much more volatile than its isomeric alcohol. He also has a repertoire of reagents that can help to detect various fragments (called radicals) in the molecule (e.g., -OH). More recently a specialized instrument, the mass spectrometer, has been developed which facilitates a unified systematic attack on structural problems. Briefly, a molecule is bombarded by an electron beam which sputters off an electron, leaving a positively charged molecule-ion. A fraction of these fragment, giving radical ions of various sizes corresponding to different modes of cleavage, often complicated by further rearrangements and reactions of fragments. Finally, the ensemble of molecule- and radical-ions is resolved by careful acceleration through electrostatic and magnetic fields.

The utility of the mass spectrometer and some examples of the logical inference employed in exploiting it are reviewed by McLafferty (1966).

The mass spectrum is a paired list of mass numbers and their relative intensities. Mass spectrometers of very high resolution have been built, capable of distinguishing between radicals of different composition but the same integer atomic weight. For example, the radical -NH, $M = 15.0110$ can be distinguished from the radical -CH$_3$, $M = 15.0215$. This capability is especially useful for determining the formula of the intact molecule. Unless we specify otherwise, however, we have in mind the more ordinary low resolution mass spectrometer which lumps together species having the same integral mass. However, more precise data are readily accommodated and avidly used by the program logic.

The stated goal of our program is then an inductive solution of the mass spectrum. That is, a molecular formula and its mass spectrum are given as data. We must induce the structure (hypothesis) that best satisfies the data. Our basic approach to this has been first to furnish the computer with a language in which chemical structure hypotheses can be expressed, then to interrogate chemists and their literature for the rules and techniques they have used in problem solving and attempt to translate these into computer algorithms. In the course of searching for these heuristics, we have in fact discovered a number of algorithms which are much more systematic than the approaches commonly used by chemists in this field.

ISOMERS

Underlying the solution of virtually every problem and subproblem in structural organic chemistry is the potential exhaustion of the list of possible isomers of a given molecule or radical. It is remarkable that while hundreds of thousands of students of elementary organic chemistry are challenged in this way every year, no algorithm for generating and verifying complete lists of isomers has hitherto been presented. Each student is left to work out his own intuitive approach to this problem, which may account for the bafflement with which very many students approach the subject upon their first exposure to it.

The core of DENDRAL is a notation for chemical structures and an algorithm capable of producing all distinct isomers and casting each of them into a canonical representation. This will be outlined in more detail further on.

The lowest level of DENDRAL might be called the topologist. This machine considers only the valence rules and elementary graph theory in constructing lists of isomers. It uses two elementary concepts, one, the center of a graph as a point of departure, and two, a recursive procedure for evaluating a radical as a way of specifying the canonical representation of a given molecule. After the center of the map is fixed, being either a bond or an atom of known valence, the radicals pendant on the center must be listed in nondecreasing value. The apical node of each radical is then regarded as a new center and the process continues recursively.

The same approach can be used to make a generator from DENDRAL. From the formula or composition list, a bond or a given species of atom is first taken as the central feature and the remaining atoms partitioned in appropriate ways, and these partitions assigned tentatively to the pendant radicals. For each radical then successive allocations are made for the apical node and then partitions are allocated to the pendant subradicals, and so forth.

TABLE 7.1   Canons of Dendral Order* (Hierarchy of Vector Valuation in Decreasing Order of Significance)

The DENDRAL-VALUE of a Radical Consists of the Vector:

COUNT

Rings by number of rings[†]
Other atoms (except II)

COMPOSITION of radical

Rings[†] by valuation of ring
    Composition, Vertex Group, Path List, Vertex List, Substituent Locations
Other atoms by atomic number (S, P, O, N,C)

UNSATURATIONS (afferent link included; ring paths excluded)

APICAL NODE

Ring Value[†]
Degree: number of efferent radicals
Composition: e.g. (S, P, O, N, C)
Afferent link: (:, :, .)

APPENDANT RADICALS if any

(nested vectors in canonical order); nil if current apex is terminal
Enantiomerism around apex (DL, D, L, unspecified) if applicable

*From J. Lederberg (1964), DENDRAL-64, NASA CR-57029, Star No. N65-13158
[†]Rings are not discussed in this paper.
Each line above is a separate cell or subcell of the vector.

Table 7.1 summarizes the order of allocation for evaluating a radical, and for generating the next structure, a procedure used recursively in the DENDRAL program in LISP. At this time, the operational program is confined to acyclic structures. However, the specifications have been detailed for a complete system, including ring structures of arbitrary complexity as well as consideration of optical isomerism (1,2). Table 7.2 lists the computation of all the isomers generated by the topologist for the formula $C_3H_7NO_2$, one of whose isomers is the common amino acid, alanine. This exercise is already at the very margin of human capability, barring the possible rediscovery of this algorithm. In practice no intelligent human has the patience to attempt to generate such a list by the intuitive process. The chemist will often then demand redundant information at this point in order to narrow the range of possibilities he is obliged to consider before he will make the effort to produce an exhaustive list.

The topologist knows only the valence rules as quasi-empirical data, that is, that four bonds must issue from each carbon atom, three from any nitrogen, two from any oxygen, and but one from hydrogen. With this very limited quota of chemical insight, the topologist produces many structures that would be regarded as absurdities by the experienced chemist, for example the radical ($\cdot$O$\cdot$NH$\cdot$OH) in no. 4 of Table 7.2. The next stage in the development of DENDRAL is then to impart a certain amount of additional chemical information taken from the real world. In doing this a definite context is implied, even if this is not immediately overt. There are probably many realms of organic chemistry, for example, at ultra low temperatures, of which we have only limited experience. The implicit context we have in fact adopted is that of the natural product, that is to say, molecular species that might be reasonably stable at ambient temperatures, and therefore stand some chance of persisting or being isolated from natural sources. However, this rule has been applied rather cautiously and the lists that will be adduced for further illustration still contain a number of items which would be regarded as quite dubious by this criterion.

The program is quite amenable to adjustment to any given set of facts. Indeed, a certain stage in the program can be switched on to interrogate the chemist to help to find the context in which various rules will be applied or not. At this stage chemical insight is given most explicitly by providing a list of forbidden substructures. Whenever these substructures are encountered during the building of a potential molecule, the generator is adjusted to ignore that entire branch of synthetic possibilities. In order to effectuate this use of a "BADLIST," a graph matching algorithm has been incorporated into the DENDRAL program. At best, however, graph matching is an expensive proposition and it soon became necessary to seek ways of economizing on redundant computation. The last

TABLE 7.2 The Isomers of Alanine, C3H7NO2, without Chemical
Common Sense*

>(ISOMERS *ALANINE)

>BADLIST
  NIL

>GOODLIST
  NIL

>SPECTRUM
  NIL

>DICTLIST
  NIL

>(ILLEGAL ATTACHMENTS)
  (NIL NIL NIL)

C3H7NO2
MOLECULES
((U . 1.) (C . 3.) (N . 1.) (O . 2.))
  1.   . C3H7   O.N = O,
  2.   . CH..CH3 CH3   O.N = O,
  3.   . CH2.CH = CH2   NH.O.OH,
  4.   . CH2.CH = CH2   O.NH.OH,
  5.   . CH2.CH = CH2   O.O.NH2,
  6.   . CH2.CH = CH2   N..OH OH,
  7.   . CH = CH.CH3   NH.O.OH,
  8.   . CH = CH.CH3   O.NH.OH,
  9.   . CH = CH.CH3   O.O.NH2,
 10.   . CH = CH.CH3   N..OH OH,
 11.   . C. = CH3 CH2   NH.O.OH,
 12.   . C. = CH3 CH2   O.NH.OH,
 13.   . C. = CH3 CH2   O.O.NH2,
 14.   . C. = CH3 CH2   N..OH OH,
 15.   . CH2.CH2.NH2   O.CH = O,
 16.   . CH2.CH2.NH2   *COOH,
 17.   . CH2.NH.CH3   O.CH = O,
 18.   . CH2.NH.CH3   *COOH,
 19.   . NH.C2H5   O.CH = O,
 20.   . NH.C2H5   *COOH,
 21.   . CH..CH3 NH2   O.CH = O,
 22.   . CH..CH3 NH2   *COOH,
 23.   . N..CH3 CH3   O.CH = O,
 24.   . N..CH3 CH3   *COOH,
 25.   . CH2.CH = NH   CH2.O.OH,
 26.   . CH2.CH = NH   O.CH2.OH,
 27.   . CH2.CH = NH   O.O.CH3,
 28.   . CH2.CH = NH   CH..OH OH,
 29.   . CH = CH.NH2   CH2.O.OH,
 30.   . CH = CH.NH2   O.CH2.OH,,
 31.   . CH = CH.NH2   O.O.CH3,

196

TABLE 7.2   (Continued)

```
32.    .  CH = CH.NH2    CH..OH OH,
33.    .  CH2.N = CH2    CH2.O.OH,
34.    .  CH2.N = CH2    O.CH2.OH,
35.    .  CH2.N = CH2    O.O.CH3,
36.    .  CH2.N = CH2    CH..OH OH,
37.    .  CH = N.CH3     CH2.O.OH,
38.    .  CH = N.CH3     O.CH2.OH,
39.    .  CH = N.CH3     O.O.CH3,
40.    .  CH = N.CH3     CH..OH OH,
41.    .  NH.CH = CH2    CH2.O.OH,
42.    .  NH.CH = CH2    O.CH2.OH,
43.    .  NH.CH = CH2    O.O.CH3,
44.    .  NH.CH = CH2    CH..OH OH,
45.    .  N = CH.CH3     CH2.O.OH,
46.    .  N = CH.CH3     O.CH2.OH,
47.    .  N = CH.CH3     O.O.CH3,
48.    .  N = CH.CH3     CH..OH OH,
49.    .  C. = CH3 NH    CH2.O.OH,
50.    .  C. = CH3 NH    O.CH2.OH,
51.    .  C. = CH3 NH    O.O.CH3,
52.    .  C. = CH3 NH    CH..OH OH,
53.    .  C = .CH2 NH2   CH2.O.OH,
54.    .  C = .CH2 NH2   O.CH2.OH,
55.    .  C = .CH2 NH2   O.O.CH3,
56.    .  C = .CH2 NH2   CH..OH OH,
57.    .  CH2.CH2.OH     CH2.N = O,
58.    .  CH2.CH2.OH     CH = N.OH,
59.    .  CH2.CH2.OH     NH.CH = O,
60.    .  CH2.CH2.OH     N = CH.OH,
61.    .  CH2.CH2.OH     O.CH = NH,
62.    .  CH2.CH2.OH     O.N = CH2,
63.    .  CH2.CH2.OH     *CONH2,
64.    .  CH2.CH2.OH     C = .NH OH,
65.    .  CH2.O.CH3      CH2.N = O,
66.    .  CH2.O.CH3      CH = N.OH,
67.    .  CH2.O.CH3      NH.CH = O,
68.    .  CH2.O.CH3      N = CH.OH,
69.    .  CH2.O.CH3      O.CH = NH,
70.    .  CH2.O.CH3      O.N = CH2,
71.    .  CH2.O.CH3      *CONH3,
72.    .  CH2.O.CH3      C = .NH OH,
73.    .  O.C2H5         CH2.N = O,
74.    .  O.C2H5         CH = N.OH,
75.    .  O.C2H5         NH.CH = O,
76.    .  O.C2H5         N = CH.OH,
77.    .  O.C2H5         O.CH = NH,
78.    .  O.C2H5         O.N = CH2,
79.    .  O.C2H5         *CONH2,
80.    .  O.C2H5         C = .NH OH,
81.    .  CH..CH3 OH     CH2.N = O,
82.    .  CH..CH3 OH     CH = N.OH,
83.    .  CH..CH3 OH     NH.CH = O,
84.    .  CH..CH3 OH     N = CH.OH,
```

TABLE 7.2 (Continued)

```
 85.   .  CH..CH3 OH    O.CH = NH,
 86.   .  CH..CH3 OH    O.N = CH2,
 87.   .  CH..CH3 OH    *CONH2,
 88.   .  CH..CH3 OH    C = .NH OH,
 89.   .  CH2.CH = O    CH2.NH.OH,
 90.   .  CH2.CH = O    CH2.O.NH2,
 91.   .  CH2.CH = O    NH.CH2.OH,
 92.   .  CH2.CH = O    NH.O.CH3,
 93.   .  CH2.CH = O    O.CH2.NH2,
 94.   .  CH2.CH = O    O.NH.CH3,
 95.   .  CH2.CH = O    CH..NH2 OH,
 96.   .  CH2.CH = O    N..CH3 OH,
 97.   .  CH = CH.OH    CH2.NH.OH,
 98.   .  CH = CH.OH    CH2.O.NH2,
 99.   .  CH = CH.OH    NH.CH2.OH,
100.   .  CH = CH.OH    NH.O.CH3,
101.   .  CH = CH.OH    O.CH2.NH2,
102.   .  CH = CH.OH    O.NH.CH3,
103.   .  CH = CH.OH    CH..NH2 OH,
104.   .  CH = CH.OH    N..CH3 OH,
105.   .  O.CH = CH2    CH2.NH.OH,
106.   .  O.CH = CH2    CH2.O.NH2,
107.   .  O.CH = CH2    NH.CH2.OH,
108.   .  O.CH = CH2    NH.O.CH3,
109.   .  O.CH = CH2    O.CH2.NH2,
110.   .  O.CH = CH2    O.NH.CH3,
111.   .  O.CH = CH2    CH..NH2 OH,
112.   .  O.CH = CH2    N..CH3 OH,
113.   .  C. = CH3 O    CH2.NH.OH,
114.   .  C. = CH3 O    CH2.O.NH2,
115.   .  C. = CH3 O    NH.CH2.OH,
116.   .  C. = CH3 O    NH.O.CH3,
117.   .  C. = CH3 O    O.CH2.NH2,
118.   .  C. = CH3 O    O.NH.CH3,
119.   .  C. = CH3 O    CH..NH2 OH,
120.   .  C. = CH3 O    N..CH3 OH,
121.   .  C = .CH2 OH   CH2.NH.OH,
122.   .  C = .CH2 OH   CH2.O.NH2,
123.   .  C = .CH2 OH   NH.CH2.OH,
124.   .  C = .CH2 OH   NH.O.CH3,
125.   .  C = .CH2 OH   O.CH2.NH2,
126.   .  C = .CH2 OH   O.NH.CH3,
127.   .  C = .CH2 OH   CH..NH2 OH,
128.   .  C = .CH2 OH   N..CH3 OH,
129.   =  CH.C2H5    N.O.OH,
130.   =  C..CH3 CH3    N.O.OH,
131.   =  CH.CH2.NH2    CH.O.OH,
132.   =  CH.CH2.NH2    C..OH OH,
133.   =  CH.NH.CH3    CH.O.OH,
134.   =  CH.NH.CH3    C..OH OH,
135.   =  N.C2H5    CH.O.OH,
136.   =  N.C2H5    C..OH OH,
137.   =  C..CH3 NH2    CH.O.OH,
```

198

TABLE 7.2 (Continued)

```
138.  =  C..CH3 NH2    C..OH OH,
139.  =  CH.CH2.OH   CH.NH.OH,
140.  =  CH.CH2.OH   CH.O.NH2,
141.  =  CH.CH2.OH   N.CH2.OH,
142.  =  CH.CH2.OH   N.O.CH3,
143.  =  CH.CH2.OH   C..NH2 OH,
144.  =  CH.O.CH3    CH.NH.OH,
145.  =  CH.O.CH3    CH.O.NH2,
146.  =  CH.O.CH3    N.CH2.OH,
147.  =  CH.O.CH3    N.O.CH3,
148.  =  CH.O.CH3    C..NH2 OH,
149.  =  C..CH3 OH   CH.NH.OH,
150.  =  C..CH3 OH   CH.O.NH2,
151.  =  C..CH3 OH   N.CH2.OH,
152.  =  C..CH3 OH   N.O.CH3,
153.  =  C..CH3 OH   C..NH2 OH,
154.  CH...  CH3   CH = NH   O.OH,
155.  C. = .  CH3   CH.NH2    O.OH,
156.  CH...  CH3   N = CH2    O.OH,
157.  C. = .  CH3   N.CH3     O.OH,
158.  CH...  CH3   CH2.OH    N = O,
159.  C.. =  CH3   CH2.OH    N.OH,
160.  CH...  CH3   O.CH3     N = O,
161.  C.. =  CH3   O.CH3     N.OH,
162.  CH...  CH3   CH = O    NH.OH,
163.  CH...  CH3   CH = O    O.NH2,
164.  C. = .  CH3   CH.OH     NH.OH,
165.  C. = .  CH3   CH.OH     O.NH2,
166.  C = ..  CH2   CH2.NH2   O.OH,
167.  C = ..  CH2   NH.CH3    O.OH,
168.  C = ..  CH2   CH2.OH    NH.OH,
169.  C = ..  CH2   CH2.OH    O.NH2,
170.  C = ..  CH2   O.CH3     NH.OH,
171.  C = ..  CH2   O.CH3     O.NH2,
172.  CH...  NH2   CH = CH2   O.OH,
173.  C. = .  NH2   CH.CH3    O.OH,
174.  CH...  NH2   CH2.OH    CH = O,
175.  C.. =  NH2   CH2.OH    CH.OH,
176.  CH...  NH2   O.CH3     CH = O,
177.  C.. =  NH2   O.CH3     CH.OH,
178.  C = ..  NH    C2H5      O.OH,
179.  C = ..  NH    CH2.OH    CH2.OH,
180.  C = ..  NH    CH2.OH    O.CH3,
181.  C = ..  NH    O.CH3     O.CH3,
182.  CH...  OH    C2H5      N = O,
183.  C.. =  OH    C2H5      N.OH,
184.  CH...  OH    CH = CH2   NH.OH,
185.  CH...  OH    CH = CH2   O.NH2,
186.  C. = .  OH    CH.CH3    NH.OH,
187.  C. = .  OH    CH.CH3    O.NH2,
188.  CH...  OH    CH2.NH2   CH = O,
189.  C.. =  OH    CH2.NH2   CH.OH,
190.  CH...  OH    NH.CH3    CH = O,
```

TABLE 7.2   (Continued)

191.	C.. =	OH	NH.CH3	CH.OH,
192.	CH...	OH	CH = NH	CH2.OH,
193.	CH...	OH	CH = NH	O.CH3,
194.	C. = .	OH	CH.NH2	CH2.OH,
195.	C. = .	OH	CH.NH2	O.CH3,
196.	CH...	OH	N = CH2	CH2.OH,
197.	CH...	OH	N = CH2	O.CH3,
198.	C. = .	OH	N.CH3	CH2.OH,
199.	C. = .	OH	N.CH3	O.CH3,
200.	C = ..	O	C2H5	NH.OH,
201.	C = ..	O	C2H5	O.NH2,
202.	C = ..	O	CH2.NH2	CH2.OH,
203.	C = ..	O	CH2.NH2	O.CH3,
204.	C = ..	O	NH.CH3	CH2.OH,
205.	C = ..	O	NH.CH3	O.CH3,
206.	N...	CH3	CH = CH2	O.OH,
207.	N...	CH3	CH2.OH	CH = O,
208.	N...	CH3	O.CH3	CH = O,
209.	N...	OH	C2H5	CH = O,
210.	N...	OH	CH = CH2	CH2.OH,
211.	N...	OH	CH = CH2	O.CH3,
212.	C....	CH3	CH3	OH	N = O,
213.	C....	CH3	NH2	OH	CH = O,
214.	C....	CH3	OH	OH	CH = NH,
215.	C....	CH3	OH	OH	N = CH2,
216.	C....	NH2	OH	OH	CH = CH2.

*This is a complete list of the topological possibilities. The restraints of BADLIST and of a filtered DICTIONARY have been relaxed. Compare with Table 7.4: the additional structures here are chemically implausible for the standard context of the intended use of DENDRAL. For example, no structures are empirically known which contain the radical (.O.NH.OH).

In these and following tables, the text is all computer output except lines prefixed with >, which are input from the teletype.

important feature merely exploits an idiosyncrasy of the DENDRAL program that makes it easy to detect linear sequences of nodes that might be on a list of illegal attachments, for example, -N-N-N or -O-O.

Of far greater generality is the use of a dictionary of solved subproblems. As soon as the program has gone a short way towards a solution of any practical problem, DENDRAL would find itself constantly redoing the same subproblems over and over again as it rebuilds radicals on one side of the

TABLE 7.3 Calling the Function (PRINDICTER) Results in a Dump of the Dictionary in Its Current State*

```
(PRINDICTER)
U00C01N01001    1.     .CH2.NH.OH
  2.     .CH2.O.NH2
  3.     .NH.O.CH3
  4.     .O.NH.CH3
  5.     .N..CH3 OH

U01C02001    1.    .CH2.CH = O
  2.     = CH.CH2.OH
  3.     = CH.O.CH3
  4.     .O.CH = CH2
  5.     .C. = CH3 O
  6.     = C..CH3 OH

U01C01N01001    1.     .CH = N.OH
  2.     = CH.NH.OH
  3.     = CH.O.NH2
  4.     .NH.CH = O
  5.     = N.O.CH3
  6.     .O.CH = NH
  7.     .O.N = CH2
  8.     .*CONH2

U00C02001    1.    .CH2.CH2.OH
  2.     .CH2.O.CH3
  3.     .O.C2H5
  4.     .CH..CH3 OH

U00C01002
(NO STRUCTURES)

U00C01001    1.    .CH2.OH
  2..   .O.CH3

U01C02N01    1.    .CH2.CH = NH
  2.     .CH2.N = CH2
  3.     .CH = N.CH3
  4.     = CH.CH2.NH2
  5.     = CH.NH.CH3
  6.     .N = CH.CH3
  7.     = N.C2H5
  8.     .C. = CH3 NH
  9.     = C..CH3 NH2

U01C01N01    1.    .CH = NH
  2.     = CH.NH2
  3.     .N = CH2
  4.     = N.CH3

U01C01002    1.    .O.CH = O
  2.    .*COOH
```

TABLE 7.3 (Continued)

```
U01C01001    1.     .CH = O
    2.     = CH.OH

U00CO2N01    1.     .CH2.CH2.NH2
    2.     .CH2.NH.CH3
    3.     .NH.C2H5
    4.     .CH..CH3 NH2
    5.     .N..CH3 CH3

U00C01N01    1.     .CH2.NH2
    2.     .NH.CH3

U00N01002
(NO STRUCTURES)

U00N01001    1.     .NH.OH
    2.     .O.NH2

U00N01    1.    .NH2

U01C03    1.     .CH2.CH = CH2
    2.     .CH = CH.CH3
    3.     =CH.C2H5
    4.     .C. = CH3 CH
    5.     = C..CH3 CH3

U01C02    1.     .CH = CH2
    2.     = CH.CH3

U01C01    1.     =CH2

U01N01002    1.     .O.N = O

U00002
(NO STRUCTURES)

U01N01001    1.     .N = O
    2.     = N.OH

U01N01    1.     = NH

U00001    1.     .OH

U01002
(NO STRUCTURES)

U01001    1.     = O

U00C03    1.     .C3H7
    2.     .CH..CH3 CH3

U00C02    1.     .C2H5
```

202

TABLE 7.3   (Continued)

U00C01   1.   .CH3

DONE
_____

*This example shows the dictionary
that was built for Table 7.4, and
contains the radicals needed to generate the molecules isomeric to
C3H7NO2. The headings encode the
compositions in the form UaaCbb
NccOdd where C, N, O have their
usual connotation of atoms, and U
stands for "unsaturations." This is
calculated as double-bond-equiva-
lents, or the number of pairs of H by
which the composition falls short of
a saturated, that is, double-bond-
free molecule.

molecules after reconstructing the other side.   In order to
avoid the waste involved in this redundancy, the program
automatically generates a list of compositions which is consulted whenever a new radical is to be generated. If the composition of the new radical appears in the dictionary, the
dictionary contents are simply copied out. If not, the problem
is solved and a new dictionary item is entered for further use
later.   Insofar as the dictionary has already been filtered with
respect to BADLIST, a great deal of effort can be saved, and
in fact the program would not be practical for molecules of
even moderate complexity were it not for this feature.   As an
example, the dictionary that has been generated in the solution
of the alanine problem is given in Table 7.3, and the filtered
list of isomers is Table 7.4.   It is also feasible and desirable
to give chemical insight into the program by overt manipulation
of the dictionary. That is to say, when a given context calls for
it, the radicals corresponding to a given composition can be
entered directly, usually with the aim of excluding certain
idiosyncratic items.   This must be done with great care, since
the list of larger radicals that may be generated later relies
upon the dictionary already established for smaller radicals.
    A serious problem encountered in practice is managing
the trade-off between the growth of the dictionary and the corresponding loss of scratch space for the LISP program to

TABLE 7.4   The Isomers of Alanine, C3H7NO2,
Restrained by Common Sense*

```
>(ISOMERS *ALANINE)

>BADLIST
 ((C (1. (N O)) (1. (N O))) ((N O) (1. C (1. (N O))))
 (C (3. C (1. (N O) (1. H)))) (C (3. C) (1. (N O) (1. H)))
 ((N O) (1. H) (1. C (3. C))) (C (2. C (1. (N O) (1. H))))
 (C (2. C) (1. (N O) (1. H))) ((N O) (1. H) (1. C (2. C)))
 (N (2. C (1. O (1. H)))) (C (2. N) (1. O (1. H))) (O (1. H)
 (1. C (2. N))) (O (1. O)) (O (1. N (1. O))) (N (1. O)
 (1. O)) (C (1. H) (1. N (2. O))) (N (1. C (1. H)) (2. O))
 (*CO* (1. O (1. H))) ((N O) (1. C (1. O (1. H)) (2. O))))

> GOODLIST
  NIL

> SPECTRUM
  NIL

>DICTLIST
  NIL

>(ILLEGAL ATTACHMENTS)
 (NIL ((N N N)) ((O) (*CH2OH*)))

 C3H7NO2
 MOLECULES
 ((U . 1.) (C . 3.) (N . 1.) (O . 2.))
  1.    . C3H7     O.N = 0,
  2.    . CH..CH3 CH3    O.N = 0,
  3.    . CH2.CH2.NH2    O.CH =0,
  4.    . CH2.CH2.NH2    *COOH,
  5.    . CH2.NH.CH3    *COOH,
  6.    . NH.C2H5    O.CH = 0,
  7.    . CH..CH3 NH2    *COOH,
  8.    . N..CH3 CH3    O.CH = 0,
  9.    . CH2.CH2.OH    CH = N.OH,
 10.    . CH2.CH2.OH    NH.CH = 0,
 11.    . CH2.CH2.OH    O.CH = NH,
 12.    . CH2.CH2.OH    O.N = CH2,
 13.    . CH2.CH2.OH    *CONH2,
 14.    . CH2.O.CH3    CH = N.OH,
 15.    . CH2.O.CH3    *CONH2,
 16.    . O.C2H5    CH = N.OH,
 17.    . O.C2H5    NH.CH = 0,
 18.    . CH..CH3 OH    CH = N.OH,
 19.    . CH..CH3 OH    *CONH2,
 20.    . CH2.CH = 0    CH2.NH.OH,
 21.    . CH2.CH = 0    CH2.O.NH2,
 22.    . CH2.CH = 0    NH.O.CH3,
 23.    . CH2.CH = 0    O.NH.CH3,
 24.    . CH2.CH = 0    N..CH3 OH,
 25.    . C. = CH3 0    CH2.NH.OH,
```

TABLE 7.4   (Continued)

26.	.	C. = CH3	0	CH2.0.NH2,
27.	.	C. = CH3	0	NH.0.CH3,
28.	.	C. = CH3	0	0.NH.CH3,
29.	.	C. = CH3	0	N..CH3 OH,
30.	.	CH.CH2.OH		CH.0.NH2,
31.	=	CH.CH2.OH		N.0.CH3,
32.	=	CH.0.CH3		CH.0.NH2,
33.	=	CH.0.CH3		N.0.CH3,
34.	C.. =	CH3	CH2.OH	N.OH,
35.	C.. =	CH3	0.CH3	N.OH,
36.	CH...	CH3	CH = 0	NH.OH,
37.	CH...	CH3	CH = 0	0.NH2,
38.	C = ..	CH2	CH2.OH	0.NH2,
39.	CH.:.	NH2	CH2.OH	CH = 0,
40.	C = ..	NH	CH2.OH	CH2.OH,
41.	C = ..	NH	CH2.OH	0.CH3,
42.	CH...	OH	CH2.NH2	CH = 0,
43.	CH...	OH	CH = NH	CH2.OH,
44.	C = ..	0	C2H5	NH.OH,
45.	C = ..	0	C2H5	0.NH2,
46.	C = ..	0	CH2.NH2	CH2.OH,
47.	C = ..	0	CH2.NH2	0.CH3,
48.	C = ..	0	NH.CH3	CH2.OH,
49.	N...	CH3	0.CH3	CH = 0,
50.	N...	OH	C2H5	CH = 0,

*This restraint is implemented by systematic graph-matching against a BADLIST which contains the worst monstrosities of fragments, as indicated in the dialogue that precedes the output table.

maneuver in.   If left unchecked the dictionary building can easily reach the point of exhausting available computing room and paralyzing the program.   A heuristic management of the dictionary would be a close analog to the human solution to this problem and is being studied at the present time.   For example, very large dictionaries could be stored on external memories, and only those segments kept in core that are needed for the current operations of the program.

These facilities have been built into the DENDRAL generator program in such a way as to leave it in a state of high efficiency.   Thus the filters are not applied at the end after the production of a larger redundant list, they are applied at the earliest possible stage in the tree building program.   When $C_3H_7NO_3$ is examined by this filtered DENDRAL generator the results of Table 7.4 are obtained.   Each of these is a moderately plausible chemical isomer.   No. 7 is the actual structure of alanine.   The order of output is the canonical DENDRAL sequence.

It may be of some interest that three of the structures in Table 7.4 have apparently not yet been reported in the chemical literature, although they would appear to be reasonable candidates for synthesis by a chemistry graduate student. With even slightly more complex molecules, one should expect to find that only a small minority of the potential structural species are in fact already known to chemical science. Without an algorithmic generator, however, it has not hitherto been possible to make any realistic estimates of the extent of empirical coverage of the theoretical expectations.

It should be perfectly obvious that again with a small increase in complexity the number of possible isomers will grow very quickly and one may have to rely upon a heuristic rather than an exhaustive approach to the generation of hypotheses apt to a given set of data.   In particular it might be desirable to use some *a priori* notions of plausibility in the generator and then to seek ways of adjusting the program so that the parameters for plausibility sequences were already sensitive to qualities in the data themselves. One approach to this uses GOODLIST, an ordered list of preferred substructures.   That is to say, we would assign the highest plausibility and therefore priority for deductive corroboration of those molecules which contain items in GOODLIST.   In order to accomplish this each GOODLIST item is regarded as a "super atom" of appropriate valence, and the corresponding subset of atoms from the compositional formula is allocated to the super atom.   Thus the very common radical -COOH, the carboxyl radical, is a very common ensemble of a double bond, a carbon atom, and two oxygen atoms, ($\cdot$C$\cdot$:OH O).   Insofar as the molecular formula permits, various numbers of these sets of atoms are assigned to carboxyl groups, and the construct -COOH is then regarded as if it were a univalent superatom.

Certain housekeeping details must be looked after to be sure of avoiding redundant representations and to reconvert the constructions to canonical form.   They will, however, no longer be in canonical sequence, but rather have some implicit order of plausibility in the sequence with which they are put out.   When alanine is subjected to such a procedure, the ordering of Table 7.5 is obtained.   It will be noted that alanine is a very early entry in this table.

```
>(SETQ GOODLIST SAVEGOODLIST)
 ((*COOH* (1. C (1. 0) (2. 0)) 100 . 0) (*CO* (2. C (2. 0))
 100. 0.) (*CHNH2* (2. C (1. N)) 100. 0.) (*CH2OH*
 (1. C (1. 0)) 100. 0.) (*NOH* (2. N (1. 0)) 100. 0.)
 (*CHNH* (1. C (2. N)) 100. 0.) (*NCH2* (1. N (2 . C))
 100. 0.))
>(ISOMERS *ALANINE)
 MOLECULES
 ((U . 0.) (C . 1.) (*COOH* . 1.) (*CHNH2* . 1.))
  1.    . CH2.CH2.NH2    *COOH,
  2.    . CH..CH3 NH2    *COOH,

 MOLECULES
 ((U . 0.) (C . 2.) (N . 1.) (*COOH* . 1.))
  1.    . CH2.NH.CH3    *COOH,

 MOLECULES
 ((U . 0.) (*CO* . 1.) (*CHNH2* . 1.) (*CH2OH* . 1.))
  1.    C = ..  0    CH2.NH2    CH2.OH,
  2.    CH...   NH2    CH2.OH    CH = 0,

 MOLECULES
 ((U . 0.) (C . 1.) (0 . 1.) (*CO* . 1.) (*CHNH2* . 1.))
  1.    C = ..  0    CH2.NH2    0.CH3,
  2.    . CH2.CH2.NH2    0.CH = 0,
  3.    CH...  OH    CH2.NH2    CH = 0,

 MOLECULES
 ((U . 0.) (C . 1.) (N . 1.) (*CO* . 1.) (*CH2OH* . 1.))
  1.    C = ..  0    NH.CH3    CH2.OH,
  2.    . CH2.CH2.OH    NH.CH = 0,
  3.    . CH2.CH2.OH    *CONH2,

 MOLECULES
 ((U . 0.) (C . 2.) (*CO* . 1.) (*NOH* . 1.))
  1.    C = ..  0    C2H5    NH.OH,
  2.    N...   OH    C2H    CH = 0,
  3.    . CH2.CH = 0    CH2.NH.OH,
  4.    . CH2.CH = 0    N..CH3 OH,
  5.    . C. = CH3 0    CH2.NH.OH,
  6.    . C. = CH3 0    N..CH3 OH,
  7.    CH...  CH3    CH = 0    NH.OH,

 MOLECULES
 ((U . 0.) (C . 2.) (N . 1.) (0 . 1.) (*CO* , 1.))
  1.    . CH2.0.CH3    *CONH2,
  2.    . CH2.CH = 0    CH2.0.NH2,
  3.    . C. = CH3 0    CH2.0.NH2,
  4.    . NH.C2H5    0.CH = 0,
  5.    . CH2.CH = 0    NH.0.CH3,
  6.    . C. = CH3 0    NH.0.CH3,
  7.    . 0.C2H5    NH.CH = 0,
```

207

TABLE 7.5 (Continued)

```
 8.      .  CH2.CH = O    O.NH.CH3,
 9.      .  C. = CH3  0    O.NH.CH3,
10.      C = ..  O    C2H5    O.NH2,
11.      .  CH..CH3  OH    *CONH2,
12.      CH...  CH3    CH = O    O.NH2,
13.      .  N..CH3  CH3    O.CH = O,
14.      N...  CH3  O.CH3    CH = O,
```

MOLECULES
((U . 1.) (*CHNH2* . 1.) (CH2OH* . 2.))
*NO ALLOWABLE STRUCTURES

MOLECULES
((U . 1.) (C . 1.) (O . 1.) (*CHNH2* . 1.) (*CH2OH* . 1.))

MOLECULES
((U . 1.) (C . 2.) (O . 2.) (*CHNH2* . 1.))
*NO ALLOWABLE STRUCTURES

MOLECULES
((U . 0.) (*CH2OH* . 2.) (*CHNH* . 1.))
*NO ALLOWABLE STRUCTURES

MOLECULES
((U . 0.) (*CH2OH* . 2.) (*NCH2* . 1.))
*NO ALLOWABLE STRUCTURES

MOLECULES
((U . 1.) (C . 1.) (N . 1.) (*CH2OH* . 2.))
```
 1.      C = ..  NH    CH2.OH    CH2.OH,
```

MOLECULES
((U . 1.) (C . 2.) (*CH2OH* . 1.) (*NOH* . 1.))
```
 1.      .  CH2.CH2.OH    CH = N.OH,
 2.      C.. =    CH3    CH2.OH    N.OH,
```

MOLECULES
((U . 0.) (C . 1.) (O . 1.) (*CH2OH* . 1.) (*CHNH* . 1.))
```
 1.      .  CH2.CH2.OH    O.CH = NH,
 2.      CH...  OH    CH = NH    CH2.OH,
```

MOLECULES
((U . 0.) (C . 1.) (O . 1.) (*CH2OH* . 1.) (*NCH2* . 1.))
```
 1.      .  CH2.CH2.OH    O.N = CH2,
```

MOLECULES
((U . 1.) (C . 2.) (N . 1.) (O . 1.) (*CH2OH* . 1.))
```
 1.      =  CH.CH2.OH    CH.O.NH2,
 2.      =  CH.CH2.OH    N.O.CH3,
 3.      C = ..  CH2    CH2.OH    O.NH2,
 4.      C = .'.  NH    CH2.OH    O.CH3,
```

MOLECULES
((U . 1.) (C . 3.) (O . 1.) (*NOH* . 1.))

208

TABLE 7.5   (Continued)

```
1.      .  CH2.O.CH3     CH = N.OH,
2.      .  O.C2H5     CH = N.OH,
3.      .  CH..CH3 OH     CH = N.OH,
4.      C.. =   CH3     O.CH3     N.OH,
```

MOLECULES
((U . O.) (C . 2.) (*CHNH* . 1.))
*NO ALLOWABLE STRUCTURES

MOLECULES
((U . O.) (C . 2.) (O . 2.) (*NCH2* . 1.))
*NO ALLOWABLE STRUCTURES

MOLECULES
((U . 1.) (C . 3.) (N . 1.) (O . 2.))
```
1.      .  C3H7     O.N = O,
2.      .  CH..CH3 CH3     O.N = O,
3.      =  CH.O.CH3     CH.O.NH2,
4.      =  CH.O.CH3     N.O.CH3,
```

*Substructures defined in GOODLIST are pre-
vented from reappearing except under the corresponding superatom. Thus the final block of
four molecules is the group containing none
of the defined superatoms: *COOH*, *CO*,
CHNH2, *CH2OH*, *NOH*, *CHNH*, *NCH2*.
In many applications, the count of a given superatom will be set to zero for a particular context, or conversely, to non-zero. For example,
the superatom *NCH2* is quite likely to be
suppressed if the chemist knows that form-
aldehyde was not used in the synthesis of the
molecule being analysed.

These computations are brought to the surface here only
in order to reveal the heuristic revision of priorities that is
available to DENDRAL. In actual problem solving, many of
these hypotheses would be rejected long before a trial molecule
was completed.

REFERENCE TO DATA

With these facilities we are now ready to attempt to apply
DENDRAL to explicit data. The actual processes in the mass
spectrometer are too complicated to be dealt with head-on in
the first instance. We therefore deal with various models of

the behavior of the mass spectrometer, the theories of mass spectrometry. To exercise the simpler logical elements of heuristic DENDRAL, we begin with a zero order theory, one which postulates that the mass spectrum is obtained by assigning a uniform intensity to each fragment that can be secured by breaking just one bond in the molecule. We neglect the splitting of bonds affecting only a hydrogen atom. To test the program we do not at first use a real spectrum, but rather the spectrum predicted by this idealized theory for some given isomer.

As before, the predicter is deeply embedded within the DENDRAL generator, so that the structure building tree is truncated at the earliest point that a violation of the theory by the data set is encountered. This leads to a very efficient set of trials, not of completed, but of tentative and partial structures when the program is given a molecular composition and a hypothetical zero-order spectrum. The essence of the program is to generate all of the partitions at a given level, and then to scan these for compatibility with the mass list of the fragments. There are also some pertinent *apriori* considerations about the partitioning of molecular compositions, and this has been used to reorder the primary partitions in the most plausible sequence. We manage the sequence with which hypotheses are tested but still retain the exhaustive and irredundant character of the generator. Owing to imperfect memory and nonstandard formats, human judgment rarely succeeds so well at this.

Each of the plausibility operations plainly should and can be related to a statement of context. For example, in setting up the GOODLIST, the chemist will be interrogated about the likelihood of certain radicals, and cues for this can also be obtained directly from the mass spectrum. For example, the program is aware that mass number 45 is almost pathognomic for the radical -COOH. Hence, this superatom will be set to zero in the absence of a signal at that mass. Conversely, in a high-resolution analysis, the occurrence of mass number 44.998 would justify fixing -COOH as nonzero.

PERFORMANCE

The description, so far, characterizes an operational

program. Its main features can be routinely demonstrated without special preparation by remote teletypewriter interactions with the PDP-6 computer at Stanford University. DENDRAL has been tested in a number of ways in an attempt to evaluate its performance as a working tool. It will, of course, vastly outdo the human chemist in such contrived but potentially useful exercises as making an exhaustive and irredundant list of isomers of a given formula (Table 7.4 shows this for $C_3H_7NO_2$). In many cases, particularly when an adequate dictionary has been previously built and no further entries are being made, the computer will output its solutions at teletype speed. The program is also slightly faster than the human operator at subgraph-matching, that is, searching a series of molecular structures for the presence of any member of a given list of forbidden embedded subgraphs. It will outdo the human by approximately 100 : 1, or perhaps better if accuracy is given due weight in converting structural representations into canonical form and testing for isomorphism.

A few real spectra have been input, with surprisingly crisp results in view of the known imperfections of the zero order theory of mass spectrometry.

Thus heuristic DENDRAL was run with data on *threonine* obtained with a Bendix time-of-flight instrument (Fig. 7.2). The program returned two solutions, *threonine*, the correct structure, and one other (Fig. 7.3). The second isomer has not, to our knowledge, been analyzed by mass spectrometry. However, its spectrum can be predicted to resemble that of *threonine* very closely in its qualitative features.

When Dendral was challenged with $C_4H_9NO_3$ under the conditions of Table 7.4 it returned 238 "plausible isomers," of which only these two satify the data according to the program's model of the theory of mass spectrometry. The inclusion of the data shortens the computation time from about 30 minutes to about 3 minutes.

It is not easy to test the exhaustiveness of the DENDRAL generator without extensive files of known structures. However, it is possible to write recursive combinatorial expressions to count the expected numbers of isomeric alkane molecules (C_nH_{2n+2}) and alkyl radicals ($-C_nH_{2n+1}$) as shown in Table 7.6. These numbers have been verified by DENDRAL for radicals through C_9H_{19} and for molecules through $C_{12}H_{26}$, after which the LISP program structure becomes too unwieldy to

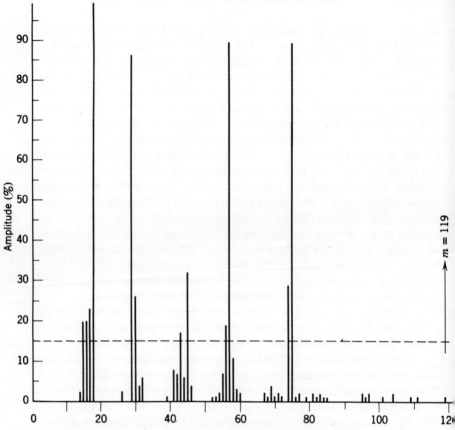

Fig. 7.2 The mass spectrum of threonine (CH...NH2 CH..CH3 OH C. = OH O) presented as a bar diagram from Martin (1965). This yielded a list of mass numbers: (15 16 17 18 29 30 43 45 56 57 74 75 119). This list was input to DENDRAL, which responded to (ISOMERS C4H9N03) with two solutions: 1. CH...NH2 CH..CH3 OH C. = OH O   threonine
2. C....CH3 OH CH2.NH2 C. = OH O   See Fig. 5.3.

Fig. 7.3   (a) Threonine, (CH...NH2 CH..CH3 OH C. = OH O), and (b) 2-Methyl, 2-hydroxy, 3-aminopropionic acid, (C....CH3 OH CH2.NH2 C. = OH O).

212

TABLE 7.6   Counting the Isomeric Alkanes and Alkyl Radicals:
C_nH_{2n+2} and C_nH_{2n+1}*

C	Alkane	Alkyl	C	Alkane	Alkyl
1	1	1	11	159	1238
2	1	1	12	355	3057
3	1	2	13	802	7639
4	2	4	14	1858	19241
5	3	8	15	4347	48865
6	5	17	16	10359	124906
7	9	39	17	24894	321198
8	18	89	18	60523	832019
9	35	211	19	148284	2156010
10	75	507	20	366319	5622109

*The figures were generated by a computer program following the algorithm of Henze and Blair (1931). Cayley's historic algorithm is incorrect, but is still quoted by a recent monograph on applications of graph theory (1965).

continue in core memory. Since there are no chemical prohibitions, the list (Table 7.7) of 75 isomeric decanes may illustrate the systematic combinatorial aspects of DENDRAL more vividly to a human reader than the preceding outputs do. Isomers are, of course, vastly more numerous for compositions containing some N and O atoms.

Facilities have been provided in the past, but are not available on our present computer system owing to hardware limitations, for providing two-dimensional graphic displays of structural maps as translations of DENDRAL notations. These programs also enabled man-computer interactions where the chemist could manipulate chemical structures to a substantial degree.

Where DENDRAL begins to be shaky is, as usual, when confronted with subtle changes of context which the user may often find difficult to communicate precisely to the program, even when he can do this readily to his fellow scientists. As far as possible we seek to get out of this difficulty by building interrogation subroutines into the program so that the chemist can provide data rather than obliging him to write new program text in the LISP language. Present efforts are concentrated on elaborating the theory of mass spectrometry as represented in

TABLE 7.7   The 75 Isomers of Decane, $C_{10}H_{22}$

(ISOMERS C10H22)

MOLECULES
((U . O.)   (C . 10.))
```
 1.    .  CH2.CH2.C3H7      CH2.CH2.C3H7,
 2.    .  CH2.CH2.C3H7      CH2.CH2.CH..CH3 CH3,
 3.    .  CH2.CH2.C3H7      CH2.CH..CH3 C2H5,
 4.    .  CH2.CH2.C3H7      CH2.C...CH3 CH3 CH3,
 5.    .  CH2.CH2.C3H7      CH..CH3 C3H7,
 6.    .  CH2.CH2.C3H7      CH..CH3 CH..CH3 CH3,
 7.    .  CH2.CH2.C3H7      CH..C2H5 C2H5,
 8.    .  CH2.CH2.C3H7      C...CH3 CH3 C2H5,
 9.    .  CH2.CH2.CH..CH3 CH3    CH2.CH2.CH..CH3 CH3,
10.    .  CH2.CH2.CH..CH3 CH3    CH2.CH..CH3 C2H5,
11.    .  CH2.CH2.CH..CH3 CH3    CH2.C...CH3 CH3 CH3,
12.    .  CH2.CH2.CH..CH3 CH3    CH..CH3 C3H7,
13.    .  CH2.CH2.CH..CH3 CH3    CH..CH3 CH..CH3 CH3,
14.    .  CH2.CH2.CH..CH3 CH3    CH..C2H5 C2H5,
15.    .  CH2.CH2.CH..CH3 CH3    C...CH3 CH3 C2H5,
16.    .  CH2.CH..CH3 C2H5      CH2.CH..CH3 C2H5,
17.    .  CH2.CH..CH3 C2H5      CH2.C...CH3 CH3 CH3,
18.    .  CH2.CH..CH3 C2H5      CH..CH3 C3H7,
19.    .  CH2.CH..CH3 C2H5      CH..CH3 CH..CH3 CH3,
20.    .  CH2.CH..CH3 C2H5      CH..C2H5 C2H5,
21.    .  CH2.CH..CH3 C2H5      C...CH3 CH3 C2H5,
22.    .  CH2.C...CH3 CH3 CH3    CH2.C...CH3 CH3 CH3,
23.    .  CH2.C...CH3 CH3 CH3    CH..CH3 C3H7,
24.    .  CH2.C...CH3 CH3 CH3    CH..CH3 CH..CH3 CH3,
25.    .  CH2.C...CH3 CH3 CH3    CH..C2H5 C2H5,
26.    .  CH2.C...CH3 CH3 CH3    C...CH3 CH3 C2H5,
27.    .  CH..CH3 C3H7      CH..CH3 C3H7,
28.    .  CH..CH3 C3H7      CH..CH3 CH..CH3 CH3,
29.    .  CH..CH3 C3H7      CH..C2H5 C2H5,
30.    .  CH..CH3 C3H7      C...CH3 CH3 C2H5,
31.    .  CH..CH3 CH..CH3 CH3    CH..CH3 CH..CH3 CH3,
32.    .  CH..CH3 CH..CH3 CH3    CH..C2H5 C2H5,
33.    .  CH..CH3 CH..CH3 CH3    C...CH3 CH3 C2H5,
34.    .  CH..C2H5 C2H5      CH..C2H5 C2H5,
35.    .  CH..C2H5 C2H5      C...CH3 CH3 C2H5,
36.    .  C...CH3 CH3 C2H5     C...CH3 CH3 C2H5,
37.  CH...   CH3    CH2.C3H7    CH2.C3H7,
38.  CH...   CH3    CH2.C3H7    CH2.CH..CH3 CH3,
39.  CH...   CH3    CH2.C3H7    CH..CH3 C2H5,
40.  CH...   CH3    CH2.C3H7    C...CH3 CH3 CH3,
41.  CH...   CH3    CH2.CH..CH3 CH3    CH2.CH..CH3 CH3,
42.  CH...   CH3    CH2.CH..CH3 CH3    CH..CH3 C2H5,
43.  CH...   CH3    CH2.CH..CH3 CH3    C...CH3 CH3 CH3,
44.  CH...   CH3    CH..CH3 C2H5    CH..CH3 C2H5,
45.  CH...   CH3    CH..CH3 C2H5    C...CH3 CH3 CH3,
46.  CH...   CH3    C...CH3 CH3 CH3    C...CH3 CH3 CH3,
47.  CH...   C2H5   C3H7    CH2.C3H7,
48.  CH...   C2H5   C3H7    CH2.CH..CH3 CH3,
49.  CH...   C2H5   C3H7    CH..CH3 C2H5,
```

214

TABLE 7.7   (Continued)

50.	CH...	C2H5	C3H7	C...CH3 CH3 CH3,
51.	CH...	C2H5	CH..CH3 CH3	CH2.C3H7,
52.	CH...	C2H5	CH..CH3 CH3	CH2.CH..CH3 CH3,
53.	CH...	C2H5	CH..CH3 CH3	CH..CH3 C2H5,
54.	CH...	C2H5	CH..CH3 CH3	C...CH3 CH3 CH3,
55.	CH...	C3H7	C3H7	C3H7,
56.	CH...	C3H7	C3H7	CH..CH3 CH3,
57.	CH...	C3H7	CH..CH3 CH3	CH..CH3 CH3,
58.	CH...	CH..CH3 CH3	CH..CH3 CH3	CH..CH3 CH3,
59.	C....	CH3	CH3	C3H7	CH2.C3H7,
60.	C....	CH3	CH3	C3H7	CH2.CH..CH3 CH3,
61.	C....	CH3	CH3	C3H7	CH..CH3 C2H5,
62.	C....	CH3	CH3	C3H7	C...CH3 CH3 CH3,
63.	C....	CH3	CH3	CH..CH3 CH3	CH2.C3H7,
64.	C....	CH3	CH3	CH..CH3 CH3	CH2.CH..CH3 CH3,
65.	C....	CH3	CH3	CH..CH3 CH3	CH..CH3 C2H5,
66.	C....	CH3	CH3	CH..CH3 CH3	C...CH3 CH3 CH3,
67.	C....	CH3	C2H5	C2H5	CH2.C3H7,
68.	C....	CH3	C2H5	C2H5	CH2.CH..CH3 CH3,
69.	C....	CH3	C2H5	C2H5	CH..CH3 C2H5,
70.	C....	CH3	C2H5	C2H5	C...CH3 CH3 CH3,
71.	C....	CH3	C2H5	C3H7	C3H7,
72.	C....	CH3	C2H5	C3H7	CH..CH3 CH3,
73.	C....	CH3	C2H5	CH..CH3 CH3	CH..CH3 CH3,
74.	C....	C2H5	C2H5	C2H5	C3H7,
75.	C....	C2H5	C2H5	C2H5	CH..CH3 CH3,

the predictor subprogram. This is giving very promising results, the chief limitations being (1) the precise definition of the rules actually used by the chemist and operant in nature, and (2) the translation of these conceptual algorithms into viable program. These two issues are, however, not as independent as might be imagined. It is the clumsiness of the program writing and debugging that impedes rapid testing of the correctness with which a rule has been formulated. In our experience each half hour of conference has generated approximately a man-month of programming effort. It is obvious that despite the simplicity of the DENDRAL notation for chemical structures, we still have a long way to go in the development of a language for the simple expression of other conceptual constructs of organic chemistry, particularly context definitions and reaction mechanisms.

Insofar as programs are also graphs and an effective subroutine may be regarded as a hypothesis that matches its intended functions, the latter being both logically deducible and operationally testable by running the subroutine, program writing may be regarded as an inductive process roughly analogous to the induction of structural formulas as solutions to sets of chemical data. We believe it may be necessary to produce a solution to this meta language puzzle before the implementation of human ideas in computer subroutines can proceed efficiently enough for the rapid and effective transfer of human insights into machine judgment. Nevertheless, by the rather laborious process that we have outlined, DENDRAL has proceeded to that stage of sophistication where it is at least no longer an occasion of embarrassment to demonstrate it to our scientific colleagues and friends who have no interest whatsoever in computers per se.

The deferral of cyclic structures will weaken the casuistic impact of the program upon chemists. However, the acyclic molecules give sufficient play for analyzing the inductive process. Furthermore, it may be advantageous to leave a blemish that diminishes the latent threat of artificial intelligence to human aspirations. However, a complete notation and specifications for cyclic DENDRAL have been documented (Lederberg, 1965) and this is being programmed now in response to the utilitarian demands of chemist friends.

BUILDING DENDRAL

DENDRAL was developed in the LISP 1.5 and 1.6 dialects. The original package was composed by Mr. William White working from the specifications summarized in Table 7.1, and a version of DENDRAL which almost worked was generated on the IBM 7090 with the help of a time-shared editing system run on the PDP-1. When the LISP system on System Development Corporation's Q-32 became available to us, we pursued a vigorous programming effort by remote teletype communication from Stanford to Santa Monica. This proved to be a very powerful and remarkably reliable system, and Mr. White and Mrs. Georgia Sutherland perfected the program (Sutherland, 1967) on that computer with a total effort of about one year.

In retrospect it is quite obvious that the program simply could never have been written and debugged without the help of the rapid interaction provided by the time-sharing system. We stress *never* advisedly, in the light of our own experience with the human frustrations involved in the typical turnaround times for error detection and error correction under the operating system for the IBM 7090. In November 1966 we moved our operations to LISP 1.5 on the PDP-6 computer installed for the Artificial Intelligence Project at Stanford. Despite the avowed close compatibility of the LISP systems, approximately 3 man-months of effort were required to transfer the program from one dialect to the other.

PATTERN RECOGNITION

As the candidate structures become more and more complex we have to abandon the idea of exhaustive enumeration of possible structures. Instead, the data are scrutinized for cues that offer any preference for certain kinds of structures as starting points. As we keep examining the problem we do find more and more ways in which such cues can be exploited. For example, an elementary pattern analysis of the period with which mass numbers are represented, for example, for gaps in the sequence of mass numbers with significant intensity around a period of about 14 mass units (CH_2), can give significant hints about the existence of a number of branch points within the molecule. If these can be limited, the extent of the necessary tree building can be drastically curtailed from first principles. Likewise, an examination of mass numbers approximating half the total molecular weight can lead to some trial hypotheses about the major partition of the molecule, which again can truncate the development. We do not, however, yet have a program sophisticated enough to make a profound reexamination of its own strategy at any level more complicated than the resetting of numerical parameters, a limitation closely related to the meta language challenge mentioned above. In sum, we find that the development of this program has not encountered very much that is fundamentally new in principle: problem solving in this field has much the same flavor as the solutions already adduced for chess, checkers, theorem proving, etc. One possible advantage of pursuing investigations in artificial intelligence and heuristic programming within this framework is that the practical utility of what has already been produced should suffice to engage the attention of a considerable number of human chemists working on practical problems in a fashion that lends itself to machine observation and emulation of their techniques.

PROGRAMMING AS INDUCTION

The game of writing programs becomes more and more an experimental science as the complexity of the programs increases. At the limit, the programmer has the insecure hope that his text will (1) run and (2) accomplish the intended goals, that is, his program is a hypothesis that needs deductive elaboration to verify it. This suggests that program writing ought to be mechanized by a process analogous to the induction of chemical hypotheses by DENDRAL and starting with mechanized observations of human techniques of problem-solving.

The pervasive role of analogy in human judgment suggests that much would be gained in artificial intelligence if a large compatible tool kit of successful programs were available both to the human and the mechanized programmer. Unfortunately, artificial intelligence researchers go to such excesses in their originality and improvisation of idiosyncratic dialects, that there is no easy way in which past successes of unpredictable relevance can be immediately tried out for a new problem. Experimental science, on the other hand, is replete with important advances that resulted from the provocative availability of a new technique waiting on the shelf to find a use. Indeed, mass spectrometry itself has exactly that history.

CHAPTER 8   *Herbert A. Simon and Richard K. Sumner*

Carnegie-Mellon University

PATTERN IN MUSIC*

One of the purposes of analysing musical structure and form is to discover the patterns that are explicit or implicit in musical works. Pattern in music is generally described in ordinary language, supplemented by technical musical terms: for example, "the movement is in sonata form," "the opening section is in the key of C major, it is followed by a section in the dominant, then a return to the original key," "the chord is a G seventh," "the slow movement is written in 3/4 time." No complete formalism has existed for describing a musical pattern precisely; its exact nature can be communicated only by writing out the music *in extenso* — the actual notes in musical notation. Although some abbreviation is achieved by such notation as figured base, all established notations set forth the notes essentially in the order of their temporal occurrence. This, as we shall see, is not at all the same as describing the pattern contained in the notes.

Ellis B. Kohs, composer and Professor of Music in the University of Southern California, has served as consultant on this project. He has helped us avoid numerous musical blunders, but should not be held responsible for those that remain. His Music Theory and forthcoming book on musical form have been major sources of insight to us, as has been also Leonard B. Meyer's Emotion and Meaning in Music. Professors Meyer, Allen Forte and Allen Newell have all supplied valuable comments on an early draft of this paper. They, too, must be held blameless for errors that remain. This research has been supported by Public Health Service Research Grant MH-07722, from the National Institutes of Mental Health.

219

1. SEQUENTIAL PATTERNS

Patterns, temporal as well as spatial, occur in many spheres of life besides music. People appear to have strong propensities, whether innate or learned, to discover patterns in temporal sequences presented by the environment, and to use these evidences of pattern for prediction. The ability and desire to discover temporal patterns undoubtedly has had great value for the survival of Man: in predicting the seasons, for example, or the weather. The urge to find pattern extends even to phenomena where one may well doubt whether pattern exists (e.g., in the movements of the stock market).

Because pattern discovery is a common, and sometimes practically important, cognitive activity, it has attracted some attention in psychology. J. Feldman, investigating ways in which people make predictions of the rise and fall in the level of business activity on the basis of data from previous time periods, observed that this predictive task is formally identical with the task of predicting a series of symbols ("check" or "plus") in the so-called binary choice or partial reinforcement experiment (Feldman, 1963). When these tasks are carried out in the laboratory, subjects behave as though the stimuli (although they are in fact random) were temporally patterned; that is, they predict "runs" of a symbol, or "alternations."

In research that began independently of Feldman's, Laughery and Gregg (1962) found similar behavior among subjects confronted with a switch-setting task (set each of four switches in a left (L) or right (R) position to turn on a single light) in which the successive correct settings formed a sequential pattern (e.g., RRRR, RRRL, RRLR, RRLL, RLRR, etc.). Subjects used notions of "same," "opposite," "change next column," and so on, to predict the next correct setting (Gregg, 1967).

Several types of items in standard intelligence tests call for the discovery and extrapolation of sequential patterns. For example, the Thurstone Letter Series Completion Test contains items like:

A B M C D M _ _

where the blanks are to be filled with letters that "reasonably" continue the sequence. Even older than letter-series completion items in intelligence tests are items calling for the extrapolation of number sequences, for example:

1 4 7 10 __ __

Simon and Kotovsky (1963), examining the behavior of subjects performing the letter-series completion task, have again found that their extrapolations are based on notions of simple periodic patterns.

When human behavior in these three rather different classes of tasks is compared, some striking similarities appear. First, in all three cases, subjects view the problem as one of finding simple temporal patterns. This seems as true of the situations where the stimuli are in fact random (the binary choice experiment; see Feldman, 1963, p. 339) as it is of those where a genuine pattern is present. With random stimuli, subjects are prepared to treat certain elements as "exceptional" if they violate what appears otherwise to be an orderly sequence. Thus, people appear to persist strongly in seeking pattern even in the presence of noise. This attitude is no doubt reinforced by the fact that most of the patterns encountered in nature must be extracted from surrounding clutter or disturbance or irregularity of one kind or another.

The second striking similarity lies in the pattern hypotheses used in the three different tasks studied by Feldman, Laughery and Gregg, and Simon and Kotovsky. The patterns in all three tasks can be attributed to a very small number of types, involving a limited range of simple relations. Thus, for the binary choice experiment, Feldman, Tonge, and Kanter (1963, p. 56) constructed a fairly successful explanation involving only the idea of "run" patterns and "alternation" patterns. Gregg (1967) has shown that notions of "same" and "next" are fundamental to the patterns used in the switch-setting experiment. Simon and Kotovsky (1963) constructed a simple formalism that allows all the letter series items, and others, to be described exactly. Their formalism is based on the notions of "alphabet," and "sequence," and the relations of "same" and "next" between pairs of alphabetic or sequential symbols. If the scheme is supplemented by arithmetic operations of subtraction and division ("differencing"), it handles the number series as well. With a little change in nomenclature, the pattern description schemes used by Feldman, Tonge and

Kanter and by Gregg and Laughery can be equated with that used by Simon and Kotovsky.

We are led by these studies to conclude that pattern-seeking is a common activity of people faced with temporal sequences, and that the vocabulary, or stock of basic concepts they have available for describing patterns is parsimonious, involving only a few elementary notions together with rules for combining them, and also is relatively independent of the specific stimulus material. Trying to outguess a roulette wheel appears to call on the same cognitive skills as taking an intelligence test. And what about listening to music?

In this paper we wish to explore the possibility that the pattern-description formalism previously applied to business-prediction, binary-choice, switch-setting, and series-completion stimuli may also be applied to musical patterns. More specifically, we wish to show that only a slight elaboration and extension of the scheme employed for these other, apparently simpler, stimuli enables us to describe with precision the pattern in musical works and their parts. Our hypothesis is that musical patterns, even when quite complex and sophisticated, involve only repeated use of the few simple components mentioned in the previous paragraphs, in particular: "alphabet," "same," "next," and rules of combination.

We shall say little here about the psychological processes that enable a listener to detect pattern in a piece of music or the processes that enable a composer to assemble a pattern. If the language of musical pattern we shall propose is adequate, it has strong implications for the nature of these processes. The theory of Simon and Kotovsky (1963), for example, includes not only a formalism for pattern description, but also a set of processes for inducting the pattern from a segment of a letter series. The musical counterpart of these processes would be a "listener" who would induct the musical pattern from the temporal sequence of sounds (or from the sheet music). In the final section of this paper, we will outline a set of processes for a "listener," but without any pretense of detailed simulation of the human processes. We will make only a few brief comments about the processes for a "composer."

Nor will we have anything to say about the reasons why certain patterns are regarded, by composers or listeners, as beautiful or interesting, or why they produce particular emotional reactions in listeners. (In general, we subscribe to

Leonard B. Meyer's (1956) views on these matters.) All of these are important questions of musical esthetics. Understanding musical pattern is a prerequisite to answering them, but not, in itself, a sufficient basis for the answer. We will limit ourselves in this paper to proposing a formalism for describing musical pattern, and to demonstrating its adequacy for describing works of music.

Our undertaking, although independent in its genesis, has an affinity with other attempts that have been made in recent years to provide formal language for the description of music. In particular, it bears a close relation to the work of Babbitt, Forte, and their students and colleagues.[1] That work, however, has focused primarily on contemporary music; and has been much preoccupied with arriving at axiomatic formulations from which theorems can be derived. Since our own interest is in description, and our viewpoint pragmatic, we can get along with relatively simple mathematical underpinnings, and with less formalism than is now the fashion.

In some respects our work is less general than other contemporary formal approaches, since it postulates a few specific relations (SAME, NEXT), derived from the psychological research on serial patterns, as the basis for its pattern descriptions. In other respects it is more general, since it claims applicability to music of any style. This latter claim remains to be evaluated—particularly with respect to the whole gamut of contemporary atonal music—but it results in our work being rather more empirical than formal. That is, we are interested in the extent to which the extant literature of music can be described by particular formalisms, not with providing formal definitions of particular classes of music or examining the consequences of such definitions.

In the next section of this paper, we will give some simple illustrations of our notions of pattern as applied to music. In Section 3, we will introduce the several elements of the formalism, illustrating them again with musical examples. In Section 4, we will discuss the processes needed for inducting the pattern from a musical score.

2. MUSICAL PATTERN—INTRODUCTION

Unlike the sequential patterns introduced above, pattern in

[1] For a recent survey of formal approaches to music with a bibliography, see Rothgeb (1966).

music is almost always multidimensional. Among the dimensions of pattern that are usually distinguished in works on music are melody, harmony, rhythm, and form. Each of these may actually have several dimensions. For example, in music with a number of voices, each voice may carry melodic and rhythmic patterns simultaneously with the others. There are additional dimensions we have not included—dynamics and orchestration, for example. For simplicity of exposition, we omit these and focus on melody, harmony, rhythm, and form. If we consider each dimension (and each voice, where appropriate) separately, we can often describe the patterns contained in it in terms not more complicated than those we have used to describe letter series. (But, as we shall see, the melodic and harmonic dimensions are not usually entirely distinct.)

For example, a very simple melodic fragment is the descending sequence of notes shown in Fig. 8.1. Interpreted in the key of C Major, it is a progression by single scale degrees from the fifth of the scale down to the tonic.

G   F   E   D   C

Fig. 8.1

A simple harmonic pattern is shown in Fig. 8.2. The notes C-E-G are repeated twice. These notes constitute the major triad on the tonic note (C) of the key of C Major. They are played in order of ascending pitch, then repeated once.

C   E   G   C   E   G

Fig. 8.2

In both examples, the similarity to the letter series is made particularly evident by use of the usual literal names for the notes. Successive notes in the melodic fragment of Fig. 8.1

are connected by the relation of NEXT in the alphabet taken backward. In the harmonic pattern of Fig. 8.2, the members of the triad are related by NEXT OF NEXT in the alphabet, forward; and the second triad is related to the first by SAME.

Fig. 8.3

To describe a rhythmic pattern (Fig. 8.3) we must introduce notation for note durations and stresses. Let us use the term "accent"(following Meyer)to denote any means of singling a note out for attention. Then long duration and heavy stress are two means commonly used to accent a note. Note durations may be indicated by selecting a particular duration (in the example, the quarter note) as the unit, and measuring other durations relative to it. In Fig. 8.3, the rhythmic pattern, in terms of durations (with the quarter note as unit), is 1-1-2. We will use an alphabet of three symbols to indicate stress: (') for main stress, ('') for secondary stress, and u for an unstressed note. The unit stress pattern in Fig. 8.3 is "-u-'. The rhythmic pattern of the example consists of the simultaneous duration and stress patterns, repeated thrice.

Finally, a form like the rondo is commonly represented by naming the individual parts, a, b, and so on, and writing:

abacada . . . .

Combining melodic, harmonic, and rhythmic elements, we show in Fig. 8.4 the score of the first four measures of Bach's *Gavotte* from French Suite #5. The music is in 2/2 time—that is, there are two half-notes to a measure.[2]

[2]To avoid fractions in analysing this music we will take the quarter note as the unit, although in the music as written the half note is the basic pulse.

Analysis will show that the basic rhythm is that given in Fig. 8.3, 1-1-2, with the three-note motive[3] beginning on the third quarter of each measure (as shown by the square braces below the score). Thus the bar-line separating the measures does not mark the beginning of the rhythmic motive, but just precedes the note with the primary stress. (The latter is the usual function of the bar—to mark stress, not to divide motives—when the two functions diverge.) Hence, the stresses as well as the durations of the rhythm conform to the pattern of Fig. 8.3.

Fig. 8.4

If we consider only the top (soprano) and bottom (base) lines, ignoring the middle one (alto), and separate the motives, we can rewrite these measures in the following recoded form (the sharp in F# is omitted):

Rhythm[4]	"u '	"u '	"u ' u	' u "u
Soprano	BGD	GEB	ECA	DCCG
Bass (pitch)	GGFF	EEDD	CCDA	FDGD
Bass (octave)	1 2 2 1	1 2 2 1	1 2 2 2	1 1 1 1
Harmony (α)	G D	e b	C D	D G
Harmony (β)	G	e	C D	G

---

[3]The term "motive" is usually used in music to refer to a short pattern. Lacking a better term, we will use "motive" both for the pattern and for its individual occurrence, even though the latter usage may appear strange to a musically trained reader.

[4]It might be debated whether the rhythm is 'u" or "u', but the distinction is not important for our analysis.

Several points need explanation here. First, we have simplified the soprano line, omitting the unaccented eighth notes. Second, we have indicated separately for the bass voice, but not for the soprano, the scale degree of each note and the octave in which it is sounded. Third, we have inducted two harmonic schemes that are implicit in the notes, and which we will now proceed to explain.

If we consider the three notes of the first chord (Fig. 8.3), we observe that they are G-D-B. These constitute the major triad on the tonic G (the key is G Major). On the next accented beat—the third chord—the notes are F#-A-D, the major triad on D. In the second motive, the corresponding chords are the E Minor (e) and B Minor (b) triads; in the third motive, C and D; in the fourth, D and G. This sequence of triads is shown as Harmony (α). The distances in scale steps from one triad to the next follow the pattern -3+1-3+1 for the first five triads, from G through C.

An even subtler, but simpler underlying pattern, employing so-called figured bass, can also be used to account for the first five chords of Harmony (α). The bass begins with a downward progression of the diatonic scale (compare Fig. 8.1), G-F#-E-D-C, with each note repeated twice. (The notes also move periodically between two octaves with the pattern 1221.) A standard figured-bass technique is to erect triads (do-mi-sol) on a sequence of bass notes, the bass notes serving alternately as the tonics (do) and thirds (mi) of their respective triads. Thus the initial G is the tonic of the G triad in Harmony (α), F# the third of D, and so on.[5] There is a clear break in the pattern in the middle of the third motive. On the main accent of that motive, the bass goes up to D, instead of down to B, then continues A-F#-D-G-D. Similarly, the sixth chord in Harmony (α) is D (followed by D-G), instead of G (3 steps below C), followed by A-E. The actual harmony in this last segment will be recognized by the musically trained as a *cadence*— usually a sequence from the dominant (here D) of the key to the tonic (here G). The cadence serves to mark a phrase ending; it is, so to speak, a punctuation mark.

Persons trained in harmony would also notice a broader structure underlying the sequence of chords (Harmony β). We will not undertake to explain this sequence, G-e-C-D-G, except to observe that it occurs frequently in tonal music, hence is familiar to musicians.

The point of all this recoding is that it reveals various elements of pattern, based on relations of SAME and NEXT on a few tonal sequences or "alphabets," incorporated in these four measures. The bass employs the alphabet of the diatonic scale, the chords, the triadic (do-mi-sol-do) alphabet, the Harmony β, the conventional sequence G-E-C-D-G. There is a rhythmic pattern of stresses "u' and durations 1-1-2. Using these alphabets, we can redescribe the music in terms of underlying patterns.

Our task in the remainder of this paper is to provide a formal, parsimonious way of representing patterns like this, and to show that our formalism requires no essentially larger stock of primitive concepts than those already employed in representing the simple letter series.

3. A FORMAL LANGUAGE FOR PATTERN DESCRIPTION

Patterns involve *periodicity* — repetition (in a generalized sense) at intervals that occur periodically (in a generalized sense). Patterns make use of *alphabets* — sets of symbols ordered in a definite sequence. Patterns can be *compound* — made up of subpatterns which can themselves be represented as arrangements of symbols. Patterns generally possess *phrase structure*, which may be explicitly indicated by various forms of punctuation. Patterns, as we have already seen, may be *multidimensional*. Repetition in pattern generally involves *variation*. In the following paragraphs we will explain each of these elements and show how the pattern-description language handles it.

Periodicity

The string "ABABABA....." can be described by the

phrase, "Alternation of 'A' and 'B'." In general, to say that a string is patterned implies that there is some way of describing it more parsimoniously than by listing its symbols *in extenso*. Even the use of "......," above, to indicate the indefinite continuation of the string, is an example of such parsimony, for the notation is applicable only to a patterned string that can be extrapolated by rule. The notation would be inadequate to describe the continuation of random string "10110010 ....."

The simplest patterns have a fixed *period*, repeating with systematic variation the sequence that consitutes the first period. We have already cited the example:

$$\text{ABM CDM EFM\_\_\_}$$

Even without the spacing, the regular repetition of the letter "M" in this sequence suggests a period of 3. With the "M's" removed, the rest of the sequence simply consists of the letters of the Roman alphabet, in their usual order. Thus, the sequence can be characterized in terms of two relations between pairs of symbols: (1) the relation of SAME, or identity, and (2) the relation of NEXT on some specified alphabet. These relations may hold among the symbols within a single period of the string: for example, the relation of NEXT between "A" and "B," and between "C" and "D." On the other hand, the relations may hold between symbols in successive periods: for examples, the relation of SAME between the "M's" of each period, and the relation of NEXT between "B" and "C," and between "D" and "E."

These relations serve to define the pattern of the example ABM CDM ..., which can be represented in algebraic notation as follows: Let us designate the symbols in the sequence by x_{ij}, where the first subscript, i, names the *period* in which the symbol occurs; the second subscript, j, the position in that period. Thus we may rewrite the above sequence:

$$x_{11} x_{12} x_{13} x_{21} x_{22} x_{23} \cdots$$

where $x_{11} = A$, $x_{12} = B$, $x_{13} = M$, and so on.

Then:

for $j = 1, 2, 3$ (There are three positions in each period.)

$x_{11} = \text{'A'}$ (The first symbol in the first period is 'A'.)

$x_{i1} = \text{NEXT}(\text{ENG}; x_{(i-1)2})$

for $i = 2, \ldots$ (For all periods beyond the first $(i = 2, \ldots)$, the first symbol in the ith period (x_{i1}) is NEXT in the English alphabet (ENG) to the second symbol in the preceding, or $(i - 1)$st, period $(x_{(i-1)2})$. Thus, $x_{21} = \text{'C'}$ is next in the English alphabet to $x_{12} = \text{'B'}$.)

$x_{i2} = \text{NEXT}(\text{ENG}; x_{i1})$

for $i = 1, \ldots$ (For all periods $(i = 1, \ldots)$ the second symbol in the ith period (x_{i2}) is NEXT in the English alphabet (ENG) to the first symbol in the same $(i$th) period (x_{i1}). Thus $x_{22} = \text{'D'}$ is next to $x_{21} = \text{'C'}$.)

$x_{i3} = \text{'M'}$

for $i = 1, \ldots$ (For all periods $(i = 1, \ldots)$, the third symbol (x_{i3}) is an 'M'. Thus, $x_{13} = \text{'M'}$.)

The four equations on the left half of the page, above, provide a precise formal definition of the pattern.

If the pattern of the example is extrapolated, we eventually reach the end of the alphabet, and cannot continue unless we define "the letter NEXT to 'Z'." In the following discussion, we will treat all of our finite alphabets as circulars—as beginning over again when the end is reached. Thus, "the letter NEXT TO 'Z'" is 'A'. This convention has great convenience for music.

The convention of circularity of alphabets permits a simple representation of the alternation of two symbols. We simply define the sequence of two symbols, '+' and '-', say, as an "alphabet," which we will call SIGN:SIGN $=+,-$. Then we can define the simple alternation:

$$+ - + - + - \ldots \ldots$$

by the relations:

$j = 1$ (There is one position $(j = 1)$ in each period.)

$x_{11} = '+'$ (The first symbol (x_{11}) is '+'.)

$x_{i1} = \text{NEXT} (\text{SIGN}; x_{(i-1)1})$ (The second and subsequent symbols $(x_{i1}, i = 2, \ldots)$ are each NEXT
for $i = 2, \ldots$ on the alphabet consisting of '+' and '-' to the symbols that precede them $(x_{(i-1)1})$.)

Since we will subsequently need notation for relations like "NEXT of NEXT" and "NEXT of NEXT of NEXT," we will abbreviate NEXT by N. We also wish to refer to strings that do not continue indefinitely, but terminate after a specified number of periods. Consider the diatonic "alphabet," C D ... A B, which we will call DIAT. In order to represent the diatonic cycle of fifths, starting with C and returning to that note, we might write:

$j = 1$ (There is one position in each period.)

$x_{11} = 'C'$ (The first note is 'C'.)

$x_{i1} = N^4 (\text{DIAT}; x_{(i-1)1})$ (Each subsequent note is four
for $i = 2, \ldots, 8$.   steps—that is, a "fifth" in musical terminology—above its predecessor on the diatonic scale.)

where $N^4 (s) = N (N (N (N (s))))$, or, more generally, $N^k (s) = N (N^{k-1}(s))$, for $k = 2, \ldots$. Thus N^2 means "NEXT of NEXT," N^3, "NEXT of NEXT of NEXT," and so on.

We will also need notation to specify the repetition of a symbol or subpattern a specified number of times. We will denote the pattern AAA, for example, by A .[3] This will enable us to describe a pattern like A BB CCC DDDD .... as: $j = 1$, $x_{i1} = (z_i)^i$, $z_1 = \text{'A'}$, $z_i = N(\text{ENG}; z_{(i-1)})$ for $i = 2$, ... In this notation we have introduced the concept of subpattern (Z_i), which we will discuss further below.

The final bit of notation we shall introduce at this point is an operator, CARRY, or C for short, to denote the carrying operation familiar in adding and multiplying numbers. Something like this is required to describe a "counting" pattern like: 1, 2, ..., 9, 10, ..., 99, 100, 101, ... The number of symbols in each period grows indefinitely. We use the alphabet DIG = 0, 1, ..., 9. Then, $x_{11} = 1$; $x_{i1} = N(x_{(i-1)1})$ for $i = 2, ...$; $x_{1j} = $ blank, for $j = 2, ...$; $x_{ij} = C(x_{i(j-1)}, x_{(i-1)j})$ for i, $j = 2, ...$, where $C(x, y)$ means performing NEXT in the column of Y, whenever we step past the end of the alphabet in the column of X. (Columns are numbered from right to left.)

Now if we denote the notes of the diatonic scale by letters, as before, and the successive octaves by integers, then the sequence of notes running up the scale can also be described by such a counting pattern: OC, OD, ..., OB, 1C, ..., 1B, 2C, and so on, where the first symbol denotes the octave, the second the note. Here $j = 2$, $x_{11} = 0$, $x_{12} = C$; $x_{i2} = N(x_{(i-1)2})$; $x_{i1} = C(x_{i2}, x_{(i-1)1})$.

Alphabets

An alphabet is an ordered set of symbols. The alphabets used in patterns are of two kinds: (1) ordered sets already defined in the culture (the Roman alphabet, the notes of the diatonic scale, the days of the week, the Arabic numerals, and so on), and (2) ordered sets that are defined *ad hoc* for the purpose of pattern construction. Thus, we defined above the *ad hoc* alphabet SIGN = +, -, and, in general, to represent the simple alternation of any pair of symbols, we define the alphabet consisting of just that pair of symbols. When we have occasion to distinguish alphabets of the two major kinds, we will refer to them as "common" and "*ad hoc*," respectively.

In music, the diatonic scales, including the major, minor, and modal, are important common alphabets. Another such alphabet is the chromatic scale.[6] Each triad, (e.g., (C, E, G)), can also be used as an alphabet in a musical pattern, as can its various inversions (e.g., (E, C, G)). The major and minor diatonic scales and their associated triads are, of course, the most widely used musical alphabets of the tonal period.

Contemporary twelve-tone music makes use of *ad hoc* alphabets, so-called tone rows, which are, in their simplest forms, permutations of the chromatic scale. However, we can think of any sequence of notes employed in a melodic motive or a vertical chord as an ad hoc alphabet. From a musical standpoint, the difference between a common and an *ad hoc* alphabet is that the listener may be assumed to have the former already stored in memory, while he must induct the latter from the music itself. Consider the sequence:

EQDFRMEQDFRMEQDFRM ......

This can be interpreted as a periodic repetition of the *ad hoc* alphabet (E, Q, D, F, R, M). At least one repetition (or a substantial portion of one) is necessary for the reader to induct that this pattern may be intended. On the other hand, the initial segment: Monday, Tuesday, ..., may already suggest that the common alphabet of days of the week is intended.

An *ad hoc* alphabet can be generated from a common alphabet by a *selection operator*, which defines a new sequence by designating the order numbers in the alphabet of the successive members of the sequence. Thus (E, Q, D, F, R, M) can be generated from the ordinary Roman alphabet by the selection operator (5, 17, 4, 6, 18, 13). The *ad hoc* sequence may contain repetitions of symbols. Thus, the operator (1, 2, 1, 3) generates (A, B, A, C) from the Roman alphabet.

Compound Symbols

As another important direction of generalization, an entire pattern can be designated, or named, by a single symbol, and

---

[6]The seven white notes on the piano, from C through B, constitute a major diatonic scale. The same notes, with some note other than C as starting point, yield other minor and modal scales. The chromatic scale consists of all 12 white and black notes.

this name used as a component in a larger pattern. Consider the pattern:

$$CQD \quad CQD \quad CQD \quad ...$$

This pattern can be described simply as

$j = 1.$ (The period is 1.)

$x_{i1} = A$, for all i, where   ($<$ ---X_i is the compound sym-
                                      bol CQD, to which we give the
$A = 'CQD'$ name A.)

This notation becomes especially convenient when there are several subpatterns, as in:

$$ABC \quad 123 \quad DEF \quad 123 \quad GHI \quad ... \quad ...$$

This is equivalent to:

$$X_1 \ Y \ X_2 \ Y \ X_3 \ Y \ . \ . \ . \ . = (X_i Y)$$

where $Y = '123'$, and

$X_i = (x_{i1} x_{i2} x_{i3})$,   ($Y$ is the compound symbol '123'.)

$x_{i1} = N(\text{ALPH}; x_{(i-1)3})$;   (X_i is a compound symbol, whose
$x_{ij} = N(\text{ALPH}; x_{i(j-1)})$,   elements proceed in sequence
$j = 2, 3; x_{11} = 'A'$ down the alphabet.)

The ability to replace subpatterns with names will be important to us in describing musical patterns. For example, when we say that a rondeau has the form *abaca* .... we mean that it is a sequence involving the subpatterns (which may be as complex as we please) *'a'*, *'b'*, *'c'*, and so on.

A more specific example can be constructed from the fragment of the Bach *Gavotte* in Fig. 8.4, considering only the first ten notes in the bass voice. We can here represent the pattern simply by

$$K_i, \quad i = 1, 2, 3,$$

where K_i is defined by

$$K_i = \left\{ \begin{array}{ll} \text{Duration:} & 1^4 \\ \text{Stress:} & ''u\,'u \\ \text{Notes:} & X^2_{(2i-1)}\,X^2_{(2i-1)}X^2_{2i} \\ \text{Octave:} & 1221 \end{array} \right\} i = 1, 2, 3$$

Where $X_1 = 'G'$, $X_i = N(\text{BDIAT}: X_{i-1})$, and BDIAT means the diatonic alphabet taken backwards (i.e., *down* the scale). The formula would predict $\left\{ \dfrac{BB}{21} \right\}$ for the 11th and 12th notes, while the actual notes are $\left\{ \dfrac{DA}{22} \right\}$, showing that the initial pattern has been interrupted and replaced by a new one (the cadence).

Phrase Structure

In oral and written prose, the listener or reader is given clues to the boundaries of periodic and aperiodic subpatterns. In English speech, these clues take the form of changes in pitch (fall in inflection at the end of words, phrases, and sentences), pauses, and accents. In written prose, they take the form of spaces and punctuation marks.

Music also contains such clues, including among them harmonic cadences, note durations, and dynamics (stress, loudness, attack). In order to have a name for all devices that can be used to mark boundaries, we will refer to them as "punctuation."

Punctuation is an aid to boundary detection, but seldom is essential for that purpose. For example, the subgroups in the following pattern are readily detected without punctuation:

ABC123DEF456GHI7.........

They would be more easily visible, however, if punctuated by spaces:

, ABC 123 DEF 456 GHI ... ...

or by commas:

ABC, 123, DEF, 456, GHI, ..., ...

or by parentheses:

(ABC)(123)(DEF)(456)(GHI)(...)(...)

Hierarchies of groups, groups within groups, can be marked by punctuation of graduated strength:

ABC 123   DEF 456   GHI ...   .
ABC, 123; DEF, 456; GHI, ...;   ....
((ABC) (123)) ((DEF) (456)) ((GHI) (...........

In the musical example of Fig. 8.4, several modes of punctuation are in evidence. Half-notes, of longer duration than the other notes, are used to terminate the rhythmic motive in its first two occurrences. The bar line is one of several conventional phrase markers. The D chord followed by G (dominant followed by tonic) that interrupts the third and replaces the fourth occurrence of the rhythmic motive is a conventional cadence that would provide a sense of completion to any ear accustomed to music of the tonal period (eighteenth and nineteenth centuries). The finality of the cadence is softened, however, by the use of eighth notes to weaken the rhythm. The cadence serves as a semicolon, so to speak, rather than a full stop.

Multidimensionality

Most of the patterns we have considered thus far consist of single sequences of symbols. As the Bach example shows, however, musical pattern is multidimensional. Not only may several notes sound simultaneously, but we must be prepared to encode the relations that hold among such simultaneous notes (harmonic or chordal relations) as well as to describe the rhythmic and dynamic patterns that accompany the patterns of pitch. In orchestrated works, we may also be concerned with patterns of tone coloration, and there are other dimensions as well.

Our language for pattern description must be general enough, then, to accommodate all of these complexities, including: (1) parallel melodic patterns, (2) the warp and weft of melodic and harmonic pattern, and (3) rhythmic pattern. In particular, we need a representation that will handle conveniently certain subtle but fundamental interactions among melody, harmony, and rhythm.

Let us designate each note by four numbers: its octave, its scale degree, its time of onset, and its duration. We will assign the number 0 to the octave below middle C. Lower octaves will be assigned negative integers; octaves from middle C (inclusive) up, positive integers. Instead of using the conventional letters or Roman numerals for scale degrees, we will also designate these by integers ranging from 0 (for C) for 11 (for B) for the 12 steps of the chromatic scale.

The first note of a piece (or of any segment we are considering) will be assigned onset 0, and the onset of each subsequent note will be the onset of its predecessor (including rests) plus the duration of that predecessor. Durations will be measured as multiples of some unit—the quarter note or eighth note, say, as convenient. Thus if the unit is the quarter note, and we consider three notes of duration 1-1-2, respectively (as the first three notes of Fig. 8.3), their onsets will be 0, $1 = (0 + 1)$, and $2 = (1 + 1)$, respectively, and the note that follows them will have onset $4 = (2 + 2)$.

For some purposes, it will be convenient to designate scale degrees relative to some note other than C—relative to the tonic associated with the key signature, for example. To designate degrees relative to D(=2), we simply subtract 2 from the degree relative to C. Likewise, we will sometimes want to talk about degrees in the diatonic major scale (numbered 0 to 6), or some other scale, instead of the chromatic scale. This conversion is also straightforward. (Chromatic degrees 0, 2, 4, 5, 7, 9, 11 become diatonic degrees 0 through 6, respectively.) Unless there is an indication to the contrary, however, scale degrees are given in the chromatic scale relative to C taken as 0. Note that the tonic, or other base of the scale is always taken as zero rather than one. This greatly simplifies the arithmetic as compared with the conventional Roman numeral notation.

With these conventions, in a piece in C Major in 4/4 time, a quarter-note C above middle C struck on the third beat of the first four-beat phrase can be denoted: (1, 0; 2, 1). The first 1 designates the octave; the 0, the C in that octave; the 2, the onset at the end of the second beat, beginning of the third; the final 1, the one-beat duration. The *Gavotte* of Fig. 8.4 is in the key of G Major. If we shift the origin of the system to the G below middle C, then the third soprano note in the *Gavotte* (D) would be denoted: (1, 7; 2, 1).

Having settled these conventions, let us return to the matter of the interaction of harmony with melody. We can use the Bach *Gavotte* to illustrate how a harmonic pattern can be combined with a rhythmic pattern to generate a melodic phrase.   Figure 8.5 shows a succession of chords, G-e-a (or chromatic 0-9-2, relative to G). For reasons we will not try to explain here, the first two chords are in !"second inversion"—that is, are written with their respective fifths (chromatic scale degree 7 relative to the tonic) as roots.

Fig. 8.5

Suppose now that we impose on these chords the rhythmic pattern of Fig. 8.3, striking the highest note (*α*) of each chord first, the middle note (*β*) second, and the lowest note (*γ*) third. The pattern may be represented:

Note	(*α*)	(*β*)	(*γ*)
Onset	0	1	2
Duration	1	1	2
Stress	"	u	'

The notes themselves are

Motive	I	II	III
Chord	0	9	2
(a)	4	0	9
(b)	0	9	5
(c)	7	4	2
Onset	0	4	8
Duration	4	4	4

The superposition of rhythm on chords generates the following series of nine notes:

Note	1	2	3	4	5	6	7	8	9
Onset	0	1	2	4	5	6	8	9	10
Duration	1	1	2	1	1	2	1	1	2
Degree	4	0	7	0	9	4	9	5	2

But these nine notes are identical with the first nine notes (ignoring the eighth notes of the second measure) in the soprano line of the *Gavotte*. (The cadence causes a modification of the subsequent notes, as we have noted previously.) We have thus generated from the harmonic pattern the melody that appears as the soprano line of the illustration. This does not prove, of course, that this is the manner in which Bach created this melodic line. (Indeed it is likely that he created it in a somewhat different way, as we mentioned earlier.) It does show that the melodies that have an underlying harmonic structure can be described parsimoniously by superimposing a rhythmic pattern on an underlying chordal structure.

Using the conventions introduced previously, and one new one ($I_2(x)$ means the 2nd inversion of chord x), the pattern of the nine soprano notes shown above can be described briefly thus:

KEY: G(MAJ) — The key is G Major.

HARM: $(I_2(0), I_2(9), 2, 0)$ — The harmony is a list of four chords:

G (2nd inver.), e (2nd inver.), a, and G.

SOPR: α_i^4 — The soprano notes follow the pattern $\alpha_i, i = 1, ..., 4$.

α_i $\begin{cases} \text{DEGR: } N(\text{DTRI: } (H_i))^3 \\ \text{DURN: } (1, 1, 2) \end{cases}$ — Three notes are chosen from the chord H_i, in succession down the tread (DTRI); their durations are ♩ ♩ ♩.

$H_i = N$ (HARM: H_{i-1}) — The chords are chosen in succession from the list HARM.

A second example, drawn this time from Bach's *Passacaglia and Fugue* in C minor, will illustrate further this scheme for factoring harmonic and rhythmic aspects of pattern. The *Passacaglia* is in 3/4 time. The opening statement of the theme (measures 1-8, see Fig. 8.6) is eight 3-beat motives in length, each motive being, rhythmically:

$$\text{Stress} \qquad u \qquad '$$
$$\text{Duration} \qquad 1 \qquad 2$$

Fig. 8.6

The opening statement consists simply of a single melodic line, thus of 16 (actually 15, because of the dotted half note in the seventh motive) independent notes. The melodic structure is very simple, for each quarter note, save the first, is on diatonic degree lower than the half note that follows it. Therefore, we can describe the pattern as follows:

KEY: C(MIN)   The key is C minor.

BASS: (4 3 5 4 2 0 4 0)   The bass accented notes consist of these scale degrees (diatonic).

STRESS: $(u\,')$ An unstressed quarter note is followed by a stressed half note; each pair is a tone preceded by the next lower tone. The tones are selected in order from BASS.

DURN: (1, 2)

DEGR: $((x_i)\,x_i)^8$

$$x_i = N(\text{BASS};\ x_{i-1})$$

EXCEPTIONS: $N(x_i) < {-}{-}0;\ N(x_8) < {-}{-}\text{TIE.}$

In Variation I (measures 9-16), there are four voices, constructed from fifteen chords whose bass tones, played in succession, form the passacaglia theme that we have just described. The first motive of Variation I is shown in Fig. 8.7. Each two-note motive has essentially the same iambic structure as before, each note serving as lowest member of an entire chord. However, a rhythmic variation is also introduced. The prevailing rhythmic units in this variation are eighth notes instead of quarter notes, so that, for convenience, we will regard the motive structure as six eighth notes instead of three quarter notes. This motive consists of two subparts of 2 and 4 eighth notes duration, respectively. We can now describe the rhythmic pattern by specifying the onset of the notes belonging to each of the two chords in each of the voices:

Chord	1	2
Chord onset	0	2
Chord duration	2	4
Sopr. onset*	1	2
Alto onset*	1	2
Ten. onset*	1	1
Bass onset*	0	0

Fig. 8.7

The rhythmic pattern described above is shown in ordinary

*In describing the pattern, the onset of the individual voices is indicated *relative* to the onset of the chord to which they belong. Hence, to determine their onset relative to the *motive*, the two numbers must be added. Thus, the second tenor note has an onset of 3 = (2 + 1) eighth notes relative to the motive. It is therefore sounded at the *end* of the third, or *beginning* of the fourth beat of the six-beat motive.

musical notation in Fig. 8.8 (β). The onsets (relative to the motive) are written below the notes. We have simplified the actual rhythmic pattern of the *Passacaglia* in one respect that is easily corrected. The soprano note in the second chord is embellished by a decoration (echappee) that is a diatonic third above the chordal tone, and occurs one sixteenth note earlier. (See Fig. 8.8 (γ).) Hence, we must replace the soprano note with a subpattern that designates both pitches and onsets relative to the embedding pattern:

	Soprano	Decoration
Degree (diat.)	0	+2
Onset	0	-1/2
Duration	2	1/2

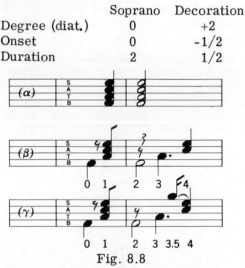

Fig. 8.8

Now the whole first variation, eight measures, is defined by the combination of the chordal sequence (based, in turn, on the 15-note melodic line) with the rhythmic pattern we have just described. (The first motive of the variation is shown in detail in Fig. 8.7).

In the next eight measures, the third variation, the melodic and rhythmic patterns remain unchanged, while a slightly different sequence of chords is constructed on the melodic line.

Variation

The pattern description scheme needs provision for flexibility in accommodating patterns which repeat with small variations.

First, by allowing names to be attached not only to complete subpatterns, but also to particular aspects of a subpattern (e.g., its harmony, or its rhythm) we can construct variations, as in the *Passacaglia*, that make rhythmic changes while the harmony remains constant, or make harmonic changes over a constant melody and rhythmic pattern.

Second, by defining intervals and time relations relative to points of origin (of pitch and time), modulations of pitch and syncopations of melodic phrase are handled readily. This coincides, of course, with the standard procedure in music whereby Roman numerals denote chords relative to the currently prevailing tonic.

Various forms of inversion and retrograde motion involve merely reversing, in direction or time, respectively, the NEXT relation that is being applied. Different inversions will arise depending on whether the tonic alphabet being used is chromatic, diatonic, or some other.

Ever freer variation can be obtained by regarding the tonal alphabet as one of the parameters that can be changed while retaining intact all or some of the other elements of a pattern. This flexibility even suggests possibilities for musical pattern that we have not yet seen exhibited in the examples of music that we have examined.

If the pattern-description scheme is to be complete, it must also provide for transformations that stretch out patterns (augmentation) or condense them (diminution) by change of rhythmic values (e.g., they may be doubled, or halved). In certain cases, particular notes or groups of notes may belong to more than one pattern element. For example, in modulating from one key to another, a pivot chord may be used that can be interpreted as belonging either to the original key or the new key.

We cannot consider all these elaborations in detail, or even present enough examples to evaluate our claim that music of a wide variety of styles can be represented formally in the notation we have introduced. Instead, we will propose in the next section a *procedure* for testing these claims—for constructing, systematically, the pattern corresponding to a musical score.

4. INDUCTION AND INTERPRETATION OF PATTERNS

Let us return for a moment to the letter-series completion

task.   To perform successfully on a letter-series test, a person must do two things: (1) examine the partial sequence presented to him, and induct from it a pattern consistent with it; (2) use the pattern to extrapolate the sequence, generating the successive symbols that belong to it.   Faced with ABM CDM ..., he must discover the pattern we described earlier, or another one that fits the sequence, and then determine that the next letters determined by the pattern are EFM ... . We will call the first task *pattern induction*, the second task *sequence extrapolation.*

Simon and Kotovsky (1963) simulated human performance in the letter-series task by constructing a pattern induction program and a sequence extrapolation program capable of handling sequences of the kinds commonly encountered in such tests.   The relation between the two programs is depicted in Fig. 8.9.

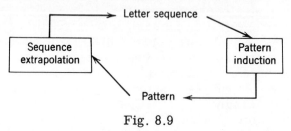

Fig. 8.9

An almost exact analogue can be constructed for the task of music analysis.   The "letter sequence" becomes the musical score; the "pattern" the musical pattern; the "pattern inductor" a program for constructing the musical pattern from the score; and the "sequence extrapolator," a program for reconstructing the score from the musical pattern. (See Fig. 8.10.)

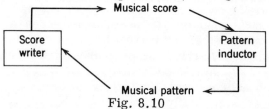

Fig. 8.10

The pattern inductor may be thought of as a "listener," since it accepts the music (or the score) as input, and detects the melodic, harmonic, and rhythmic relations implicit in it. The score writer may be thought of, less accurately, as a "performer." In actual fact, of course, performers are given scores, which they translate from written to aural form, rather than patterns, so this analogy is really not precise. The real score writer is the composer, who (we would hypothesize) first composes the pattern, then produces the score from it.

The adequacy of the descriptive scheme we have outlined in this paper may be tested by undertaking to construct such pattern inducting and score writing programs. The score writer, while the less interesting of the two, is the simpler to construct, and can be used to test whether proposed descriptions of specific pieces of music are accurate and complete. The score produced by the score writer, when it is given the pattern as input, can be compared directly and note for note with the actual score. Inadequacies in the description will show up as discrepancies between the two. We are currently constructing such a score writer, but it is not yet completely debugged. It consists of two parts. One (still under construction) transforms the pattern into an internal representation of the score; the other (now complete) prints the score from the internal representation.

Rhythm as Cue to Pattern

Some aspects of the performance of the pattern inducting program for music have been hand simulated, but construction of the actual computer program has not yet begun. We can sketch here the approach that is being taken.

First, the larger segments of a piece of music can often be delimited by the presence of conventional punctuation: double bars, key signatures, changes in tempo, and so on. By this means, sections, each four to sixteen measures long, say, are identified.

Second, experiments with a variety of musical styles indicate that rhythmic variations are the simplest cues for delimiting the smaller motives and phrases. Consider, as a simple example, a Beethoven *Dance*, of 16 measures. (The first eight measures are shown in Fig. 8.11.) A double bar occurs at the end of the eighth measure, dividing the piece into two parts. The durations of the soprano notes in the first eight measures are as follows (the eighth note is taken as unit):

1 + 1 + 4 + 1 + 1 + 4 + 1 + 1 + 1 + 1 + 1 + 1 + 1 + 1 + 1 + 1 + 1
+ 1 + 1 + 1 + 4 + 1 + 1 + 4 + 1 + 1 + 1 + 1 + 1 + 1 + 2 + 4

Scanning this sequence from left to right, we find the first occurrence of the longest note (4), then continue to scan to find the next occurrence of the same duration. We now match for identity the patterns from these starting points, first moving left from the longest note (4). In this way we find two groups of (1 + 1 + 4), with total duration of six each.

Fig. 8.11

Continuing to scan, we find two more patterns of the same kind (1 + 1 + 4), whose origins are separated from the earlier patterns by a duration of 12, a multiple of six. We might now rewrite the sequence thus:

$$(1+1+4)^2 (1+1+1+1+1+1) (1+1+1+1+1+1) (1+1+4)^2$$

$$(1+1+1+1+1+1) (2+4)$$

But two of the remaining segments are made up of sequences of six eighth notes each, so we can rewrite again:

$$(1 + 1 + 4)^2 ((1)^6)^2 (1 + 1 + 4)^2 (1)^6 (2 + 4)$$

It is now not difficult to see that this section has the rhythmic form ABAC, where: $A = (1 + 1 + 4)^2$, $B = ((1)^6)^2$, $C = ((1)^6(2 + 4))$.

In the second half of the *Dance* (not shown here), all notes in the soprano, except in the final measure, are eighth notes, hence do not help us to find the pattern. In the bass, however, we find

$$((\underline{2} + 2 + 2)^3 (2 + \underline{2} + \underline{2}))^2$$

where the underlining denotes rests.

In this example, as in many others, the alphabets of durations are *ad hoc*, that is, $(1 + 1 + 4)$ or $(2 + 2 + 2)$—but stress and duration alphabets are commonly drawn from a small pool of familiar patterns used in both music and poetry—for example, the iambic $(\frac{u'}{12})$ of waltz time, in its simplest form.

Harmonic Cues to Pattern

The *Dance* of Fig. 8.11 also provides simple examples of how the pattern inductor could discover harmonic elements of pattern. The key Signature, final notes, and absence of accidentals allow the inference that the music is written in the key of D Major—that is, that the primary relevant alphabet of scale degree is the diatonic scale with D as 0.

If the pattern inductor examines the soprano notes in the groups we called "A" above, it finds that the first three all constitute the same sequence (with shift of octave): $(0 + 2 + 4)$. But this is a familiar subsequence, the major triad on the tonic. Thus, these notes can be generated by the NEXT operator on the common triadic alphabet, starting from the tonic. The fourth sequence is a simple permutation of the same notes: $(2 + 4 + 0)$. In a similar manner, the groups in "B" can be generated by NEXT downward on the diatonic alphabet, starting from G (3). The soprano notes in "C" require a little more subtle interpretation, for they do not form a major triad. We will return to them presently.

If the pattern inductor now examines the eight segments of bass notes corresponding to the pattern elements in the soprano, it finds comparable simplicity. To interpret these patterns, let us consider the triadic alphabet on the diatonic scale as not stopping with 4 (the "fifth" in usual musical terminology), but continuing upward by diatonic thirds: 0, 2,

4, 6, 1, 3, 5. In this way we obtain the major seventh chord, ninths, elevenths, and thirteenths. In each pattern of six eighth notes in the dance, exactly three scale degrees appear. In the first two measures, and in the fifth, sixth, and eighth, they are (from low to high) 0, 2, 4, that is, the tones of the major triad on D. In the three remaining measures they are 4, 1, 3, that is, 0, 4, 6 *relative to A*.

We recall that a selection operator generates a sequence from an alphabet by designating the order numbers in the alphabet of the successive members of the sequence. Thus, from the alphabet (1, 4), the selection operator (1 + 1 + 2) generates the sequence (1 + 1 + 4). Consider now the selection operator (1 + 3 + 2 + 3 + 1 + 3) on the alphabets (0, 2, 4), and (0, 4, 6), respectively. In the first case, it generates the sequence (0 + 4 + 2 + 4 + 0 + 4); in the second case, the sequence (0 + 6 + 4 + 6 + 0 + 6). But these are precisely the sequences of notes that occur in the bass voice of the dance (the two patterns taken relative to D and A, respectively). The pattern produced by this particular selection operator is well known in music of the late eighteenth and early nineteenth century; it is the so-called "Alberti bass."

If we review the analysis to this point, we find that all the notes of both soprano and bass in measures 1, 2, 5, 6 and 8 belong to the major triad on D, while the bass notes of measures 3 and 4, and soprano and bass of measure 7 belong to the triadic alphabet of A. We can therefore associate a scale degree, or "chord" with each subpattern, obtaining the harmonic pattern: 0 + 0 + 4 + 4 + 0 + 0 + 4 + 0. Again this is a simple (and common) musical in which the harmony moves from tonic to fifth, then from tonic to fifth and back.

The induction strategy outlined here parallels closely the one used for letter series, where the pattern induction program first detected the periodicity of the pattern (which corresponds to detection of motive boundaries), then proceeded to describe the relations that defined the pattern.

The pattern thus induced from the musical example of Fig. 8.11 is shown in Fig. 8.12. The smallest pattern elements are designated by the Greek letters ρ (for rhythmic patterns) and π (for melodic patterns). There are three of the former and six of the latter in the soprano and bass lines, taken together, of the eight measures. (Thus, considering rhythm and melody of both voices, this part of the notation achieves a

$$\begin{pmatrix} M_i^2 \\ (i=0) \end{pmatrix} \begin{pmatrix} S \begin{bmatrix} (\rho_2,\ \pi_3(i))^2 \\ (i=6,\ 0) \\ B:\ \beta_2 \end{bmatrix} \end{pmatrix} \begin{pmatrix} M_i^2 \\ (i=0,\ 2) \end{pmatrix} \begin{pmatrix} \text{Degree: } 4 \\ S:\ \rho_2,\ \pi_5 \\ B:\ \beta_2 \end{pmatrix} \begin{pmatrix} \text{Degree: } 0 \\ S:\ \rho_2,\ \pi_6 \\ B:\ \beta_1 \end{pmatrix}$$

(with Degree: 4 over first M_i^2, Degree: 4 over third M_i^2)

where

$$M_i = \begin{pmatrix} \text{Degree: } 0 \\ S:\ \rho_1,\ \pi_1(i) \\ B:\ \beta_1 \end{pmatrix}$$

ρ_1 = Duration: $(1,\ 1,\ 4)$

ρ_2 = Duration: $(1)^6$

ρ_3 = Duration: $(2,\ 4)$

$\beta_1 = \pi_2,\ \rho_2$

$\beta_2 = \pi_4,\ \rho_2$

π_1 = Degree: $(i,\ (N(\mathrm{DIAT}))^2)$

π_3 = Degree: $(i,\ (N(\mathrm{BDIAT}))^5)$

Q = Select: $(1,\ 3,\ 2,\ 3,\ 1,\ 3)$

π_2 = Degree: $Q(0,\ 2,\ 4)$

π_4 = Degree: $Q(0,\ 4,\ 6)$

π_5 = Degree: $Q(2,\ 6,\ 4)$

π_6 = Degree: $(0,\ 0)$

Fig. 8.12

compression from 32 to 9 independent elements) The Greek letters β name two combinations of rhythm and melody that are repeated several times in the bass voice. The pattern named M is a combination of soprano and bass patterns that occurs, with parameterized variation, in measures 1, 2, 5, and 6. The top part of Fig. 8.12 shows the pattern for the entire eight measures described in terms of these more elementary components.

CONCLUSION

In this paper we have presented a scheme for describing music in terms of underlying pattern. A pattern language was introduced which is a slight extension of a formalism that has been used previously to describe patterns in certain intellectual aptitude tests and psychological laboratory tasks. Examples were presented to show how the language would be used for the description of tonal music.

A program is under construction that will translate pattern

descriptions into printed music in order to test the accuracy and adequacy of the formal language. A second program was described in outline that will induct the pattern description from the printed score. The pattern description language we have described may prove useful both in psychology and in music theory. As a tool in psychology, it can be used to try to arrive at an understanding of the cognitive activity of the music listener. As a tool of music theory, it may be used to provide rigorous descriptions of musical pattern as a prerequisite for the characterization and comparison of style. In the more distant future, it may provide an interesting basis, different from those employed heretofore, for experiments in musical composition by computer.

CHAPTER 9   *John R. Hayes*

Carnegie-Mellon University

STRATEGIES IN JUDGMENTAL RESEARCH

This conference has brought together a very diverse group
of participants. They come from many different parts of the
country and many different research traditions. They have
studied judgment in such areas as chemistry, music, clinical
decision-making, classifying warships, and setting odds. With
such a group, there is very little overlap in specifics. None
of the papers for example, develops any fact which is either
helpful or embarrassing to any of the others. The papers can't
be integrated into a tightly knit whole. Their variety however,
does offer us an opportunity to take a broad view of the area
of judgmental research.

When one stands back to look at the conference, several
generalizations emerge from the particulars. First, the participants have employed three distinct research strategies.
Two of them, the "black box" strategy and the "process tracing"
strategy are traditional, and one, the "program-first" strategy
is quite new. Second, certain surprising weaknesses inherent
in the "black box" strategy are just being brought to general
attention. Finally, the "process tracing" strategy, which has
long been neglected, is going through a period of development
in which new analytic tools are being invented and old ones are
being refined.

THE STRATEGIES

The "black box" strategy, employed by Hoffman and Edwards, treats the judgmental process as if it were a mechanism
sealed in an unopenable box. The aim of the strategy is to infer
the nature of the mechanism by observing the relations between

251

the box's informational inputs and the judgments which constitute its output. The "black box" strategy has long been in vogue with behavioristically oriented psychologists. (See Forehand, [1966] for an interesting discussion of this relationship.)

The "process tracing" strategy, on the other hand, has long been out of vogue with behavioristically oriented psychologists. The characteristic feature of this strategy is that it goes beyond input-output analysis and attempts to obtain measures of the events occurring between input and output. Thus, the process tracers insist on opening the black box to watch the mechanism inside while it is working. The analysis of verbal protocols is the most common technique used to obtain process information, but other more exotic measures, such as eye movements (Winikoff, 1967), have been used as well.

The use of verbal protocol analysis suggests an unfortunate parallel to the Introspectionist School—a parallel which has undoubtedly discouraged some from adopting the process tracing strategy. The parallel is unfortunate because it is quite misleading. The Introspectionists and the process tracers use protocol data in radically different ways. The Introspectionists were attempting to discover the elementary images and feelings which they believed to be the constituents of the mind. They collected their protocols from observers who were carefully trained to recognize these constituents when they turned up. The process tracers, on the other hand, are attempting to find processes of thought rather than contents of consciousness. They collect their protocols by asking relatively naive observers to describe what they are doing. Kleinmuntz's paper provides an excellent example of the process tracing strategy.

The "program-first" strategy, employed here by Simon, represents an interesting new approach to psychological investigaton.   Given the problem of analyzing a judgmental task, the initial impulse of the "program-firster" is not to rush to the psychological laboratory for new input-output relations or for new protocols.   Rather, it is to try to write a computer program designed to perform the task in a way that fits the currently available data.

The difference between pursuing this strategy and doing artificial intelligence work is one of intent. The "program-first" strategist is primarily concerned with discovering the processes of human cognition whereas the artificial intelligence expert is interested in discovering the best process for accomplishing a given task.

The rationale of the program-first strategy is this. In trying to understand how humans accomplish a given task, it helps a great deal to have available for comparison other systems which accomplish the same task. A computer program is an especially good system to have available for comparison because it is so well specified. It can suggest very precise questions to ask of the human system and can provide very precise answers for questions posed by the human system. I have in mind the following sorts of dialogue.

Q. Humans exhibit behavior A. Doesn't that imply that they have process X?
A. No. My program exhibits behavior A also and it certainly doesn't have process X.
Q. My medical diagnosis program is confused if the patient has more than one disease. What about people?
A. Physicians find these situations confusing too.
Q. Our program is bothered by dirty thoughts. Do humans have this trouble also?
A. No, they seem to enjoy them.

In addition to providing this sort of specific dialogue, the program can serve a more general guiding function. Perhaps this is best explained by geographical analogy. Having a couple of programs which perform a task we are interested in analyzing is like having the reports of a couple of explorers who have investigated a region we want to explore. Their routes through the territory may be different from ours. Nevertheless, they help us to form a crude map on which we can locate the major hazards, and from which we can calculate the probable length of our journey.

Now is Simon indeed a "program firster" rather than simply an artificial intelligence buff? I think so. His paper contrasts strongly with those of Cattell and Lederberg who fall clearly in the artificial intelligence area. Cattell is interested in providing artificial means for identifying clusterings in data. Lederberg is interested in generating programs which will enumerate classes of chemical compounds. Neither appears particularly concerned with human procedures for accomplishing these same tasks. Simon differs a good deal from these two. First he chooses components for his model with a sharp eye to the psychological literature. The elements "same,"

254 Formal Representation of Human Judgment

"next," "sequence," and "alphabet" have all been found useful in earlier studies of human response to temporal patterns. Second, he claims that his analysis "... has strong implications for the nature of ..."the human listening and composing processes. It seems clear that his interest is to illuminate human cognitive processes rather than to replace them.

CRITICISM OF THE BLACK BOX STRATEGY

Criticism of the black box strategy is hardly new. Skinner (1953) has long opposed this strategy. He holds that it is at best a waste of time to try to infer the nature of an unseen process from its input-output relations. If the process is really unseen, he argues, it can't help us to predict observable behaviors. It is better to describe the functional relations between input and output, and avoid inferences about process. Such inferences are risky in his view, because they are all too frequently mistaken for explanations. Proponents of the black box strategy have argued that these risks are worth taking. They hold that inferences about process, while they are sometimes wrong, and sometimes empty, often provide conceptual tools which are extremely useful in understanding data.

Recently, criticisms of the black box strategy have appeared which are of a different and more damaging kind. These criticisms have pointed out certain inherent ambiguities in the relation of a process to its output which have been widely overlooked. They have shown that in some important cases, it is genuinely impossible to infer the nature of the process from an input-output analysis.

Green has summarized one line of argument in his penetrating comment on Hoffman's paper. The essential point of the argument is this. While multiple regression analysis, and analysis of variance provide us with models for describing our data, we must not assume that these models also describe the process which generated the data.

Many different models can be fit to the same data. The standard analytic techniques arbitrarily choose one of these models as *the* description but clearly any of the others would be equally valid. Analysis of variance and multiple regression analysis have a built in bias for linear models. Thus, in the instance cited by Green, data generated by a completely nonlinear process was assigned a predominantly linear descriptive model. This is not, of course, a criticism of analysis of variance. It is simply an illustration of the limitation of input-output analysis for revealing the nature of the underlying process.

While the arguments that Green presents were published as long ago as 1961, they have still not received sufficient attention. If as clever and informed a researcher as Hoffman has failed to appreciate their significance, certainly many more have also.

Another line of argument which leads to the same conclusion as that reached by Green has been pursued by Newell.[1] Newell notes that one can't necessarily infer the nature of a computer from the computer's output, that is, from the set of computations that the computer will perform. Computers with very different internal mechanisms may be exactly equivalent in the sense that they solve the same set of problems and they fail to solve the same set of problems. This has been proved, for example, for Turing machines.

A Turing machine is a simple sort of abstract computer. It has a moveable tape which is marked off into cells. The tape can be placed under a scanner which looks at the content of one cell. On the basis of what it sees, the machine takes one of three actions:

1. It erases what it sees and writes something else.
2. It moves the tape one unit left or right.
3. It stops.

Surprisingly enough, a very large class of functions is computable by machines of this sort, namely all of the partially recursive functions. If we were to get ourselves a much fancier set of Turing machines with several scanners and a tape that moved in two dimensions, the set of functions that we could compute would be exactly the same as with the simpler machines (Mendelson, 1964). Thus, the output of the Turing machine can't be used to identify its internal structure.

Both lines of argument show that the relationship between process and output is ambiguous. This doesn't mean that the black box strategy is useless for identifying process. Two devices which have different output can't be the same. Input-output analysis, then, can help us to make distinctions among

[1] Personal Communication.

processes. The arguments do show, however, that in the search for underlying process, input-output analysis must be supplemented by other techniques.

THE DEVELOPMENT OF THE PROCESS
TRACING STRATEGY

Newell and his associates have been working to develop new process tracing techniques. Winikoff (1967) has done interesting work on eye movement protocols in cryptoarithmetic and chess problems. Nevertheless, the analysis of verbal protocols is still the primary process tracing technique.

One must exercise considerable care in collecting and interpreting verbal protocols. Kleinmuntz's paper illustrates both the strengths and the pitfalls of protocol analysis. The strength is dramatically illustrated in the analysis of MMPI judgments. The interpretation of the protocols proved quite direct. The judges were asked for their judgmental rules, and the rules which they stated were put into a model which was tested by simulation. Not only did these rules prove sufficient to yield judgments (After all, they might not have if the subjects had said things like, "I do it by feel." or "Well, he just looks like a microcephalic."), they actually gave a rather good approximation of the performance of the human judge. To construct such a model without the use of a verbal protocol would clearly have been much more difficult.

Kleinmuntz's analysis of the neurologist's judgments seems far less successful than his analysis of MMPI judgments. He claims for example, that the tree diagrams he presents represent the diagnostic search strategies employed by his subjects. Unfortunately, there is some ambiguity as to what the diagrams actually represent. At best, the tree diagram is a segment of the subject's fixed search tree in which the answer to each question determines the question which the subject will as next. At worst, the diagram simply illustrates that any sequence of yes-no questions at all, whether they are generated by a search strategy or not, can be represented by such diagrams. See Fig. 9.1, for example. Examination of Kleinmuntz's sample protocols suggests that the truth lies somewhere between these two extremes. In many cases, though, the subjects do seem to be jumping from topic

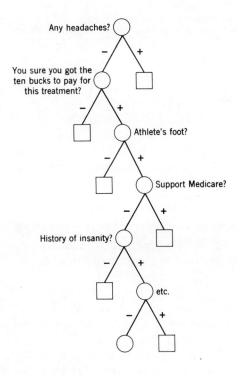

Fig. 9.1

to topic rather than pursuing a single line of questioning. Kleinmuntz also claims that the sequence of questions procedes from general to specific. Here again there is ambiguity because Kleinmuntz has not provided us with a clear definition of generality.   Consider the following sequence of questions and answers:

Q. What is the nature of your complaint?
A. Pains.
Q. Where is the complaint?
A. In the stomach.

The questions certainly seem to proceed from general to specific, starting out with an unspecified pain and narrowing it down to a stomach ache. But now consider another sequence of questions:

Q. Where is the complaint?
A. In the stomach.
Q. What is the nature of the complaint?
A. Pains.

This sequence also seems to proceed from general to specific. That is, it narrows down a vague stomach complaint to a stomach ache. In the sequences above, it seems that what really goes from general to specific is not the set of questions, but rather our state of knowledge about the subject. If we assume that the answers to our questions don't destroy information about the subject, then all questions must by this criterion proceed from general to specific. If Kleinmuntz has some other definition of generality in mind he has not made it plain.

I emphasize these points because they illustrate the pitfall which can entrap even a sophisticated interpreter of protocols. Protocols are sometimes really difficult to interpret and the techniques for dealing with the difficulties are not yet very far advanced. DeGroot (1965) has suggested some rule to observe in protocol collection, and Hayes (1965) has made use of stringent experimental controls to keep protocols simple. Newell (1966) has been very active in developing techniques for analyzing obtained protocols. The technique of computer simulation is an extremely powerful tool, as Kleinmuntz's paper shows, for evaluating the results of protocol analysis. The development of these and other techniques will presumably continue to increase the power of the process tracing strategy.

Edwards might well object to all this. In fact, I imagine that I can hear him now.

EDWARDS: "A pox on all your process tracing. Remember, I'm interested in discovering the underlying processes, too. But your damn protocols always seem so fuzzy. Give me a good solid output every time and to hell with the protocols. I'd rather fight than switch."

HAYES: "Of course, of course." (Soothingly)

EDWARDS: "I've always remembered the words of my old professor who said to me, 'Ward, my boy, you must appreciate how clever it is of this little stone to know the laws of gravity. But to understand the stone, you will do better to study its behavior rather than its thoughts.'"

HAYES: "But isn't that missing Green's point. No matter how fuzzy the information is, you still need it to help you resolve the ambiguities between process and output. Anyway, if you really work hard at it the protocols needn't be so fuzzy."

EDWARDS: "Look, I'm not just being cantankerous. I've tried protocol analysis and I've found out what psychologists have been finding out ever since the Wurzburg School. With a simple judgment, you get very little protocol. There just doesn't seem to be anything nontrivial for the subject to report on. I couldn't take your advice even if I wanted to, so if you guys want me to change my ways you better tell me more about how to do it."

HAYES: "That is certainly a fair argument. Probability judgments may, alas, be an area in which process tracing just isn't practical. But I haven't given up on it yet. Piaget (1951) has found that children's protocols do give some interesting information. He claims that the protocols reveal a sequence of stages in the development of the child's ability to make probability judgments. By relating these stages to other aspects of cognitive development, he is able to make some interesting inferences about the nature of the judgmental process. Incidentally, Piaget finds that young children tend to be very 'conservative' (in your sense, not his)."

EDWARDS: "Well, I hope that you are right about protocols providing us with solid data in this area, but I suspect that you aren't."

HAYES: "Thanks and I hope that your judgment is conservative."

In summary, the broad view that we have taken of judgmental research has shown us a field undergoing rapid change. New research strategies are being invented and old strategies are being criticized and sharpened. New techniques are being invented to implement the strategies. These changes are ones that promise to accelerate our understanding of human judgment. Prospects in this field, then, appear bright.

REFERENCES

Anderson, N. H.   Test of a model for opinion change. Journal of Abnormal and Social Psychology, 1959, **59**, 371-381.

Anderson, N. H.   Note on weighted sum and linear operator models. Psychonomic Science, 1964, **1**, 189-190.

Anderson, N. H., & Ann Jacobson.   Effect of stimulus inconsistency and discounting instructions in personality impression formation. Journal of Personality and Social Psychology, 1965, **2**, 531-539.

Aumann, R. J.   Subjective programming. In M. W. Shelly and G. L. Bryan (Eds.) Human Judgments and Optimality, New York: John Wiley & Sons, 1964.

Beach, L. R.   Accuracy and consistency in the revision of subjective probabilities.   IEEE on Human Factors in Electronics, 1966, **7**, 29-37.

Beach, L. R., & L. D. Phillips.   Subjective probabilities inferred from estimates and bets. Journal of Experimental Psychology, 1967, **75** (3) 354-359.

Brunswik, E.   Systematic and Representative Design of Psychological Experiments.   Berkeley: University of California Press, 1947.

Busacker, R. G., & T. L. Saaty.   Finite Graphs and Networks: An Introduction with Applications.   New York: McGraw-Hill, 1965.

Cattell, R. B. r_p and other coefficients of pattern similarity.   Psychometrika, 1949, **14**, 279-298.

Cattell, R. B.   The principal culture patterns discoverable in the syntal dimensions of existing nations.   Journal of Social Psychology, 1950, **32**, 215-253.

Cattell, R. B.   Factor Analysis. New York: Harper, 1952.

Cattell, R. B.   Personality and Motivation Structure and Measurement. New York: World Book, 1957.

Cattell, R. B.   Group theory, personality, and role: A model for research. In F. Geldard (Ed.) Defense Psychology. New York: Pergamon Press, 1963.

Cattell, R. B.   (Ed.) Handbook of Multivariate Experimental Psychology. Chicago: Rand McNally, 1966.

Cattell, R. B., H. Breul, & H. P. Hartman.   An attempt at more refined definition of the cultural dimensions of syntality in modern nations. American Sociological Review, 1952, **17**, 408-421.

Cattell, R. B., & M. A. Coulter.   Principles of behavioral taxonomy and the mathematical basis of the taxonome computer program. The British Journal of Mathematical and Statistical Psychology, 1966, **19**, 237-271.

Cattell, R. B., & M. A. Coulter.   The taxonome program for finding types as stats and aits. British Journal of Mathematical and Statistical Psychology, 1966, **19**, 281.

Cattell, R. B., & H. J. Eber.   The Sixteen Personality Factor Questionnaire (3rd ed.). Champaign, Illinois: Institute for Personality and Ability Testing, 1966.

Cattell, R. B., P. Rican, & J. Jaspars.   Plasmode 30-10-5-2 for experimentation with factor analytic procedures. Multivariate Behavioral Research, 1968 (in press).

Cattell, R. B., & D. F. Tatro.   The personality factors, objectively measured, which distinguish psychotics from normals. Behavior Research Therapy, 1966, **4**, 1-13.

Cattell, R. B., D. F. Tatro, & E. Komlos.   The diagnosis and inferred structure of paranoid and non-paranoid schizophrenia from the 16 P.F. profile. Indian Psychological Review, 1964, **1**, 52-61.

Chesterton, G. K.   Robert Browning. London: Macmillan, 1903.

Clarkson, G.   Portfolio Selection: A Simulation of Trust Investment. Prentice-Hall, 1962.

Cohen, J.   Behavior in Uncertainty, New York: Basic Books, 1964.

DeGroot, A. D.   Thought and Choice in Chess. The Hague: Mouton, 1965, 373-374.

Dudycha, A. L., & J. C. Naylor.   The effect of variations in the cue R matrix upon the obtained policy equation of judges. Educational and Psychological Measurement, 1966, **26**, 583-603.

Edwards, W.   Human Processing of Equivocal Information ESD-TDR-64-601, University of Michigan, Institute of Science and Technology, Report 3780-23-F, April, 1965.

Edwards, W.   Nonconservative Probabilistic Information Processing Systems, ESD-TR-66-404, University of Michigan, Institute of Science and Technology Report 5893-22-F, December, 1966.

Edwards, W., H. Lindman, & L. D. Phillips.   Emerging technologies for making decisions. New Directions in Psychology II, New York: Holt, Rinehart, & Winston, 1965.

Edwards, W., H. Lindman, & L. J. Savage.   Bayesian statistical inference for psychological research. Psychological Review, 1963, **70**, 193-242.

Feigenbaum, E. A., & J. Feldman (Eds.).   Computers and thought. New York: McGraw-Hill, 1963.

Feldman, J.   Simulation of behavior in the binary choice experiment. Proceedings of the Western Joint Computer Conference, 1961, **19**, 133-144.

Feldman, J.   Simulation of behavior in the binary choice experiment. In Feigenbaum, E. A., & Feldman, J. (Eds.) Computers and Thought, New York: McGraw-Hill, 1963, p. 329-346.

Feldman, J., & A. Newell.   A note on a class of probability matching models. Psychometrika, 1961, **26**, 333-337.

Feldman, J., F. Tonge, & H. Kanter.   Empirical explorations of a hypothesis-testing model of binary choice behavior.   In Hoggatt, A. C., & Balderston, F. E. (Eds.) Symposium on Simulation Models, Cincinnati: South-Western Publishing Company, 1963.

Forehand, G. A.   Epilogue: Constructs and strategies for problem solving research.   In B. Kleinmuntz (Ed.) Problem Solving: Research, Method and Theory.   New York: John Wiley & Sons, 1966.

Gibson, W. A.   Proportional profiles and latent structure. Psychometrika, 1956, **21,** 135.

Grebstein, L.   Relative accuracy of actuarial prediction, experienced clinicians, and graduate students in a clinical judgment task.   Journal of Consulting Psychology, 1963, **27,** 127-132.

Gregg, L. W.   Internal representations of sequential concepts.   In B. Kleinmuntz (Ed.) Concepts and the Structure of Memory, John Wiley & Sons, 1967, p. 107-142.

Griffith, R. M.   Odds adjustment by American horserace bettors. American Journal of Psychology, 1949, **63,** 290-294.

Halbower, C. C.   A comparison of actuarial versus clinical prediction to classes discriminated by MMPI.   Unpublished doctoral dissertation. Minneapolis: University of Minnesota Press, 1955.

Hammond, K. R.   Probabilistic functioning and the clinical method. Psychological Review, 1955, **62,** 255-262.

Hammond, K. R., Carolyn J. Hursch, & F. J. Todd.   Analyzing the components of clinical inference.   Psychological Review, 1964, **71,** 438-456.

Hammond, K. R., & D. A. Summers.   Cognitive dependence on linear and nonlinear cues.   Psychological Review, 1965, **72,** 215-224.

Hathaway, S. R.   A coding system for MMPI profiles.   Journal of Consulting Psychology, 1947, **11,** 334-337.

Hathaway, S. R., & J. C. McKinley.   The Minnesota Multiphasic Personality Inventory Manual.   (revised ed.) New York: Psychological Corporation, 1951.

Hayes, J. R.   Problem topology and the solution process, Journal of Verbal Learning and Verbal Behavior, 1965, **4,** 371-379.

Hays, W. L.   Statistics for Psychologists.   New York: Holt, Rinehart, & Winston, 1963.

Helm, C. E., & L. R. Tucker.   Individual differences in the structure of color-perception.   American Journal of Psychology, 1962, **75,** 437-444.

Henze, H. R., & C. M. Blair.   The number of isomeric hydrocarbons of the methane series.   Journal of American Chemistry Society, 1931, **53,** 3077-3085.

Hoffman, P. J.   The paramorphic representation of clinical judgment. Psychological Bulletin, 1960, **57,** 116-131.

Hoffman, P. J., P. Slovic, & L. G. Rorer.   An analysis of variance model for the assessment of configural cue utilization in clinical judgment. Psychological Bulletin, 1968 (in press).

Hoggatt, A. C., & F. E. Balderston. (Eds.) Symposium on Simulation Models.   Cincinnati: South-Western Publishing Company, 1963.

Holzinger, K. J., & H. Harman.   Factor analysis.   Chicago: University of Chicago Press, 1941.

Horn, J. L.   Significance tests for use with r_p and related profile statistics.   Educational and Psychological Measurement, 1961, **2,** 363-370.

Horst, P.   Current problems in linear and configural prediction.   Unpublished manuscript, University of Washington, September, 1964.

Humphrey, G.   Thinking.   John Wiley & Sons, 1951.

Hursch, Carolyn J., K. R. Hammond, & J. L. Hursch. Some methodological considerations in multiple-cue probability studies. Psychological Review, 1964, 71, 42-60.

Jane's Fighting Ships. London: Jane's Fighting Ships Publishing Company, 1964-1965.

Johnson, D. M. The Psychology of Thought and Judgment, Harper, 1955.

Jung, C. G. Psychological Types. London: Routledge and Kegan Paul, 1923.

Kleinmuntz, B. The college maladjustment scale (Mt): Norms and predictive validity. Educational and Psychological Measurement, 1961, 21, 1029-1033.

Kleinmuntz, B. MMPI decision rules for the identification of college maladjustment: A digital computer approach. Psychological Monographs, 1963, 77, No. 14 (Whole No. 577), (a).

Kleinmuntz, B. Personality test interpretation by digital computer. Science, 1963, 139, 416-418, (b).

Kleinmuntz, B. Profile analysis revisited: A heuristic approach. Journal of Counseling Psychology, 1963, 10, 315-324.

Kleinmuntz, B. (Ed.) Concepts and the Structure of Memory, New York: John Wiley & Sons, 1967.

Kleinmuntz, B. Sign and seer: Another example. Journal of Abnormal Psychology, 1967, 72, 163-165.

Knox, R. E., & P. J. Hoffman. Effects of variation of profile format on intelligence and sociability judgments. Journal of Applied Psychology, 1962, 46, 14-20.

Kogan, N., & M. A. Wallach. Risk Taking. New York: Holt, Rinehart & Winston, 1964.

Laughery, K. R., & L. W. Gregg. Simulation of human problem-solving behavior. Psychometrika, 1962, 27, 265-282.

Lazarsfeld, P. F. Latent structure analysis and test theory. In Gulliksen, H., & S. Messick (Eds.) Psychological Scaling: Theory and Applications. New York: John Wiley & Sons, 1960.

Lederberg, J. DENDRAL-64. S system for computer construction, enumeration and notation of organic molecules as tree structures and cyclic graphs. Part I. Notational algorithm for tree structures. NASA CR-57029. STAR No. N65-13158, 1964.

Lederberg, J. DENDRAL-64. Part II. Topology of cyclic graphs. NASA CR-68898. STAR No. N66-14074, 1965.

Lederberg, J. Topological mapping of organic molecules. Proceedings of National Academy of Science, U. S., 1965, 53, 134-139.

Lederberg, J. A general outline of the DENDRAL system. Systematics of organic molecules, graph topology and Hamilton circuits. NASA CR-68899. STAR No. N66-14075, 1966.

Mahalanobis, P. C. On the generalized distance in statistics. Proceedings at National Institute of Science, Calcutta, 12, 49-55.

Marks, P. A. An assessment of the diagnostic process in a child guidance setting. Psychological Monographs, 1961, 75, No. 3 (Whole No. 507).

Martin, N. An investigation of the mass spectra of twenty-two free amino acids. Instrumentation Research Laboratory, Department of Genetics, Stanford University School of Medicine. Technical Report No. IRL-1035, 1965.

Martin, H. T., Jr.   The nature of clinical judgment.   Unpublished doctoral dissertation, Washington State College, 1957.

Marx, M. H.   The general nature of theory construction.   In Marx, M. H. (Ed.)   Theories in Contemporary Psychology, New York: Macmillan, 1963.

McLafferty, F. W.   High-resolution mass spectrometry.   Science, 1966, 151, 641-649.

McQuitty, L. L.   Rank order typal analysis.   Educational and Psychological Measurement, 1963, 23, 55-61.

Meehl, P. E.   Clinical versus Statistical Prediction.   Minneapolis: University of Minnesota Press, 1954.

Meehl, P. E.   Wanted—A good cookbook.   American Psychologist, 1956, 11, 263-272.

Meehl, P. E.   A comparison of clinicians with five statistical methods of identifying psychotic MMPI profiles.   Journal of Counseling Psychology, 1959, 6, 102-109.

Meehl, P. E., & W. G. Dahlstrom.   Objective configural rules for discriminating psychotic from neurotic MMPI profiles.   Journal of Consulting Psychology, 1960, 24, 375-387.

Mendelson, E.   Introduction to Mathematical Logic.   Princeton: Van Nostrand, 1964.

Messick, S., & D. N. Jackson.   Individual differences in social perception.   Research Bulletin No. 23, Pennsylvania State University, 1961.

Messick, S., & N. Kogan.   Personality consistencies in judgment: Dimensions of role constructs.   Multivariate Behavioral Research, 1966, 1, 165-176.

Meyer, L. B.   Emotion and Meaning in Music.   Chicago: University of Chicago Press, 1956.

Naylor, J. C., & R. J. Wherry, Sr.   The use of simulated stimuli and the "JAN" technique to capture and cluster the policies of rater.   Educational and Psychological Measurement, 1965, 25, 969-986.

Newell, A.   Comment on Kleinmuntz' "Profile Analysis Revisited: A Heuristic Approach."   Journal of Counseling Psychology, 1963, 10, 322-324.

Newell, A.   On the Analysis of Human Problem Solving Protocols.   Paper delivered at the International Symposium on Mathematical and Computational Methods in the Social Sciences, Rome, July, 1966.

Newell, A., & H. A. Simon.   An example of human chess play in the light of chess playing programs.   In Weiner N., & J. P. Schade (Eds.)   Progress in Biocybernetics, Vol. 2, Amsterdam: Elsevier, 1965.

Peterson, C. R., & L. R. Beach.   Man as an intuitive statistician.   Technical Report No. 4, University of Michigan, 1966.

Peterson, C. R., W. M. DuCharme, & W. Edwards.   Sampling distributions and probability revisions.   Journal of Experimental Psychology, 1968 (in press).

Peterson, C. R., & L. D. Phillips.   Revision of continuous subjective probability distributions.   IEEE Transactions on Human Factors in Electronics, 1966, 7, 19-21.

Peterson, C. R., R. J. Schneider, & A. J. Miller.   Sample size and the revision of subjective probabilities.   Journal of Experimental Psychology, 1965, 69, 522-527.

Peterson, C. R., Z. J. Ulehla, A. J. Miller, L. E. Bourne, & D. W. Stilson. Internal consistency of subjective probabilities. Journal of Experimental Psychology, 1965, 70, 526-533.

Phillips, L. D. & W. Edwards. Conservatism in a simple probability inference task. Journal of Experimental Psychology, 1966, 72, 346-354.

Phillips, L. D., W. L. Hays, & W. Edwards. Conservatism in complex probabilistic inference. IEEE Transactions on Human Factors in Electronics, 1966, 7, 7-18.

Piaget, J. & B. Inhelder. La Génese de L'Idee de Hasard Chez L'Enfant. Paris: Presses University France, 1951.

Pitz, G. F. & Helen Reinhold. Payoff effects in sequential decision making. Journal of Experimental Psychology, 1968 (in press).

Radner, R. Mathematical specification of goals for decision problems. In Shelly, M. W. & G. L. Bryan (Eds.) Human Judgments and Optimality. New York: John Wiley & Sons, 1964.

Restle, F. Psychology of Judgment and Choice. New York: John Wiley & Sons, 1961.

Rigby, F. D. Heuristic analysis of decision situation. In Shelly, M. W. & G. L. Bryan (Eds.) Human Judgments and Optimality. New York: John Wiley & Sons, 1964.

Robinson, G. H. Continuous estimation of a time-varying probability. Ergonomics, 1964, 7, 7-22.

Rorer. L. G., & P. Slovic. The measurement of changes in judgmental strategy. American Psychologist, 1966, 21, 641-642 (abstract).

Rothgeb, J. Some uses of mathematical concepts in theories of music. Journal of Music Theory, 1966, 10, 200-215.

Sarbin, T. R. A contribution to the study of actuarial and individual methods of prediction. American Journal of Sociology, 1943, 48, 593-602.

Savage, L. J. The Foundations of Statistics. New York: John Wiley & Sons, 1954.

Schum, D. A., I. L. Goldstein, & J. R. Southard. Research on a simulated Bayesian information-processing system. IEEE Transactions on Human Factors in Electronics, 1966, 7, 37-48.

Shelly, M. W., & G. L. Bryan. (Eds.) Human Judgments and Optimality. New York: John Wiley & Sons, 1964.

Shelly, M. W., & G. L. Bryan. Judgments and the language of decisions. In Shelly, M. W., & G. L. Bryan, (Eds.) Human Judgments and Optimality. New York: John Wiley & Sons, 1964.

Simon, H. A., & K. Kotovsky. Human acquisition of concepts for sequential patterns. Psychological Review, 1963, 70, 534-546.

Skinner, B. F. Science and Human Behavior. New York: Macmillan, 1953.

Slovic, P. Cue-consistency and cue-utilization in judgment. American Journal of Psychology, 1966, 79, 427-434.

Sokal, R. R., & H. A. Sneath. Principles of Numerical Taxonomy. New York: Freeman and Company, 1963.

Stephenson, W. The Study of Behavior: Q-technique and Its Methodology. Chicago: University of Chicago Press, 1953.

Sutherland, G. DENDRAL- A computer program for generating and filtering chemical structures. Stanford Artificial Intelligence Project, Memo No. 49, 1967.

Toda, M. Measurement of subjective probability distribution. Division of Mathematical Psychology, Institute for Research, State College, Pennsylvania, University Park,   Rept. 3, April, 1963; Decision Sciences Lab. Electronic Systems Division, USAF, L. G. Hanscom Field, Mass., ESD-TDR-63-407, July, 1963.

Todd, F. J. A methodological study of clinical judgment. Unpublished doctoral dissertation. University of Colorado, 1964.

Thurstone, L. L. Multiple Factor Analysis. Chicago: University of Chicago Press, 1947.

Tucker, L. R. A suggested alternative formulation in the development by Hursch, Hammond, & Hursch, and by Hammond, Hursch & Todd. Psychological Review, 1964, 71, 528-530.

Tucker, L. R., & S. Messick. An individual differences model for multidimensional scaling. Psychometrika, 1963, 28, 333-367.

Uhl, C. N., & P. J. Hoffman. Contagion effects and the stability of judgment.   Paper read at Western Psychological Association, Monterey, California, 1958.

Walters, H., & D. Jackson. Group and individual regularities in trait inference: A multidimensional scaling analysis. Multivariate Behavioral Research, 1966, 1, 145-164.

Welsh, G. S. An anxiety index and an internalization ratio for the MMPI. Journal of Consulting Psychology, 1952, 16, 65-72.

Wiggins, Nancy. Individual viewpoints of social desirability. Psychological Bulletin, 1966, 66, 68-79.

Wiggins, Nancy, & P. J. Hoffman. Three models of clinical judgment. Journal of Abnormal Psychology, 1968a, 73, No. 1, 70-77.

Wiggins, Nancy, & P. J. Hoffman. Dimensions of profile judgments as a function of instructions, cue-consistency and individual differences. Journal of Multivariate Behavioral Research, 1968b, January, 3, No. 1.

Wilcoxon, F. Some Rapid Approximate Statistical Procedures. Connecticut: Cyanimid, 1949.

Winikoff, A. W. Eye movements as an aid to protocol analysis of problem solving behavior. Ph.D. dissertation, Department of Electrical Engineering, Carnegie Institute of Technology, 1967.

Woodworth, R. S., & H. Schlosberg. Experimental Psychology (revised ed.) Holt, Rinehart & Winston, 1954.

Wortman, P. M. Representation and strategy in diagnostic problem solving. Human Factors, 1966, 48-53.

Yntema, D. B., & W. S. Torgerson. Man-machine cooperation in decisions requiring common sense. IRE Transactions on Human Factors in Electronics, 1961, HFE-2, 20-26.

Author Index

269

Subject Index

271